Prompting HTML and CSS for Frontend Development

Build Responsive Websites, Semantic Layouts, Accessible Interfaces, and Modern UI Components Faster with AI Prompt Engineering

Olatunde Adedeji

www.orangeava.com

First Published: May 2026

Published By: Orange Education Pvt Ltd, AVA®

Address: 9, Daryaganj, Delhi, 110002, India

275 New North Road Islington Suite 1314 London,
N1 7AA, United Kingdom

ISBN (PBK): 978-93-49887-45-9
ISBN (E-BOOK): 978-93-49887-74-9

Scan the QR code to explore our entire catalogue

www.orangeava.com

Get a Free eBook

We hope you're enjoying your recent book purchase! Your feedback is incredibly valuable to us and helps other readers discover books that truly make a difference.

If you found this book useful or enjoyable, we'd greatly appreciate it if you could leave a short review with a 5-star rating on Amazon. Your review supports our work and allows us to reach more learners worldwide.

As a thank-you, we're happy to offer you a **free digital copy of this book** plus a **30% discount code** for your next purchase on our official websites:

www.orangeava.com

www.orangeava.in (For the Indian Subcontinent).

☑ **How it works:**

Leave your review on Amazon, take a screenshot of the confirmation or use the following link to submit the claim and email it to **info@orangeava.com.** Once received the required detail, we will send your rewards within 24 hours, **along with one month free subcription to the book on AVA SkillShelf!**

Claim Form
https://rebrand.ly/4d2477

Thank you for your support—it truly means a lot to us.

Downloading the code bundles and colored images

Please follow the links or scan the QR codes to download the ***Code Bundles and Images*** of the book:

https://github.com/ava-orange-education/Prompting-HTML-and-CSS-for-Frontend-Development

The code bundles and images of the book are also hosted on ***https://rebrand.ly/c6cf8f***

In case there's an update to the code, it will be updated on the existing GitHub repository.

Errata

We take immense pride in our work at **Orange Education Pvt Ltd,** and follow the best practices to ensure the accuracy of our content to provide an indulging reading experience to our subscribers. Our readers are our mirrors, and we use their inputs to reflect and improve upon human errors, if any, that may have occurred during the publishing processes involved. To let us maintain the quality and help us reach out to any readers who might be having difficulties due to any unforeseen errors, please write to us at:

errata@orangeava.com

Your support, suggestions, and feedback are highly appreciated.

Dedicated to

My Father, Amos Ojo Adedeji-

Though the Tools and Technologies Change, the Values You Instilled in Me Remain Constant.
You are Eternally Loved and Remembered.

About the Author

Olatunde Adedeji is a principal Full-Stack Software Engineer and AI Solutions Architect with over 15 years of experience developing scalable, user-centric enterprise applications. As the founder of MoWebsite, he has led the design and delivery of cloud-native platforms as well as AI-enabled products across Fintech, Healthtech, Edutech, and SaaS industries. He specializes in MERN stack, Python/Django, and high-performance backend architecture integrated with modern AI workflows.

Olatunde is a Udacity Certified Agentic AI Professional and an Oracle Certified Generative AI Professional, focusing his expertise on grounded Retrieval Augmented Systems (RAGs), agentic workflows, and prompt engineering.

His work bridges the gap between technical depth and real-world business impact through the mastery of tools such as Django, Flask, FastAPI, React, Vue, Docker, and Kubernetes. Beyond his engineering and architectural roles, Olatunde enjoys a quiet life with his wife, Adedoyin, and loves playing chess or spending quality time with his two lovely daughters, Michelle and Mabel!

You can explore more of his work at olatundeadedeji.com.

About the Technical Reviewer

Dr. Sudin Baraokar is a globally recognized AI and DeepTech leader with a Doctorate in Computer Science from Canterbury University, UK, and a Bachelor's in Computer Engineering (Honors) from the University of Mumbai. He is a Quantum Architect and AI expert specializing in enterprise-scale AI/ML systems, Generative AI (LLMs/SLMs), Retrieval-Augmented Generation (RAG), and advanced data pipelines. His technical expertise spans Hugging Face, LangChain, Databricks, and MLOps, with extensive experience deploying cloud-native AI solutions across AWS, Azure, and GCP.

With leadership roles at SBI, Barclays, IBM, and GE, Dr. Baraokar has served as Chief Innovation Officer, Enterprise Architect, and IT Advisor. He currently advises global organizations and academia on AI and digital transformation, while mentoring deep-tech startups and serving as a Certified Independent Director.

He has driven large-scale transformations, including modernizing SBI's core banking systems to handle 1.5 billion daily transactions and building the YONO AI Autonomic Banking Super App with over 50 million users. His work also includes developing Barclays' Global Innovation Platform, GE's Industrial Digital Cockpit, and IBM Watson AI solutions for global banking.

A prolific innovator, Dr. Baraokar has worked across 70+ technologies spanning AI, blockchain, fintech, cybersecurity, quantum computing, and IoT. He also founded the Bankchain Alliance, uniting more than 30 banks for emerging technology solutions.

Dr. Baraokar has trained over one million professionals and mentored 1,000+ startups. A global keynote speaker and recipient of over 100 awards, he actively researches future technologies while pursuing interests in music, sports, and philanthropy.

Acknowledgments

This book represents a creative and technical exploration into the future of web development. Translating natural language into clean code has been a challenge, and at the same time, a rewarding experience. This would not have been possible without the unrelenting support of many. My sincere appreciation goes to the editorial team at Orange Education Pvt. Ltd., whose expertise and dedication ensured the success of this book. A special thank you to Sumit Rawat, his soft but strict management of the timeline was the key to bringing this book to life in record time.

I am also deeply grateful to the developers, educators, and open-source contributors who shape our digital ecosystem. Specifically, I want to recognize the teams behind Visual Studio Code, GitHub, ChatGPT, and GitHub Copilot. These tools are not just utilities; they are the catalysts changing how we think, build, and ship interfaces, and they inspired many of the workflows explored in the pages of this book.

Beyond the technical support, I am greatly thankful to my mentors, colleagues, and clients whose interactions have refined my perspective as a full-stack engineer and author. Each experience contributed meaningfully to the practical lens through which I view the modern web.

Finally, I want to thank my family. Their patience and belief in my work kept me committed from the initial idea to the final manuscript! To my amazing wife, Adedoyin, and my beautiful daughters, Michelle and Mabel: Thank you for providing the emotional stability and inspiration that every line of code always requires.

Preface

This book sits at the intersection of AI prompting and frontend development. We are entering a new phase; for years, building interfaces meant manually crafting every HTML tag, every CSS selector, and every responsive adjustment. Today, the emergence of AI-assisted prompting is fundamentally changing that workflow. Designers and developers can now describe an interface in natural language, and receive structured, styled code in return. This shift is not replacing frontend development; it is transforming how we approach it.

This book was written to help developers, product designers, and other digital creators understand this shift clearly and practically. Prompt HTML and CSS shows how to turn ideas into well-structured, maintainable, and accessible frontend code using prompt-based workflows. Rather than treating Artificial Intelligence (AI) as a shortcut, this book presents it as a development partner, the one that requires direction, judgment, and high standards. In modern frontend development, the primary skill is no longer just writing markup and styles from scratch; it is learning how to navigate AI toward useful outputs and how to refine those results into production-ready digital art.

The goal of this book is simple: To help you move from concepts to building interface faster without losing code quality. Along the way, you will learn how to write effective prompts, generate semantic HTML, create responsive CSS, build reusable components, experiment with visual prompting tools, refine AI-generated output, and deploy finished work to the web. We also emphasize accessibility and clean code, because speed alone is not enough; professional engineering still requires clarity, usability, and intent.

This is a hands-on guide for creators at any level. Thus, whether you are just beginning or an experienced professional, trying to modernize workflows, this book meets you at the intersection of web fundamentals and AI-assisted development.

Across 13 progressive chapters, this book covers the full frontend development lifecycle. It starts with the foundations of AI communication and environment setup, moves into the execution of semantic and responsive layouts, and concludes with production refinement, where you will master visual tools and deployment strategies to ship high-quality web interfaces.

Chapter 1: Introduction to Prompt-Driven Web Development

This chapter introduces the emerging practice of prompt-driven frontend development, and explores how Artificial Intelligence (AI) is reshaping the way developers write HTML and CSS. You will learn to see prompting as a critical skill that complements traditional expertise, while tracing the technological evolution from manual coding to AI-augmented workflows.

Chapter 2: Tools and Setup for Prompt-Based Development

Before generating code, you will align your development environment with modern AI-augmented workflows by setting up essential tools like ChatGPT and GitHub Copilot. This chapter ensures that you can effectively integrate these tools into Visual Studio Code to increase productivity and reliably test your HTML and CSS output.

Chapter 3: Prompt Engineering for HTML and CSS

This chapter explores the principles of crafting effective prompts that produce clean, semantic, and responsive code through clarity and context. You will master the core techniques such as few-shot prompting and prompt chaining to progressively refine your results, and debug ambiguous instructions.

Chapter 4: Core HTML with AI Assistance

In this chapter, you will use AI tools to build the foundational structure of a web page by organizing content with semantic elements such as headers, navigation, and main sections. This approach helps you create logical layouts that improve accessibility and SEO, while maintaining high standards for structural clarity.

Chapter 5: Content-Specific HTML with AI

This chapter focuses on generating interactive and media-rich web content, such as structured forms and data tables, through practical AI assistance. You will practice incorporating accessibility best practices directly into your prompts to ensure that your digital experiences remain inclusive from the start.

Chapter 6: Styling with Prompt-Based CSS

In this chapter, you will explore how AI accelerates the styling process using traditional CSS and utility-first frameworks like Tailwind CSS. The chapter demonstrates how to construct modern layout systems such as Flexbox and Grid, while ensuring your designs adapt fluidly to various screen sizes.

Chapter 7: Advanced CSS Techniques with AI Assistance

This chapter introduces advanced styling features to enhance the visual richness of your interfaces through smooth transitions and eye-catching animations. You will learn to refine prompts to style UI elements dynamically, using AI to bring static components to life with polished effects.

Chapter 8: Building UI Components

In this chapter, you will learn how to break down a user interface into modular, reusable components like navigation bars, cards, and modals using prompt-based workflows. This chapter demonstrates strategies for producing consistent patterns and styled variations of the same component with minimal manual effort.

Chapter 9: Applied Prompt Workflows

This chapter transitions into real-world interface building through structured case studies, moving from initial design ideas to functional layouts. You will build projects such as a fintech landing page and an IoT dashboard to understand how to move fluidly between ideation and implementation.

Chapter 10: Visual Prompting in Design Tools

In this chapter, you are introduced to visual prompting, the practice of guiding tools like Framer AI to prototype layouts using natural language commands. This section explores the best practices for structuring prompts that respect visual hierarchy, while identifying the current limitations in AI-powered design tools.

Chapter 11: From AI Code to Live Website

This chapter guides you through the deployment pipeline to turn your generated code into a fully functional, publicly accessible website. You will learn to clean up the AI-generated code to meet industry standards and use platforms like GitHub and Vercel to launch your project.

Chapter 12: Refining AI-Generated Code

In this chapter, you will explore the crucial process of identifying and correcting AI hallucinations or inconsistencies to meet professional standards. This chapter teaches techniques for optimizing performance and accessibility compliance, ensuring that your final drafts are polished and production-ready.

Chapter 13: AI-Driven Frontend Mastery and Future Readiness

This is the final chapter that focuses on maintaining clean and sustainable code, while building a personalized prompt library to boost your long-term productivity. You will learn strategies to embrace evolving AI ecosystems confidently, and stay relevant in the ever-changing developer's job market!

DID YOU KNOW

Did you know that Orange Education Pvt Ltd offers eBook versions of every book published, with PDF and ePub files available? You can upgrade to the eBook version at **www.orangeava.com** and as a print book customer, you are entitled to a discount on the eBook copy. Get in touch with us at: **info@orangeava.com** for more details.

At **www.orangeava.com**, you can also read a collection of free technical articles, sign up for a range of free newsletters, and receive exclusive discounts and offers on Print Books and eBooks.

PIRACY

If you come across any illegal copies of our works in any form on the internet, we would be grateful if you would provide us with the location address or website name. Please contact us at **info@orangeava.com** with a link to the material.

ARE YOU INTERESTED IN AUTHORING WITH US?

If there is a topic that you have expertise in, and you are interested in either writing or contributing to a book, please write to us at **business@orangeava.com**. We are on a journey to help developers and tech professionals to gain insights on the present technological advancements and innovations happening across the globe and build a community that believes Knowledge is best acquired by sharing and learning with others. Please reach out to us to learn what our audience demands and how you can be part of this educational reform. We also welcome ideas from tech experts and help them build learning and development content for their domains.

REVIEWS

Please leave a review. Once you have read and used this book, why not leave a review on the site that you purchased it from? Potential readers can then see and use your unbiased opinion to make purchase decisions. We at Orange Education would love to know what you think about our products, and our authors can learn from your feedback. Thank you!

For more information about Orange Education, please visit **www.orangeava.com**.

Table of Contents

CHAPTER 1
Introduction to Prompt-Driven Web Development

Introduction

Prompt HTML *and* CSS, at their core, aims to have a hands-on, prompt-first approach that transforms your ideas into semantic, styled interfaces. This chapter kickstarts with the introduction of the emerging practices in prompt-driven frontend development. It explores how Artificial Intelligence (AI), specifically Large Language Models (LLMs) such as ChatGPT and GitHub Copilot are reshaping the way developers write HTML and CSS, moving beyond manual coding, into a new era of natural language-based interaction. You will discover prompting as a critical skill that complements traditional frontend expertise, expanding on what is possible with prompt-based workflows.

The chapter also provides a historical and technological context, tracing the evolution of web development from hand-coded HTML/CSS in text editors, through the rise of visual builders and low-code/no-code platforms, to today's AI-augmented workflows. We shall illustrate how prompt-driven development is not just a trend, but the next logical step towards more intuitive and efficient tools for building the Web. Furthermore, you are encouraged to rethink your web development role: from sole code author to orchestrator of AI-assisted systems that guide outcomes through well-crafted prompts. The chapter concludes with the introduction of hands-on, outcome-driven structure of the book, identifying who the book is for, and previewing the real-world projects that you will be able to build by the end of this book. It is a hands-on approach that offers a forward-looking perspective on how development environments are evolving from IDEs to browser-based, prompt-driven interfaces, and what this shift means for the future of frontend development.

After reading this chapter, you will be able to explore the evolution of HTML and CSS and explain how low-code and no-code tools paved the way for AI-assisted frontends. You will trace the key AI capabilities in modern web development and pinpoint the challenges and opportunities they introduce. You will articulate why a prompt-driven approach can streamline HTML/CSS generation and bridge the gap between design intent and code. You will also see how the developer's role is shifting toward prompt engineering, orchestration, and quality governance. You will learn how this book aligns with your goals and how to use its structure and exercises effectively. Finally, you will visualize the practical deliverables; UI blueprints, prompt workflows, and production-ready components, which you will build by the end of the book.

Structure

In this chapter, we will cover the following topics:

- A Brief History of HTML and CSS
- The Rise of Low-Code and No-Code Tools
- Overview of AI in Frontend Development
- Rethinking the Development Environment
- Challenges and Opportunities in AI-Driven Web Development
- Why Use Prompts for HTML/CSS
- The Changing Role of Developers
- Who Should Read This Book
- How to Use This Book
- What Readers Will Build by the End

A Brief History of HTML and CSS

The modern World Wide Web established from the union of HTML's structural clarity and CSS's expressive elegance has blossomed into a universe of dynamic interfaces, immersive media, and seamless interaction. Each day, we build upon this digital foundation, weaving layouts with Flexbox, orchestrating animations with keyframes, and adapting designs through responsive media queries. Still, rarely do we pause to honor the profound simplicity beneath this creative craft. These languages, once revolutionary in their intent, have become so deeply woven into the fabric of development that their origins are often eclipsed by their ubiquity. We forget that what Tim Berners-Lee and Håkon Wium Lie gave us were not merely tools, but a transformative paradigm; one that separated structure from style and, in doing so, redefined how humanity creates, shares, and experiences information on a global scale.

HyperText Markup Language (HTML) and Cascading Style Sheets (CSS) technologies have transformed the web from a research tool into the vibrant, interactive medium we now know it to be. Understanding their origin offers more than a technical narrative. It unveils a story of innovation, collaboration, and the relentless pursuit of a universal language for ideas. In this section, we will explore the history of HTML and CSS, the underlying technology to the present Web.

The Foundations beneath the Surface

Before HTML and CSS, the Internet existed as a decentralized network of computers, primarily used by researchers and military institutions. While protocols like TCP/IP, FTP, Telnet, and SMTP enabled communication and data transfer, the web-like navigation we know today was clearly absent.

In this fragmented ecosystem, there were bold attempts at linking information meaningfully and some of the events were as follows:

- Vannevar Bush's 1945 *Memex* envisioned a personal device that allowed users to browse linked documents.
- Ted Nelson, in the 1960s, coined the term *hypertext*, and conceptualized Project Xanadu, which aimed to implement non-linear writing and interlinked documents.
- Douglas Engelbart, in 1968, demonstrated the revolutionary *Mother of All Demos*, showcasing early hypertext systems, the mouse, and video conferencing.

However, none of these systems had global reach, scalability, or wide adoption. But here is the seed of the web, ENQUIRE. In 1980, Tim Berners-Lee, while working as a software consultant at CERN, built a personal knowledge management system called ENQUIRE. As Berners-Lee recalls in his book, *Weaving the Web*, ENQUIRE was designed to help organize relationships between people, software, and documentation at CERN. Let us examine the core features and functionality of the ENQUIRE prototype at the time, as outlined here:

- Broke information into individual units called nodes, each representing a specific concept or piece of knowledge.
- Linked these nodes together using typed, bi-directional connections, which described the relationship between ideas in both directions, allowing users to see how pieces of information were related contextually.
- Enabled users to build and explore a flexible, evolving web of knowledge, much like how modern tools similar to Roam Research or Obsidian help users link notes and ideas to support deeper thinking and learning.

In essence, ENQUIRE was a conceptual forerunner to the modern *linked thinking* tools used for personal knowledge management. Though limited to Berners-Lee's own use, ENQUIRE was conceptually radical, it planted the seeds of a system that would link ideas- charitable and commercial, across the globe. Next, we shall discuss the invention of the Web.

The Invention of the World Wide Web (1989–1991)

In 1989, upon returning to CERN, Berners-Lee revisited the core ideas of ENQUIRE, this time combining them with the emerging global infrastructure of the Internet. He proposed a system that allowed documents to link to each other through Universal Resource Identifiers (URLs), served via Hypertext Transfer Protocol (HTTP), and rendered using a markup language, HTML.

By 1991, the first web page was published on a NeXT computer at CERN. It explained what the World Wide Web was and how to use it. This foundational system includes HTML for structuring information, HTTP for communication and URL as the addressing system.

Berners-Lee emphasized simplicity and openness. As he wrote in *Weaving the Web*, *"The dream behind the Web is of a common information space in which we communicate by sharing information."*

With the foundational concepts in place, Berners-Lee needed a simple, accessible way to format and link content on the web. This thinking led to the creation of HTML, the first markup language for the Web.

The First Markup for the Web

HTML was inspired by the Standard Generalized Markup Language (SGML), but was simplified for practical use. It used tags like `<h1>`, `<p>`, `<a>`, and `<img>` to structure content.

The first HTML specification (1991) had only 18 tags, and focused on the following:

- Headings and paragraphs
- Lists
- Hyperlinks (`<a href>`)
- Inline images

This lean design made HTML easy to learn and implement, a crucial factor for early adoption. By 1993, Marc Andreessen and colleagues at NCSA released Mosaic, the first graphical web browser. Mosaic's popularity spurred a race among tech companies to build their own browsers. As commercial interest exploded, Netscape and Microsoft Internet Explorer began adding proprietary tags like `<blink>`, `<marquee>`, and `<font>`. This era, known as the browser wars, introduced non-standard HTML extensions that created chaos for developers and fractured web compatibility. Amid this chaos, Berners-Lee formed the World Wide Web Consortium (W3C) in 1994 to guide web standards.

While HTML handled structure and linking, it lacked visual design tools, prompting the need for a better way to style web pages. This gap led to the development of CSS, which marked a turning point in the visual evolution of the Web.

The Styling Revolution

While HTML allowed documents to be structured and hyperlinked, early web pages looked stark. Designers used tables, inline fonts, and spacer GIFs to simulate layouts, often leading to bloated and inaccessible code. Let take a quick look at the first website on the Internet as developed by Tim Berners-Lee:

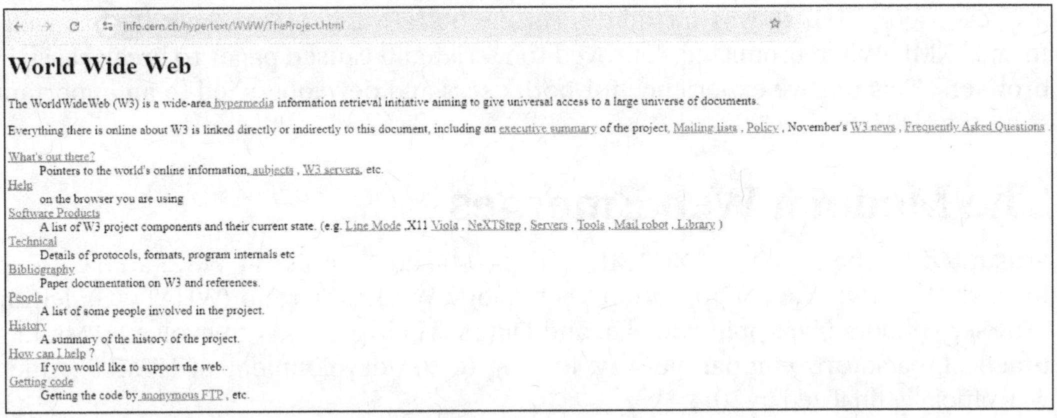

Figure 1.1: *Screenshot Showing the Image of the First Website on the Internet*

In 1994, Håkon Wium Lie, then working with Berners-Lee at CERN, proposed Cascading Style Sheets (CSS), a separate language for styling web pages. The proposal addressed the growing need for visual control over web content. CSS separated content (HTML) from presentation, allowing developers to define colors, fonts, margins, and layout properties in a central style sheet. It also introduced the cascading rules, giving priority to the most specific styles.

CSS1 was officially released in 1996, and CSS2 followed in 1998, introducing positioning, z-index, and media types. But browser support was inconsistent, Internet Explorer supported only parts of the standard, and Netscape Navigator was even less compliant. It was only after the Web Standards Project (WaSP) formed in the late 1990s did pressure mount for browsers to adhere to CSS specifications. As Dave Raggett noted in his W3C account, collaboration was the key: "*The Web had grown so quickly that no single person or organization could steer it... cooperation across industry and academia became vital.*"

With the turn of the millennium, the Web had moved beyond simple pages of formatted text, HTML4 and its XML-based successor, XHTML, ushered in a new era in which the very tags we used began to carry the meaning as well as style, setting the stage for today's rich, machine-understandable semantic Web.

HTML4, XHTML, and the Rise of Semantics

Prior to HTML4, earlier versions of HTML like HTML+, HTML 2.0, and HTML 3.2 established a solid foundation for structuring web content but offered limited design and interactive capabilities. These versions were largely focused on basic formatting and linking, with little standardization for layout or scripting. However, in 1997, HTML4 added major improvements like tables, forms, and scripting support. Accessibility features such as *alt text and* internationalization support were added. But as the web matured, developers misused HTML for layout instead of structure, again polluting the separation of concerns CSS was meant to solve. To address HTML's lax syntax and improve rigor, XHTML was introduced in 1999. XHTML is HTML rewritten as well-formed XML. While promising, it proved too strict and caused pages to break easily in browsers. This tensive experience for both users and developers led to an important shift, the HTML5 and CSS3.

The Modern Web Emerges

Frustrated by the rigidity of XHTML, and the stalled progress at W3C, a new group formed: Web Hypertext Application Technology Working Group (WHATWG), led by browser vendors like Apple, Mozilla, and Opera. Their goal was to evolve HTML in a practical, backward-compatible way, leading to the development of HTML5, which was officially finalized in 2014.

HTML5 laid the groundwork for contemporary web applications by introducing native support for audio and video through the `<audio>` and `<video>` elements, integrated graphics capabilities via the `<canvas>` element and Scalable Vector Graphics (SVG), as well as a suite of new semantic tags including `<article>`, `<section>`, `<header>`, and `<footer>`. Additionally, it offered powerful web APIs to support features such as geolocation, offline storage, and real-time communication. In parallel to these advancements, CSS3 marked a significant departure from previous styling conventions. Released in modular form, CSS3 introduced transformative capabilities such as Flexbox and Grid for sophisticated layouts, media queries to facilitate responsive design across devices, and dynamic visual effects through transitions, animations, and transformations. CSS3 also enabled developers to utilize custom properties, commonly known as CSS variables, and greatly expanded typographic possibilities with features like @font-face and integration with Google Fonts. Collectively, HTML5 and CSS3 empowered developers to build rich, interactive, and highly responsive web applications directly in the browser, eliminating the need for external plugins or complex workarounds. Together, HTML5 and CSS3 enabled complex, interactive applications in the browser without plugins or hacks.

With component-driven frameworks like React, Vue, and Svelte gaining popularity, developers began styling components inside JavaScript. Libraries like styled components and Emotion brought CSS into the JS ecosystem, a controversial, yet powerful trend. At the same time, Web Components standardized via Shadow DOM and HTML templates promised reusable, and encapsulated HTML/CSS/JS units, an echo of ENQUIRE's modular nodes.

Now, with AI tools now generating code from prompts, HTML and CSS have graciously entered a new golden era. Designers and developers are increasingly capable of using natural language to scaffold pages, while tools like GitHub Copilot and Framer abstract the boilerplate. Beneath these tools still lie the bedrock languages of the web: HTML and CSS.

From ENQUIRE's semantic nodes in 1980 to today's dynamic web apps and AI-powered design systems, the journey of HTML and CSS reflects humanity's deep desire to connect, organize, and share knowledge.

In *Weaving the Web*, Berners-Lee writes:

"The Web is not a network of computers; it is a network of people."

HTML and CSS gave this network its language and style; simple, yet powerful tools that turned linked documents into a global conversation.

As we stand at the threshold of new paradigms like AI-driven interfaces, immersive WebXR, decentralized identity, the humble markup and style languages remain as relevant as ever. HTML and CSS are the lingua franca of the digital world, a legacy of open collaboration and the relentless pursuit of human connection.

As web technologies like HTML5 and CSS3 matured and the capabilities of the browser expanded, attention began to shift toward simplifying the development process itself, paving the way for the rise of low-code and no-code tools.

Next, we shall be discussing the rise of low-code and no-code tools. This is important because it highlights the evolving nature of web development. Today, even non-technical users can participate in the global digital ecosystem.

The Rise of Low-Code and No-Code Tools

The idea of low-code and no-code starts long before these terms were coined. In the days of Visual Basic, Delphi, and PowerBuilder, when developers were already trying to speed up applications building by dragging and dropping pieces instead of hand-writing every line of codes. That spirit evolved through model-driven ideas in the 2000s, and in 2014 Forrester, an independent market research and advisory firm gave it a name: low-code. Almost alongside that broader movement, no-code platforms like Bubble began pushing the idea further. Bubble's co-founder Josh Haas, after watching his non-technical partner Jody Apap struggle to launch and sustain *KeywordSmart*, a platform that helps photographers and image asset managers catalog, find, and maintain their photo libraries. Without an engineer, he left that project in 2012 with the explicit goal of building a visual platform so domain experts could create full web applications themselves with no traditional programming knowledge.

Forrester has been one of the loudest voices of the low-code and no-code movement. It is believed that these platforms let teams move faster by blending professional developers and business users, cutting down the time it takes to get apps to end users. However, this book introduces a prompt-augmented low-code and a prompt assisted no-code. This is a frontend development approach where developers use visual building blocks to assemble interfaces quickly and invoke natural-language prompts to generate, customize, or extend underlying HTML/CSS/JS or component logic. It combines the speed of visual composition with the precision of prompt-generated code for behaviors the visual builder does not natively support.

Interestingly, when aEleanor H. Brooks, the managing partner at Brooks & Finley Law, found herself waiting weeks for a dashboard that would give her real-time insight into client intake, she did something different: she opened *Budibase*, dragged prebuilt widgets into place, connected them to internal data, injected a sliver of custom CSS to align branding, and had a working, deployable tool by afternoon. That one afternoon erased a two-month backlog. It shifted operational decision-making closer to the frontline and carefully illustrated a fundamental change in who gets to build software. Low-code and no-code platforms have not simply added new tools to the developer's toolbox, they have reshaped the topology of software creation, moving agency out of central engineering queues into the hands of those closest to problems. This decentralization is both amazing and strategic. It promises speed, inclusion, and alignment, while demanding new kinds of oversight and collaboration.

Democratizing Creation and Collapsing Timelines

The recent surge in low-code/no-code adoption is more than a passing trend; it is a structural realignment in how organizations deliver digital capabilities. Enterprises facing chronic backlogs, talent shortages, and rapidly shifting requirements are turning to these platforms to unlock latent capacity. What once required requests routed through traditional dev schedule and weeks of sprints now begins with business users visually composing applications. Forward-looking companies are launching structured citizen development programs to give non-technical employees clear responsibilities while reducing the risks of unapproved tool use. Meanwhile, recent studies show that low-code/no-code technologies are becoming central tools, not a peripheral to the delivery strategies of digital transformation initiatives, a core delivery model.

Visual Abstraction with HTML and CSS under the Hood

Low-code and no-code tools often look like effortless composition, dragging a hero section into place, wiring a form to a backend in a few clicks, but what they produce is not mystical. Underneath the visual layer is a familiar, standards-based web technology: HTML gives the structure, CSS controls the presentation, and JavaScript adds interactivity. Platforms like Webflow make the design-to-code process transparent, your visual layout is instantly converted into clean, production-ready HTML and CSS that you can export. A designer can visually assemble a responsive landing page, and the system emits semantic <section> elements, accessible `<img>` tags with alt text, and well-scoped styling. The result is HTML and CSS powered website that can live beyond the platform if needed. That apparent simplicity comes with a catch. When the underlying structure is treated as a black box, you get what practitioners called *HTMLHell:* disorganized interfaces that are hard to maintain, hurt accessibility, obscure your intent, and even slow performance. Low-code/no-code tools reduce many traditional mistakes, but they do not eliminate the need for thoughtful oversight. Front-end enthusiasts, developers, and architects need to act as stewards verifying that exported markup preserves semantic clarity, that custom CSS does not introduce regressions, and that accessibility is built in from the start instead of tacked on later. Business professionals can push the boundaries of what can be composed visually; however, it is a collective responsibility of the designers, frontend developers and architects to oversee the moment when a visual asset or prototype gets turned into a production code. Exported markup can only succeed in live environment if the output is interpretable, standards-aligned, and clean. Clear conventions, documented structure, and collaboration between creators and technical reviewers ensure that what looks simple on the surface remains robust, performant, and sustainable underneath.

In a nutshell, the rise of low-code and no-code development marks a cultural and technical inflection point. Low-code/no-code is reshaping how work gets done by lowering build barriers and tightening feedback loops. The real power shows up when business users, developers, designers, and governance partners collaborate on shared standards backed by HTML/CSS as the durable foundation. The invitation to you and organizations is clear: audit one key backlog item for low-code/no-code acceleration, pair a business user with an engineer in a co-creation experiment and embed governance early on with transformation that balances freedom and responsibility.

Next, we shall discuss AI in the frontend development. As AI-driven tools become more sophisticated, they are reshaping every phase of frontend development as well, from automating repetitive tasks to enhancing design and accessibility.

Overview of AI in Frontend Development

Frontend development is changing in real time. What used to mean manually assembling HTML, hand-tuning CSS, and endless circling between design and Quality Assurance (QA)—designs iteration, has become a co-creative process with intelligent assistants. Artificial intelligence is not a background curiosity anymore; it is stepping up as a co-author, editor, and validator in modern interface building. For a frontend enthusiast or mid-level developer, this is not a minor tool upgrade. It is a disruptive shift in how we develop frontend. You would discover that your afternoon-long chores like scaffolding responsive layouts, producing accessible markup, and enforcing consistent theming are now routinely accelerated or augmented by models that understand plain language, infer design intent, and emit production-ready code. And if you are a beginner, you are one of the core audiences for this book. Nearly everyone is quietly witnessing a rewrite of how UIs are conceived and delivered: simple autocomplete has given way to context-aware suggestions, which are evolving into prompt-driven composition engines spanning design-to-code pipelines. This evolution has two practical implications. First, learners can climb the curve faster. A well-crafted prompt acts as a live scaffold for internalizing semantics, layout strategies, and style system conventions. Second, experienced developers are relieved of repetitive plumbing or HTML/CSS weaving and can invest more deeply in system coherence, extensibility, performance tuning, and mentoring non-technical associates. The excitement is real, but so is the responsibility. Lasting productivity depends on knowing how these AI capabilities interact with HTML and CSS, how to prompt them effectively, and how to validate their output and ensure that it remains semantic, accessible, secure, and aligned with broader architectural intent.

Translating Intent to Interface

At its core, AI in frontend development is collapsing the distance between idea and implementation, turning plain-language intent into structured, styled, production-ready UI faster. You can describe a hero section with a gradient background, a clear call to action, and a mobile-first layout. These are well examined and implemented in this course of this book. An AI assistant can emit semantic HTML with appropriate <section> hierarchy and headings, scaffold responsive CSS using Flexbox or Grid, and surface accessibility improvements like alt text suggestions and contrast checks, all in a few iterative prompts. These models have absorbed common patterns from web best practices and can be steered to match conventions such as BEM-style class naming, CSS custom properties, or theme variants like dark/light mode. The value goes beyond the pure generation. Modern tooling increasingly couples suggestion with validation: accessibility-aware extensions remind builders about compliance as they work, and intelligent nudges flag semantic or structural issues before they become entrenched. This kind of augmented pair programming embeds awareness, semantic correctness, ARIA usage, and performance trade-offs into the composition loop instead of leaving it as an afterthought.

The benefits become concrete in everyday work. Imagine Michelle, a frontend developer at a growing SaaS startup with two years of experience. She was tasked with a promotional landing page that included a responsive product comparison module and an accessible signup form. Traditionally, laying out the comparison, writing utility styles, and iterating for mobile behavior would have consumed three to four hours plus testing. This time, she opened her AI assistant and prompted: "*Generate a two-column comparison section with headers, icons, subtle hover transitions, and an accessible signup form beneath; responsive for mobile with a stacked fallback.*" Within twenty minutes, she had a clean HTML/CSS skeleton. She followed up with requests for a reduced-motion variant and a dark theme. The output arrived with semantic markup, aria annotations, and CSS variables for theming. After a quick integrity review, her standard guardrail pass, and she shipped. The campaign that followed saw a 12% lift in form completions, and her build time shrank by over 75%. Michelle's takeaway: "AI *did not replace my judgment. It let me prototype, validate, and polish in the same window. I spent more time refining the experience instead of wrestling with base layout.*"

That example highlights the dual contribution of AI: speed and scaffolding. It does not eliminate the need to understand HTML and CSS. It amplifies learning. When developers inspect generated output, they see structure, trace style origins, and internalize conventions by editing, turning suggestions into hands-on lessons. The real leverage comes from the AI-human partnership: intelligent generation guided by human judgment, with oversight ensuring that output is semantic, accessible, and aligned with broader design and architectural intent.

Turning Design Intent into Actionable Markup

The difference between an AI assistant that generates noise and one that delivers usable frontend markup comes down to how you ask. In this context, prompt engineering means translating visual intent, behavior expectations, and technical constraints into clear, actionable instructions. In *Chapter 3: Prompt Engineering for HTML and CSS*, we unpack methods, patterns, and refinement tactics in depth, but a few practical principles up front will help you get better output faster.

- **Be specific.**

  Do not say *build a form*. Say instead:

  "*Create a signup form with three fields—email, password, and an 'agree to terms' checkbox. Show inline errors beneath invalid inputs. Include aria-describedby for help text and disable the submit button until all fields are valid.*" The model cannot infer everything. The more concrete you are about structure, behavior, and accessibility, the closer the first pass will be.

- **Iterate.**

  Prompting is a conversation, not a one-off magic wand sentence. Start with a base prompt, inspect what is returned, then layer your follow-ups:

  " *Simplify the CSS to remove unused selectors.*"

"Add a reduced-motion variant."

"Adjust the layout so the comparison columns stack on narrow screens."

- **Anchor in context.**

  Give examples or conventions you want the output to follow. For instance, *"Use utility-style class names like mb2, employ CSS custom properties for colors, and favor semantic elements (<section>, <h2>) over div."* This helps the model align with your existing design system style.

- **Chain prompts.**

  Break the work into stages: one pass generates semantic HTML, the next applies theming (dark/light, reduced motion), and a third makes it responsive or adds accessibility annotations. Each step conditions the next, keeping complexity manageable.

The exploration of deeper techniques is expected in *Chapter 3: Prompt Engineering for HTML and CSS*, but the core takeaway now is this, prompt engineering is not a single perfect phrasing. It is a dialogue pattern. Each prompt is an experiment in expressing intent; the model's output becomes feedback that shapes your next input.

Rethinking the Development Environment

The mechanics of integrating AI into your frontend development flow is hinged on the tools and orchestration around them. At the heart of many developers', toolkits are intelligent pair programmers like GitHub Copilot, ChatGPT and conversational assistants that sit in the editors' interfaces. These tools provide recommendations as you type, suggest entire component scaffolds, and can even infer appropriate CSS based on preceding markup. But the most effective AI partnerships treat AI as a collaborator, and not a substitute. Developers boost its output by giving it context like file history, naming conventions, surrounding code and guiding it with focused corrections. This allows human developers to supply anchors and selective corrections. Beyond in-editor copilots, ChatGPT, a growing ecosystem of specialized AI-powered utilities complements and extends this capability. You can come across a curated collection of these tools catalog on a wide array of assistance, from snippet generation to UI composition to documentation synthesis.

Design-to-code pipelines increasingly incorporate AI into major steps. Emerging offerings like Google's Stitch, announced at Google I/O 2025 allow you to supply textual descriptions or reference sketches and receive full UI variants with corresponding HTML/CSS output. Stitch can iterate conversationally, adjust themes, and export to formats compatible with design tools or direct application embedding, blurring the boundary between brainstorming and implementation.

Workflows that maximize AI's utility tend to interleave human validation checkpoints. A typical cycle starts with intent capture a brief description of the component or layout, followed by prompt-driven generation. You can then ensure a quick integrity guard review to validate semantics and accessibility, with necessary customization. Then, you can finally integrate the code into a version control pipeline. This *prompt-iterate-validate* rhythm brings discipline to what might otherwise be a loose experiment. For beginners, the entry point often begins with simple browser-based interfaces or IDE plugins that expose the model's suggestions directly. As your comfort grows, you add on more advanced patterns like using AI to generate accessible form components, asking for performance-optimized CSS, or auto-creating variants for internationalization. The detailed exploration of these platforms, extension points, and best practices appears in *Chapter 2, Tools and Setup for Prompt-Based Development*. The discussion will reflect a blending of design, coding, and machine-mediated insight in a typical developers daily routine.

Having re-imagined the modern development environment, we will now explore the challenges and opportunities that AI-driven web development brings.

Challenges and Opportunities in AI-Driven Web Development

AI-driven web development sits at the intersection of human creativity and machine intelligence, with the promise to reshape how we build, deploy, and maintain modern applications. This transformation brings its own set of challenges to overcome and breakthroughs to celebrate. In this section, we will explore both sides of the coin using real world illustrations that allow developers- beginners, mid-level well as business owners mapping out their digital strategy.

Let us start discussion with the AI-Markup integration complexity!

Integrating AI into Markup and Styles

Integrating AI-driven capabilities into traditional markup and styling workflows presents both, technical hurdles and strategic opportunities. Most legacy codebases rely on static HTML templates, CSS preprocessors, or CSS-in-JS architectures designed long before AI-assisted frontends became feasible. Introducing model-driven features such as on-the-fly layout generators or automated style recommendations often demands refactoring monolithic components and disentangling deeply nested style dependencies. You can treat AI-generated snippets like any other external resource and pull them in with pure HTML and CSS. Let us examine a simple pattern using an **`<object>`** tag for the HTML and a **`<link>`** for the CSS:

```
<!DOCTYPE html>
<html lang="en">
<head>
<meta charset="UTF-8" />
<title>AI Hero Section (</title>
<!-- 1. Pull in AI-generated CSS as an external stylesheet -->
<link
rel="stylesheet"
href="https://api.example.com/layout.css?prompt=Clean, tech-startup
style with subtle animation"
onerror="this.disabled = true"
  />
<style>
    /* 2. Fallback styles if AI CSS fails to load */
    #hero-fallback {
      background: #eee;
      padding: 2rem;
      text-align: center;
      font-family: sans-serif;
      color: #333;
    }
</style>
</head>
<body>
<!-- 3. Embed AI-generated HTML snippet -->
<object
    id="ai-hero"
    type="text/html"
    data="https://api.example.com/layout.html?prompt=Clean, tech-startup
style with subtle animation"
    width="100%"
    height="400"
    style="border:none"
>
<!-- 4. Fallback content if the <object> can't load -->
<div id="hero-fallback">
<h1>Welcome to Our Site</h1>
<p>Your default hero section has appeared. </p>
</div>
</object>
</body>
</html>
```

In the previous code, when the page loads, the browser first fetches the AI-generated CSS via a standard `<link>` tag pointing to your layout service. If that stylesheet fails to load, or contains errors, the `onerror` attribute automatically disables it, so it will not break your existing styles. At the same time, you include a small inline `<style>` block with basic hero-section rules so your site still looks polished even without the AI's enhancements. Next, you embed the AI's HTML snippet inside an `<object>` tag, which pulls in the fragment scoped with its own class names like `.ai-hero` and `.ai-cta`, and keeps it isolated from your main document's markup. If the AI endpoint cannot deliver valid HTML, or is unreachable, the browser falls back to the static `<div>` you placed inside the `<object>`, ensuring that your hero section always renders something functional. By treating AI snippets as self-contained widgets loaded via HTML includes, you get dynamic, on-demand layouts and theming while keeping your static HTML/CSS codebase clean and stable.

Relying on AI endpoints for pure HTML and CSS embeds brings both hurdles and promise: on one hand, you risk flickering unstyled content or broken layouts when the service is slow or returns conflicting class names, and you must guard against leaking any user data in your prompts; on the other, you unlock the power of instant theming and modular updates, simply tweaking a URL query can restyle your hero section or card component without touching local files, and by providing lightweight inline fallbacks you ensure a solid baseline experience even if the AI is unavailable, all without the overhead of JavaScript or complex build pipelines.

Next, we shall discuss quality, bias and explainability, part of challenges and opportunity of AI driven web development. Before you roll out AI-generated styles, it is essential you ensure quality, mitigate bias, and maintain explainability, so that every output aligns with your brand standards and accessibility goals.

Quality, Bias, and Explainability

Generative AI models, by virtue of being trained on large, diverse web data, inherently carry the biases of their original data sources. When applied to CSS theming or markup generation, these biases can manifest as default design choices, such as color palettes skewed toward trendy neon or dark-mode aesthetics, typography scales optimized for headlines rather than body text. Even you can have the spacing conventions tailored to desktop rather than mobile layouts. Such defaults risk clashing with established brand guidelines, undermining visual coherence, and even compromising accessibility. For instance, an AI might pick very bright text colors that are easy to read, but proves to be tiring on the eyes over time, or it might space letters so widely that they break the layout. Without mechanisms to catch and fix these biases early, you will end up constantly cleaning up AI outputs instead of guiding them towards the right design style. A real-world example of this issue occurs when an e-commerce platform uses an AI-powered widget to apply themes to its product cards. The model, having ingested thousands of fashions and retail sites, overuses neon highlights and giant headline fonts. Shoppers in one region see product cards in bright yellow green, clashing with the brand's earth tones, and text so big that descriptions get cut off or buttons drop out of view. This mismatch not only confuses customers, but also creates more support tickets and forces design rollbacks. To fix this, the team adds metadata to each card request that only allows approved colors and font sizes. The quick patch adds metadata to each request to enforce approved colors and font sizes, but it does not reveal how the model makes decisions. A better approach is to include a *style card* with every AI snippet, listing the exact hue, saturation, font size, line-height, and spacing ranges used. With that info, teams can spot outliers like low contrast backgrounds and tweak allowed scales. A central prompt-tuning dashboard then lets non-technical stakeholders adjust prior hue ranges, or spacing rules through an easy UI instead of rewriting the code.

Over time, this approach yields compounding benefits. Designers retain creative control and can trust that AI-driven suggestions will adhere to brand equity and accessibility standards. Developers swap one-off metadata hacks for a single middleware layer that enforces style rules and flags policy breaches. This gives stakeholders a clear audit trail of every design decision, vital for compliance. By pairing AI theming with built-in explainability and bias checks, teams can innovate on demand without losing consistency or brand integrity. With those guardrails on quality, bias, and explainability in place, the next priority is protecting form inputs and user-generated content.

Protecting Form Inputs and User-Generated Content

When AI features like autocomplete or content generation touch form fields, whether suggesting addresses, filling in contact details, or drafting emails, they typically send whatever you type names, street numbers, private notes off to external AI servers for processing. If this sensitive information is not explicitly scrubbed first, it can end up logged in plain text on those servers or in intermediary logs, creating a serious risk of data leaks and non-compliance with privacy regulations like GDPR, CCPA, or HIPAA. Users might unknowingly expose their home addresses, medical details, or private conversations, therefore erode trust and invite potential legal penalties. A short-term workaround is to introduce a proxy layer within your application: before any data leaves the browser, the proxy strips out or masks Personally Identifiable Information (PII), then forwards only the minimal context such as city names or zip codes to the AI endpoint. Once the AI returns its safe suggestions, the proxy re-injects them client-side. While effective, this scrub-and-forward adds extra maintenance and latency.

A more robust, long-term strategy is hybrid inference. You deploy sensitive workloads like address completion or payment data handling on privately hosted or on-premises AI models kept within your secure network perimeter. Less sensitive tasks, such as generating themed HTML email templates or marketing copy, can still leverage scalable cloud hosted AI. You can then complement this setup by tokenizing user inputs in the browser, replacing real strings with reversible placeholders, so that actual PII never leaves the client. Together with end-to-end encryption, strict sanitization rules, and clear data-flow boundaries, these measures let teams harness AI's speed and personalization benefits for forms and content without compromising user privacy or regulatory compliance. Now is the time to optimize performance and control costs by caching AI-generated styles and throttling inference calls.

Caching Styles and Throttling Inference

Real-time AI requests for styling like generating CSS on every hover or viewport change, cause noticeable delays often 0.5 s per action and skyrocket API costs. Modern design tools aim for on-the-fly AI enhancements, but these calls can interfere with the fast feedback loops pivotal to designers and content creators. For example, a headless CMS saw a 300 % monthly cost spike and sluggish live previews until engineers added a context-hash cache using page slug, user ID, and viewport width) to reuse previous HTML/CSS blobs instead of making redundant API calls. To reduce both latency and expenses, teams should:

- Cache intelligently with the implementation of client- or proxy-side caching with smart keys, so identical AI prompts hit the cache instead of the API.
- Batch rapid UI events like typing, slider drags, breakpoint tweaks into single inference requests rather than one per event.
- Run smaller, specialized local models for common layout patterns and reserve cloud-hosted LLMs for complex or unique prompts.
- Track cache hit rates, API usage, and median response times, then adjust TTLs, throttle thresholds, and distillation coverage based on real metrics.

This combined approach restores instant feedback, smooth out UI interactions, and keeps the cloud bills in check. By balancing caching, rate-limiting, and local inference, teams can deliver AI-powered design tools that feel instant and remain cost-effective. Now, we will discuss how tracing broken styles back to the model ensure reliability, you need a clear observability strategy that lets you trace broken styles back to the exact AI prompt and model version that generated them.

Tracing Broken Styles Back to the Model

Generative AI introduces a new layer of complexity into frontend pipelines, one that traditional debugging tools were not built to address. Browser developer consoles can highlight CSS specificity clashes, show JavaScript exceptions, or even step through execution with breakpoints, but they offer no visibility into the upstream AI processes that produced a malformed snippet. When an AI-generated block of CSS keyframes is missing a closing brace or contains invalid property names, the browser simply drops the entire rule or fails silently, leaving layouts broken or animations stalled without any clear error message. Dev teams can spend hours digging through components, utility functions, or build configs, only to find a bad AI response like a truncated payload was the real culprit. Without prompt-level diagnostics, every broken style turns into a detective story across tools, preprocessors, caches, and sanitizers. Traditional dev tools cannot link broken CSS or animations back to the AI prompt, so teams waste hours chasing unrelated code paths. By logging each prompt, response time, HTTP status, and running CSS validity checks, a team found a 500-ms timeout was truncating keyframes; increasing the timeout and retrying partial results restored the carousel overnight. So, treat AI as first-class telemetry, log prompts and outputs with metadata and validation results, define service level objective, automate alerts on threshold breaches and then drilldown dashboards linking failures to exact prompt, model version, and environment.

Next, we shall discuss how building a team of frontend developers skilled in prompt engineering and AI best practices not only fills critical talent gaps but also unlocks opportunities for faster prototyping, smarter design systems, and truly interactive web experiences.

Talent and Skill Gaps

Bridging traditional web development and conversational AI means teaching developers to write prompts that deliver clean HTML and maintainable CSS. This calls for intuition and accessibility expertise. Without it, teams deploy bloated, nested code with verbose styles. For example, junior devs used mobile-first CSS grid card with hover effect and got inefficient CSS until pairing with senior designers and prompt-engineering workshops to specify breakpoints, semantic wrappers, and ARIA tags. To upskill at scale, organizations can embed AI-for-CSS modules into their internal learning platforms. These might include interactive sandboxes where developers iterate on prompts and immediately preview generated HTML/CSS, complete with linting and a11y warnings. Complementing these sandboxes with low-code AI editors that suggest prompt improvements flagging missing alt attributes or proposing more concise grid definitions helps democratize prompt expertise without demanding a deep dive into machine-learning theory. Over time, a culture of prompt review and shared best practices transforms prompt engineering from a niche skill into a core competency, empowering frontend teams to harness AI creatively and responsibly.

Having discussed some of the key challenges and opportunities in AI-Driven web development, it is time to explore the real advantages of leveraging prompts to generate HTML and CSS in frontend development.

Why Use Prompts for HTML/CSS

Whether you are a beginner, mid-level developer, or simply a curious learner of UI, turning ideas into real browser-rendered interfaces is often a major challenge in frontend development. Imagine you need a responsive comparison block, a themed card, or an accessible form, only to get bogged down in nested containers, class-name management, breakpoints, and semantic markup. Prompts remove much of these frictions. Instead of struggling with syntax, you can simply describe your intent in plain language. An AI-assisted system then returns structured HTML and CSS that matches your vision. This is not a shortcut around craftsmanship; it is a force multiplier. By translating your ideas into machine-readable prompts, you can scaffold usable markup instantly and learn as you go. This gives you speed and control in equal measure. The deeper opportunity is that this interaction can shift how you build mental models. Instead of memorizing every layout trick up front, you can prompt for a semantic structure, inspect the returned code, ask follow-up questions to understand why certain tags were chosen, and then iterate, turning each prompt into a compact, embedded tutorial.

How AI Helps with HTML and CSS

The current generation of AI tools has internalized many recurring patterns of web layout, styling, responsiveness, and accessibility. When prompted effectively, they can synthesize semantic HTML structures, compose CSS for both desktop and mobile breakpoints, and apply theming coherently to all in a matter of seconds. A clearly phrased request like "Generate a two-column product comparison section with icons, hover transitions, and an accessible signup form below; ensure mobile fallback stacks gracefully" yields markup with appropriate elements, heading hierarchies, aria annotations, and CSS using modern layout techniques such as Flexbox or Grid. Beyond new layouts, AI helps refactor and optimize the existing code: it can simplify over-specific selectors, convert hardcoded values into CSS variables or BEM class names, and suggest performance tweaks to reduce repaints. It also flags a11y issues, missing form labels, contrast failures, or improper heading order and offers compliant fixes on demand, training your intuition as you work.

Illustratively, consider Mabel, a mid-level frontend developer at a fast-growing e-commerce startup. Her task was to build a reusable product card component that displayed images, price comparisons, ratings, and an "`Add to Cart`" call to action; it had to adapt across viewport sizes and support a high-contrast theme for accessibility. Instead of starting with boilerplate, she opened her AI assistant, fed it a concise prompt: "*Create a responsive product card with an image on the left, product details on the right, rating stars, and a primary* CTA; *support a toggleable high-contrast mode and stacking layout for mobile*" and received structured HTML and CSS in less than ten minutes. She followed up with "*Refactor class names to follow* BEM *conventions and extract colors into CSS variables*, then asked for "*a version with reduced motion for users who prefer it.*"

The resulting implementation required only a quick review and minor manual polish. The component rolled out across three product categories, reducing build time from what would have been two days to less than four hours, and internal A/B tracking showed a 9% increase in engagement for the high-contrast variant. Mabel noted, "Prompts did not do the thinking for me; they gave me a scaffold I could interrogate, improve, and own."

Next, we will discuss the changing role of developers. As AI takes on more of the repetitive and boilerplate work, developers are shifting from solely writing code to orchestrating AI-driven workflows, curating prompts, and focusing on higher-level design and strategy.

The Changing Role of Developers

Obviously, developers are not being pushed out, instead, roles are shifting. Today's engineers increasingly act as curators and enablers: you build the scaffolds, create reusable extensions, define safe APIs, and manage the handoffs that let non-technical creators assemble pieces into resilient systems. Developers' real leverage is in handling complexity, managing integration points, assuring quality, and augmenting visual platforms with custom logic that the drag-and-drop layer cannot encapsulate alone. At the same time, the frontier is expanding as artificial intelligence moves to assist in composing user interfaces, data structures, and application behavior. New tools can infer data models from plain descriptions, suggest interface patterns, auto-generate styling themes, and even turn natural-language requirements into working application logic. That accelerates the journey from idea to software, collapsing friction, but speed without structure brings risk. AI can propose a component or scaffold, but it cannot replace the human judgment needed to ensure that the output is semantic, accessible, secure, and consistent with broader architectural intentions. The future will favor ecosystems where intelligent assistance is paired with standards-aware oversight and thoughtful stewardship. This is exactly why the conversations this book matter. It is not just a catalog of features and capabilities, it a hands-on guide for building shared understanding between the developers, builders, and the AI layer. Through examples, checklists, discussion prompts, and decision frameworks, this book helps you to establish lightweight guardrails and review checkpoints that cushion rapid composition with constructive oversight. You then know when to accept AI suggestions, when to refactor, and when to escalate to a developer. Embedding prompt templates and evaluation criteria, so that AI-generated output is solicited and assessed in ways that align with semantic and performance expectations.

Who Should Read This Book

This book is for anyone who cares about building user interfaces faster, smarter, and with more intention, whether you are just beginning your frontend journey, already shipping components as a mid-level developer, or a designer/enthusiast curious about how prompt engineering can bridge vision and code. You do not need ML expertise; one requires only the curiosity about using your natural language as precise instructions, and a willingness to collaborate with AI. If you have ever had difficulty with responsive layouts, accessibility tweaks, or theme consistency, or if you are a product manager or tech lead aiming to scale quality and reduce cognitive overhead, this book is for you.

How to Use This Book

This book is designed for hands-on, prompt-first approach use. It is recommended to work through it as you go, rather than simply reading it straight. Master the Prompt–Refine–Validate cycle by pasting a sample prompt into your AI assistant, reviewing the HTML and CSS it returns, and tweaking your prompts. Each chapter presents clear objectives, adaptable prompt recipes, quick exercises, and tips to help you build your own prompt catalog. Clone the companion GitHub repo to explore how we arrived at the projects we built in this book. You can also add generated components to your project, run accessibility checks, and compare variants. Stop regularly to apply what you learnt to real code in your own codebase. As you practice, you will use prompts not just to generate isolated snippets but to enforce consistency across related UI components. The book's framework will serve as both a checklist and your creative scaffold.

What Readers Will Build by the End

By the end of this book, you would have transformed ad-hoc prompt experiments into a repeatable frontend workflow. You will not only learn to plan complete UI blueprints with prompts, but moreover, to turn those blueprints into three real-world projects, a responsive personal bio page, a modern fintech landing page, and an IoT dashboard component layout. Along the way, you will review and iterate on AI-generated interfaces against accessibility, responsiveness, and branding standards, building a library of prompt-driven components like cards, forms, headers, comparison blocks with semantic HTML and CSS-variable theming such as light/dark modes. You will also implement a *Prompt–Refine–Validate* guardrail, integrate these workflows into visual tools like Framer, and assemble a custom prompt recipe catalog that enforces your project's naming conventions and design tokens. After reading this book, you will own a reproducible, production-ready pipeline for AI-assisted frontend development.

Conclusion

In this chapter, we began by introducing the concept of prompt-driven web development and tracing the history of HTML and CSS through the rise of low-code and no-code tools that set the stage for AI in the frontend. We then re-thought the development environment by examining the challenges and opportunities AI brings to web workflows and explained why prompts offer a clear path to generating HTML and CSS that matches design intent. We explored how the developer's role is shifting from hand-crafting every line of code to orchestrating AI-assisted pipelines, and clarified who will benefit most from this book, and how to get the most out of its hands-on structure. Finally, we looked ahead to the concrete deliverables you will build like UI blueprints, prompt workflows, and production-ready components, so that you know exactly what skills you will walk away with by the end of this book. In the next chapter, we will explore tools and setup for prompt-based development environment.

Points to Remember

- Prompt-driven web development uses AI (LLMs) to turn natural-language intent into semantic HTML, shifting developers from sole authors to orchestrators.
- The web's evolution: ENQUIRE -WWW (HTTP/URL/HTML) - HTML/CSS standards via W3C -HTML5/CSS3 - component frameworks or Web Components - today's AI augmented workflows.
- Low-code-no-code democratizes UI creation, prompt-augmented low-no-code blends visual composition with prompt generated code speed with oversight.
- AI in frontend translates intent to interface, generating responsive, accessible markup; value comes from Prompt–Refine–Validate (PRV) and human review.
- Effective prompting: be specific, iterate, anchor conventions, and chain prompts like structure -theming – responsiveness- a11y.
- Tooling is shifting toward AI collaborators in IDEs and design-to-code pipelines; guardrails such as version control, reviews, a11y checks remain essential.
- Integrating AI snippets safely, managing bias/brand consistency, protecting PII, caching/throttling inference, and adding AI telemetry for traceability.
- Why prompts for HTML/CSS: faster scaffolding, clearer bridge between design intent and code, and a learning aid that reinforces semantics/a11y.
- Developer role is expanding to curation, governance, and prompt/catalog stewardship rather than only hand-coding layouts.

- Expected outcomes: UI blueprints, prompt workflows, PRV guardrails, a prompt-recipe catalog, and three projects (bio page, fintech landing, IoT dashboard layout).

Multiple Choice Questions

1. Which milestone most directly paved the way for AI-assisted frontends?
   a. Introduction of HTML5's`<canvas>`element
   b. The rise of low-code/no-code tools
   c. Adoption of server-side rendering frameworks
   d. The invention of CSS preprocessors
2. Which amongst the following is a core benefit of a prompt-driven approach to HTML/CSS generation?
   a. It replaces all manual coding instantly.
   b. It eliminates the need for version control.
   c. It bridges design intent and code through natural-language instructions.
   d. It guarantees zero runtime bugs.
3. Modern AI tools like GitHub Copilot or ChatGPT can be prompted to:
   a. Compile JavaScript into machine code.
   b. Generate semantic HTML with responsive breakpoints and ARIA annotations.
   c. Replace a site's entire backend.
   d. Automatically deploy to production.
4. How is the developer's role changing in an AI-driven frontend workflow?
   a. From writing HTML/CSS manually to orchestrating and refining AI prompts
   b. From building UIs to exclusively writing backend APIs
   c. From using version control to relying on AI for state management
   d. From accessibility auditing to ignoring a11y entirely
5. Which deliverable should you expect to build by the end of the book?
   a. A database schema for an AI log store
   b. A prompt-recipe catalog enforcing your project's naming conventions
   c. A real-time 3D renderer in WebGL
   d. An email marketing automation sequence

6. Prompt–Refine–Validate primarily helps you:
    a. Write complex SQL queries.
    b. Vet AI-generated markup before it goes live.
    c. Cure performance issues in images.
    d. Manage user authentication.
7. Which statement best describes prompt blueprints?
    a. Wireframes drawn by AI in a graphics editor
    b. Natural-language plans that outline your UI's structure before coding
    c. CSS variables grouped by color scheme
    d. A Git branching strategy for AI projects

Answers

1. b
2. c
3. b
4. a
5. b
6. b
7. b

Key Terms

- **Prompt-driven web development:** Building UIs by instructing AI to emit semantic HTML/CSS from natural language.
- **Prompt–Refine–Validate (PRV):** Workflow to generate, iterate, and quality-check AI output before shipping.
- **Prompt engineering:** Writing structured, contextual instructions and follow-ups to steer AI toward the desired code.
- **ENQUIRE:** Tim Berners-Lee's 1980 hyperlinked knowledge system that foreshadowed the Web.
- **World Wide Web (WWW):** Open system combining URLs, HTTP, and HTML to publish and link documents.
- HTML and CSS: Structure and presentation layers of the Web; separation enables clean semantics and styling.

- **W3C/WaSP:** Standards body and advocacy group that pushed browsers toward interoperable HTML/CSS.
- **WHATWG/HTML5**: Pragmatic evolution of HTML adding semantics, media, canvas, and modern APIs.
- **CSS3:** Modular CSS era with Flexbox, Grid, media queries, animations, custom properties, web fonts.
- **Semantic HTML:** Meaningful elements/structure that improve a11y, SEO, and maintainability.
- **Accessibility (a11y)/ARIA**: Inclusive design practices and attributes to aid assistive technologies.
- **Web Components/Shadow DOM**: Standard for encapsulated reusable UI elements.
- **Design-to-code pipeline:** Tools that turn descriptions or designs into runnable HTML/CSS.
- **Bias and explainability in AI theming:** Ensuring AI-generated styles follow brand/a11y rules and are auditable.
- **Caching and throttling:** Reuse results and batch events to cut latency and cost of style generation.
- **AI telemetry/observability:** Logging prompts, model versions, and validations to trace broken styles.
- **BEM/CSS variables:** Naming convention and theming primitives often requested in prompts for maintainability.

CHAPTER 2
Tools and Setup for Prompt-Based Development

Introduction

With the introduction of the prompt-based web development well solidified with a historical perspective, we will be discussing tooling and development environment set up in this chapter. It is widely believed that the quality of workmanship is, to a significant extent, a function of the tools employed. In prompt-based frontend development, your tools include both your physical workspace, editor, extensions, browsers and your AI collaborators like ChatGPT and GitHub Copilot. The better the setup is, the smoother is the conversation between a human and the machine. In this chapter, the tools and setup for prompt-based development are explored. We will build a lean, dependable frontend environment where ChatGPT can help you with your frontend development goals and refactor big chunks of code if necessary while Copilot slips in to polish the small details right in your editor.

Think of it like pairing a senior architect with a lightning-fast intern; each has their own specialty, and together the whole workflow is smooth, and objectives are realized. You will not just install things and move on. You will actually implement a small mini healthcare appointment page as hands on project, wire up the right extensions, and tweak settings so you spend less time fixing AI quirks and more time shipping features. We will walk through a prompt-first loop, starting with a structured prompt spec in ChatGPT, iterating on feedback, then letting Copilot fill in the gaps and patterns inline. You will learn how to preview your work instantly, test across devices, and bake in accessibility and performance from the start. By the end of this chapter, you will have a ready-to-go workspace that feels almost unfair, where AI is not just a novelty, but a consistent, reliable coding partner.

After reading this chapter, you will be able to configure a modern frontend workspace optimized for AI assistance with ChatGPT and GitHub Copilot. You will set up a minimal, robust project scaffold that provides consistent structure for an AI-generated code. You will identify which tasks ChatGPT handles best, large-scale generation, audits, refactors, and where Copilot shines with inline completions, micro-variants, and repetitive patterns. You will use spec-first prompts to steer AI toward accessible, semantic, performant HTML/CSS, and add file-scope intent comments to keep Copilot on-brand and within constraints. You will preview, debug, and harden components with live reload and Chrome DevTools, then run responsive and accessibility checks at golden breakpoints. Finally, you will complete a guided project that ties all tools together, delivering a healthcare minimalist appointment page to test workflow steps you can improve the book progress and reuse in future project.

Structure

In this chapter, we will discuss the following topics:

- Setting up Your Development Environment
- Using ChatGPT for Frontend Development
- Optimizing Development with GitHub Copilot
- Improving Workflow with Visual Studio Code Extensions
- Previewing, Testing AI-Generated HTML and CSS

Setting up Your Development Environment

Before we start firing off prompts and building responsive layouts, we need to bring workspace into the combating mode. The development environment in software development is the combined workspace of tools and configurations used to create, test, and refine code before it is released. Therefore, it is necessary to set up some tools and extensions; a minimal, battle-tested kit so that you can move fast with your frontend development. Let us start with the installation of core tools for the project we plan to build in this book.

Installing Core Tools

This set of tools are must-have stack to support the frontend we are building in this book. Even if your focus is mainly HTML and CSS, some of these tools will save you hours later. Let us start with installing the VS Code!

Installing VS Code

Visual Studio Code (VS Code) is a frcc, lightweight, cross-platform code editor created by Microsoft. It supports IntelliSense, debugging, Git, extensions, and multiple languages. These steps allow you to install as follows:

- Download from www.code.visualstudio.com.
- Choose and run installer (Windows/macOS/Linux).
- Follow setup prompts, accept defaults.
- Then, launch VS Code after installation.

The following screenshot shows the image of the VS Code download page:

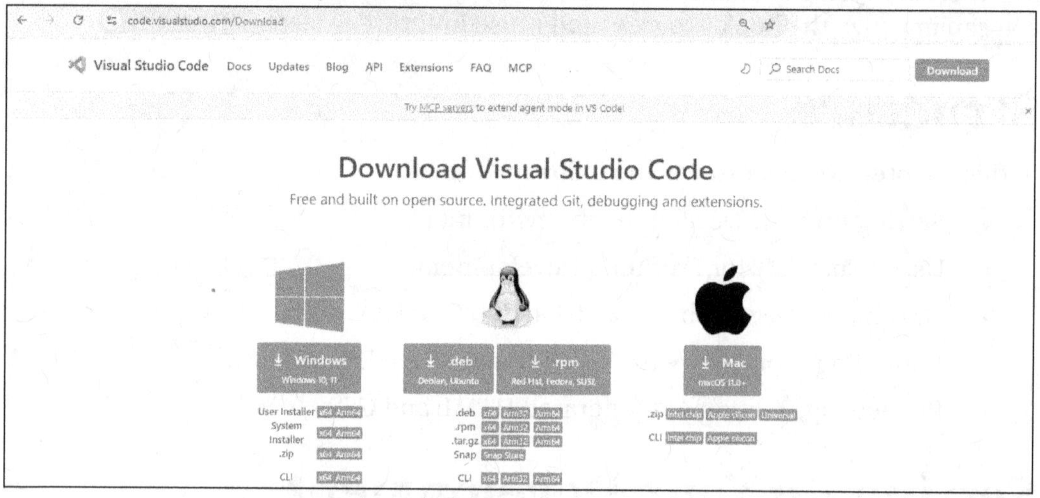

Figure 2.1: *Node.Js Download Page*

The VS code is ideal for web development, scripting, and coding with speed and customization. This tool represents our main Independent Development Environment (IDE).

Installing Node.js

Let us now install Node.js. Even with HTML and CSS-only projects, Node.js gives us access to live preview servers, an extension we are installing shortly, CSS linters, and lightweight test runners.

The following screenshot is used to test Node.js installation and Node Package manager:

In the terminal, run `node -v`, then `npm -v`

Figure 2.2: *Test Node.js Installation and npm*

Git and GitHub

Git and GitHub are version control tools used in modern software development. Git tracks code changes, while GitHub provides cloud hosting for collaboration. GitHub Pages also lets you host static websites, like project demos for free. This is perfect for sharing projects with teammates or clients. Let us follow a step-by-step installation and setup:

1. **Installing Git**

   Windows: Download from www.git-scm.com and run the installer. Maintain the default settings during installations.

   macOS: Use Homebrew with brew install git or download from Git's website.

   Linux:

   ```
   sudo apt update && sudo apt install git  for Debian/Ubuntu
   sudo dnf install git for Fedora
   ```

2. **Configuring Git**

   After installing Git, open your terminal, and set your username and email as default used in commits.

   ```
   git config --global user.name "Your Name"
   git config --global user.email"email@example.com"
   ```

   Configuring Git allows you to customize your workflow, ensures proper credit for your work, and prevents common issues like line endings, merge conflicts. It is a one-time setup that saves time and also from many of the hassles later!

3. **Choosing Browsers**

   Choosing the right browser is a part of the smart choice of software development tools setup. You decide your browser suite like Google Chrome as primary browser, then plus Firefox or Safari for quick cross-browser checks. When choosing a browser for frontend development, Google Chrome is the most popular choice due to its powerful built-in DevTools, extensive extensions, and reliable JavaScript debugging. Its Lighthouse tool helps audit performance, accessibility, and SEO, while the Device Toolbar makes responsive testing easy. However, never rely solely on Chrome, always test in at least one other browser, such as Firefox or Safari, to catch rendering inconsistencies. Firefox, for example, has excellent CSS Grid/Flexbox inspectors, while Safari is crucial for debugging iOS/macOS-specific issues. Cross-browser testing ensures that your AI-generated (or, manually written code) works everywhere, as subtle differences in rendering engines can break layouts unexpectedly. For best results, develop in Chrome, but verify in multiple browsers early and often.

***Tip**: If you are on Windows, enable Windows Subsystem for Linux (WSL) for smoother dev tooling especially if you follow a lot of tutorials written for macOS/Linux.*

Hopefully, you are following along, and make sure you have got all these tools installed and working before moving on. In the next section, we will set up a minimal project scaffold that we will keep reusing for every example in the book. This keeps all your AI prompts grounded in the same folder structure and helps both ChatGPT and Copilot think in context.

Setting up a Minimal Project Scaffold

So, this will be your prompt playground, a folder you will keep coming back to, whenever we test ideas, tweak layouts, or run experiments in this book. By keeping one clean, reusable scaffold, you save yourself from re-creating the same boilerplate every time.

In a step-by-step approach, let us set it up:

1. **Creating working directory**

   Create a folder somewhere easy to find in your local machine like a `C:\prompt-first-dev`.

Figure 2.3: *Creating Project Directory*

2. **Adding files to the directory.**

   Inside the prompt-first-dev directory, create these following files:

```
├ index.html
├ styles.css
├ script.js
├ .editorconfig
├ .prettierrc
├ .stylelintrc.json
├ package.json
```

3. **Initializing `package.json` file and installing dependencies.**

   The **`package.json`** file is the backbone of any Node.js or frontend project. It defines project metadata like name, version, author, dependencies, along with the libraries that your project needs, and scripts to automate tasks for development, testing, and deployment. Inside your terminal, run `npm init -y` and update the scripts section as follows:

```
{
  "name": "prompt-first-dev",
  "private": true,
  "scripts": {
    "dev": "npx live-server --quiet --no-browser",
    "format": "npx prettier . --write",
    "lint:css": "npxstylelint \"**/*.css\"",
    "test:ui": "playwright test"
  }
}
```

Let us briefly understand the scripts section:

- **`dev`**: Starts a zero-config local server with live-server and no browser popup.
- **`format`**: Auto-formats code with Prettier.
- **`lint:css`**: Lints CSS files using Stylelint.
- **`test:ui`**: Runs Playwright for cross-browser UI testing.

Now, let us install the dependencies as follows: `npm install --save-dev live-server prettier stylelint playwright`

4. **Tweaking project config files**

   Let us start with the **`.prettierrc`** that helps us keep formatting consistent; even AI likes predictable code:

   ```
   { "singleQuote": true, "tabWidth": 2, "printWidth": 100 }
   ```

   Then, update **`.stylelintrc.json`** to catch bad CSS before it bites you as follows:

   ```
   {
     "extends": ["stylelint-config-standard"],
     "rules": { "color-no-invalid-hex": true }
   }
   ```

   Finally, the **`.editorconfig`** prevents formatting weirdness, when AI generates cross-platform code. Update as follows:

   ```
   end_of_line = lf
   insert_final_newline = true
   ```

So far, the preceding steps allow your project to have clear formatting rules and linting in place. We are intentionally guiding the AI to generate a code that fits the exact style from the start and save us time for cleaning up later.

Next, we will select some set of extensions in the VS Code to allow the combo of ChatGPT + Copilot to work at their best.

Getting VS Code Extensions Installed

Now, we install some of the right Extensions for AI-powered development. The goal is not to install all the extensions possible, but to install the few that can turn AI help into a shippable code with less friction. From the project directory terminal, enter code as depicted in the following screenshot:

***Figure 2.4**: Opening VScode from Terminal*

Install `GitHub Copilot`, `GitHub Copilot Chat`, `Prettier`, `Stylelint`, `HTMLHint`, `Live Server`, `Auto Rename Tag`, `CSS Peek`, `Color Highlight`, `GitLens`, and `Error Lens`by searching by the name in the Extensions panel. To open extensions panel, click on the panel, or use the keyboard shortcut in Windows- *Ctrl*+*Shift*+X.

Let us briefly discuss what each of the extensions does:

- **GitHub Copilot + Copilot Chat:** Provides AI-powered code completions as you type and answers technical questions directly in your editor, reducing context switching.
- **Prettier:** Automatically formats a code on save, ensuring consistent style across AI-generated and manual code to keep pull requests clean.
- **Stylelint:** Lints CSS/Sass in real-time, catching invalid properties, redundant selectors, or accessibility issues before they cascade into bigger problems.
- **HTMLHint:** Validates HTML structure, warning about missing alt text, deprecated tags, or improper nesting that AI might overlook.
- **Live Server:** Auto-refreshes your browser as you edit, letting you instantly see how AI-generated HTML/CSS renders without manual reloading.
- **Auto Rename Tag:** Syncs opening/closing tags automatically when renaming, preventing broken markup when restructuring AI's HTML output.
- **CSS Peek:** Quickly navigate from HTML class attributes to their CSS definitions and back, speeding up debugging when tweaking AI's styles.
- **Color Highlight:** Displays visual swatches next to hex/rgb/hsl values in your CSS, making it easier to verify color palettes suggested by AI.
- **GitLens:** Supercharges Git blame/diffs, helping you review and understand AI-generated changes line-by-line before committing.

- **Error Lens:** Highlights errors/warnings inline next to the problematic code, highlighting issues from linters or compilers immediately.

These extensions bridge the gap between AI suggestions and a production-ready code with an early catching of the errors — Stylelint, HTMLHint, Error Lens, maintain consistency; Prettier, Auto Rename Tag, speeds up iteration with Live Server, CSS Peek and also improves visibility.

Here, we update the VS Code **`settings.json`** snippet to optimize how they work together, especially for an AI-generated code:

1. Open VS Code settings, *Ctrl + , (that is Ctrl + plus+comma at the same time)*, then click the **`Open Settings (JSON)`** icon.

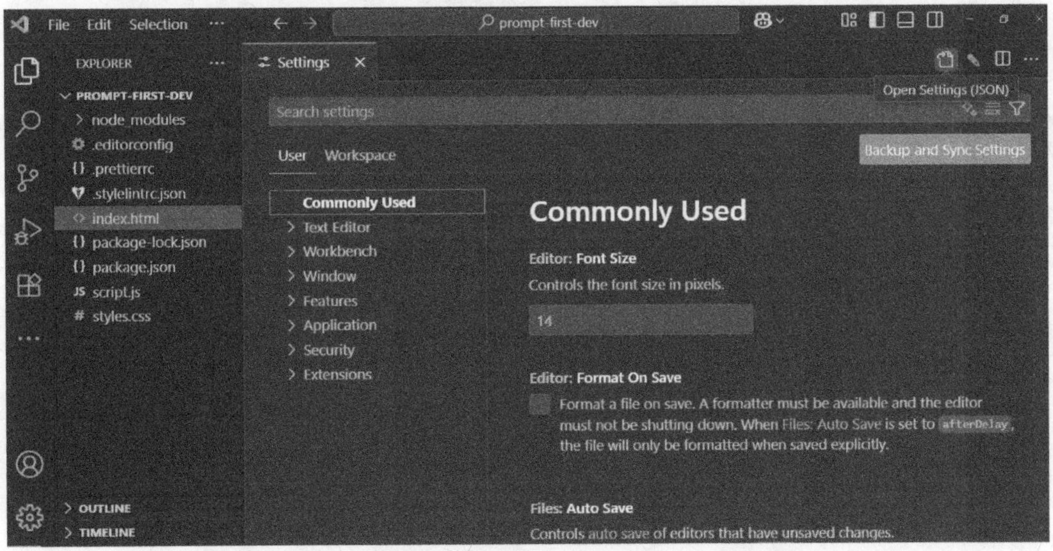

***Figure* 2.5**: VScode Workspace and Open Settings JSON

2. Then, paste the snippet into your **`settings.json`**:

```
{
  "editor.formatOnSave": true,
  "editor.codeActionsOnSave":{"source.fixAll.stylelint": "explicit" },
  "editor.inlineSuggest.enabled": true,
  "git.confirmSync": false,
  "files.eol": "\n",
  "prettier.singleQuote": true,
  "prettier.printWidth": 100
}
```

No restart is needed, as the update take effect immediately.

Now, let us test what we have done so far. Inside the project directory in the GitHub, copy and paste content, **`index.html`** and **`style.css`** files. Right click the **`index.html`** and open with a Live Server. The following screenshot shows the displayed page:

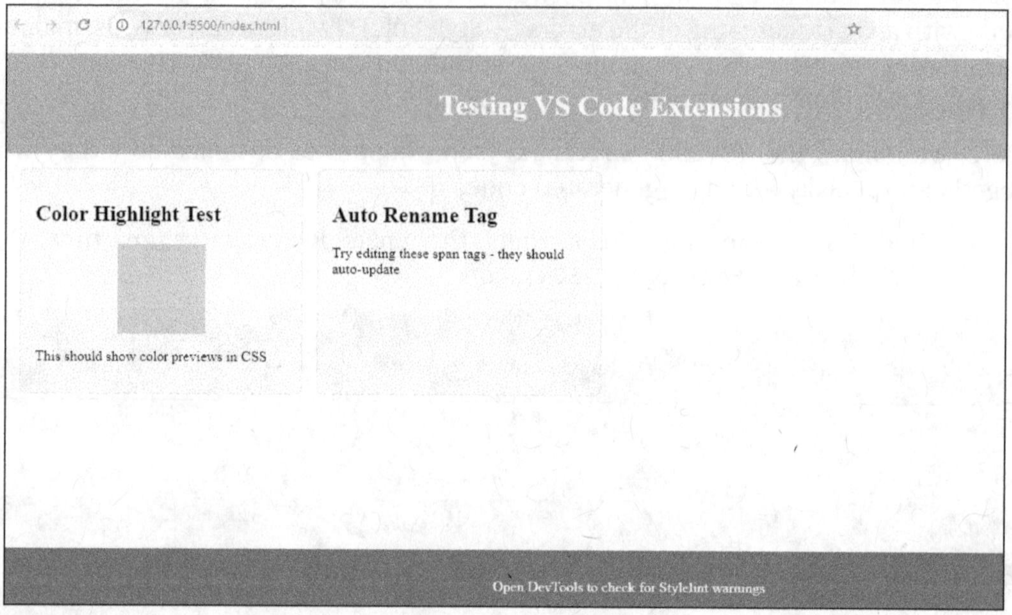

***Figure 2.6**: Testing VS Code Extensions*

Alternatively, you can run **`npm run dev`** in the project terminal and access the index page from http://127.0.0.1:5500. The command uses live-server to serve the folder and auto-reload on save.

Now that your VS Code setup is optimized for AI-assisted workflows, let us explore how ChatGPT can speed up your frontend development process. While extensions like GitHub Copilot excel at code completion, ChatGPT shines in explaining complex concepts, generating boilerplate code, debugging assistance and providing architecture advice.

Let us explore the **`prompt->paste-> save->verify`** approach to frontend development.

Using ChatGPT for Frontend Development

Now that your development environment is set up with the right tools like VS Code extensions, linters, and automation scripts, it is time to explore how ChatGPT can accelerate your frontend workflow. While Copilot is the strongest at inline completions, ChatGPT helps you reason through the whole work: plan components, fix layout quirks, and is output organized, best-practice HTML and CSS.

Let us examine ChatGPT's key strengths in frontend development, starting with architecture guidance.

Architectural Guidance

In web development, structure comes before code and styling. Treat ChatGPT as an interface architect that helps you design markup that scales. ChatGPT does not just spit out snippets; it mirrors the judgment of an experienced peer, favoring semantic HTML, sound accessibility choices, and responsive patterns from the start. This human-ChatGPT partnership provides markup rationale, alternatives, and trade-offs, not just tags. To get the most out of ChatGPT, begin with a clear, constraint-rich spec content, roles, breakpoints, interactions and then ask for code that fits those boundaries. For instance, if you want ChatGPT to generate HTML/CSS, you can start with something like:

```
“You are a senior frontend developer. Generate accessible, semantic HTML
+ modern CSS.
Context:
- Page/Component: <what is it?>
- Audience/Brand vibe: <tone, feel>
- Constraints:
  - No frameworks (plain HTML/CSS)
  - Mobile-first, responsive (>=320px)
  - Use CSS variables, BEM naming, and container queries where helpful
  - Meet WCAG AA contrast, keyboard navigable
  - Keep CSS < 200 lines if possible
Deliverables:
1) Single HTML file with external styles.css
2) Brief checklist verifying responsiveness and a11y
“
```

In *Chapter 3: Prompt Engineering for* HTML *and* CSS, we will explore more on prompt engineering. In a nutshell, AI thrives better when you give it a box to work inside. No constraints mean a verbose, bloated, or inconsistent output. Clear constraints usually result in a lean, focused, and an almost production-ready code.

The idea of role framing, senior frontend developer produces better architectural choices. Context ensures that ChatGPT adapts tone, structure, and styling to your project and constraints force the ChatGPT to think lean and avoid bloat. Finally, the deliverables list allows you to control the format, not the model.

Tip: *Save this as a snippet in ChatGPT or your notes app. Use it as your project seed prompt every time. You will notice output quality improve immediately.*

Optimizing Development with GitHub Copilot

With your architecture solidified through ChatGPT's guidance, GitHub Copilot becomes your precision tool for execution, the perfect complement to ChatGPT's strategic thinking. ChatGPT comes to one's mind when you think big moves like structure, semantics, and accessibility strategy versus Copilot with micro moves for fast and accurate keystrokes. Copilot keeps you in flow by predicting what you will type next, not by redesigning your app. In practice, Copilot shines when you are expanding CSS rules, repeating HTML fragments, generating state variants, writing quick docs, or propagating small refactors. Start a selector like **`.pricing-card {`** and it completes spacing, typography, and a grid/flex pattern that matches the nearby code. Let us examine an example of Copilot style's suggestions from the screenshot as follows:

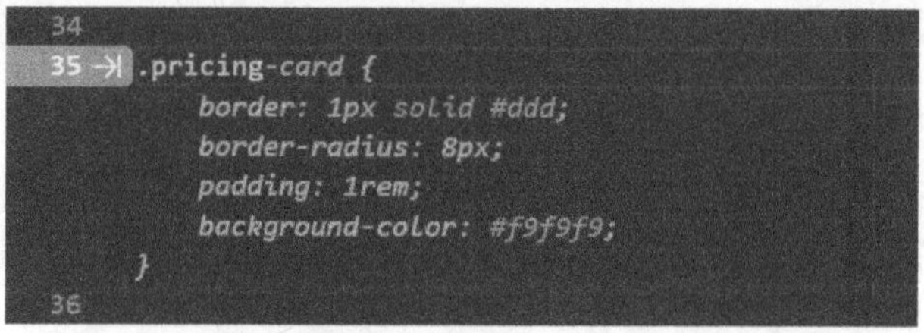

***Figure** 2.7: Testing Copilot Auto Suggestions*

GitHub Copilot is highly suggestible, a tiny file-scope intent comment acts like a mission briefing for your frontend development. If you drop something like `/* BEM naming; CSS variables; prefer @container; respect prefers-reduced-motion; low specificity, no !important */` at the top of your **`styles.css`**. You will notice it reaches for **`var(--brand)`** instead of hex values, it offers **`@container`** over generic **`@media`**, and proposes the right set of selectors. We will see this in action in subsequent chapters.

Note: *During major refactors, temporarily disable Copilot until the new structure stabilizes. It is like turning off power tools during delicate measurements.*

Now that we have discussed how Copilot handles the micro-moves and ChatGPT shapes the big-moves, let us explore how tuning Visual Studio Code with the right extensions, formatters, linters, testers, and workflow helpers turn the best practices into defaults, cut context-switching, and keep feedback instant.

Improving Workflow with Visual Studio Code Extensions

Building on the big moves versus micro moves model, we need Visual Studio Code extensions that transform conceptual guidance into active editor enforcement. These tools serve as the connective tissue between strategic planning and tactical execution, keeping Copilot's rapid-fire suggestions aligned with project standards while hardening ChatGPT's architectural blueprints against technical debt. These extensions were discussed previously. They create a safety net that tightens the feedback loop at every stage, from initial scaffolding to final review. GitHub Copilot + Copilot Chat keep you in flow with inline completions and quick, scoped answers, perfect for the micro moves we discussed. Prettier acts as the silent enforcer, automatically standardizes formatting across both AI-generated and manual code to ensure consistent style. Stylelint serves as our CSS sentry, intercepting invalid properties, specificity creep, and accessibility anti-patterns in real time. When working with HTML scaffolds from ChatGPT, HTMLHint provides a significant validation of semantic structure, catching missing alt text, deprecated elements, and problematic nesting before they become issues.

For immediate visual feedback, Live Server creates a seamless testing environment that refreshes with every change, making it effortless to verify the impact of both Copilot suggestions and manual tweaks. Auto Rename Tag eliminates one of the most common refactoring headaches by keeping HTML tags synchronized, particularly valuable when restructuring AI-generated markup. CSS Peek and Color Highlight optimize the styling workflow, enabling instant navigation between class definitions and visual verification of color values—critical when evaluating AI-proposed design choices. The review process benefits equally from thoughtful tooling. GitLens brings transparency to code evolution, clearly showing authorship and changes at the line level, an essential feature when auditing AI contributions. Error Lens takes this further by surfacing lint warnings directly in the editor gutter, transforming potential issues into contextual, actionable notifications. Together, these extensions create an environment where strategic direction from ChatGPT and tactical execution via Copilot can flourish while maintaining strict quality control, precisely the workflow professional developers need to ship production-grade code with confidence.

Next, we prove the UI actually works. Treat AI-generated HTML/CSS as a hypothesis: render it, poke it, and test it.

Previewing, Testing AI-Generated HTML and CSS

As previously stated, always treat AI-generated HTML/CSS as a hypothesis and prove it fast. Start by rendering exactly what the model produced, then pressure test responsiveness, semantics, and accessibility before you polish visuals. Try to keep the loop tight-preview, poke, fix, repeat so Copilot handles micro edits while your tools enforce standards. The goal is not to be perfect on first render; it is to secure rapid confidence that the scaffold is correct and safe to ship.

Let us work with this minimalist prompt for the previewing purpose. Copy and paste this prompt into your ChatGPT:

Prompt:

"You are a senior frontend developer. Produce beautiful, colorful, accessible, semantic HTML and modern, minimal CSS for a MINI HEALTHCARE APPOINTMENT PAGE.

Brand: Healthworx (text logo only)

Requirements:

- Plain HTML + CSS (no JS, no frameworks)

- No sidebar, no disclaimers/legal footer

- Three tabs for care types (e.g., Family Medicine, Pediatrics, Dental)

- CSS-only tabs (radio-based), keyboard reachable; visible :focus-visible

- Mobile-first (>=320px); responsive layout

- Use <main>, <header>, <section>; include a "Skip to content" link

- No provider links or booking CTAs; show a few non-clickable <time> slots in each tab

- Use CSS variables and BEM naming; low specificity; no !important

- WCAG AA contrast; system font stack

- ≤ ~200 lines of CSS; include an intent header comment

Deliverables: /index.html and /styles.css only"

Then, update the **`index.html`** and styles.css in your project directory. Open the Healthworx project in VS Code and launch Live Server. Change color in styles.css, save, and confirm hot-reload. This is your tight loop for micro edits. The following mini appointment page screenshot is produced from the prompts-`index.html` and `styles.css`:

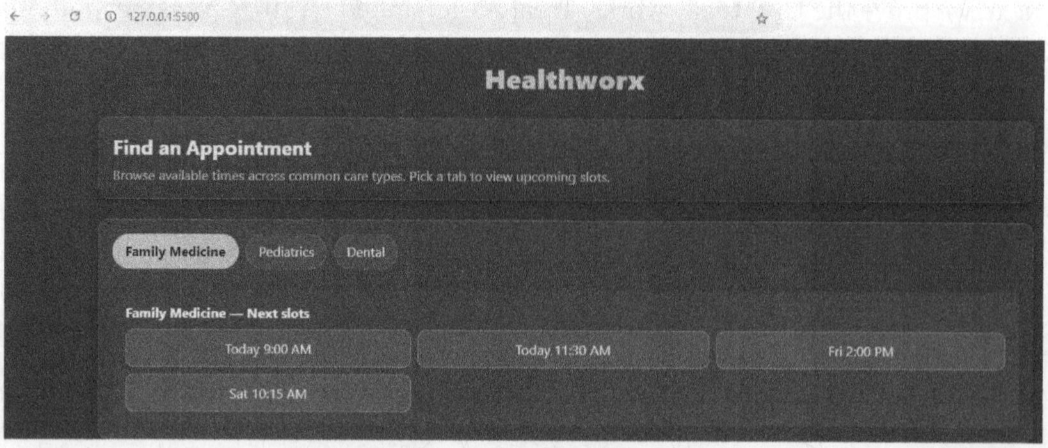

Figure 2.8: AI Generated Code Page

Let us do housekeeping, starting with the baseline sanity checks while focusing on structure and wiring:

DevTools Verification

1. Check for 404 errors on styles.css: Open Chrome DevTools (F12 or *Ctrl+Shift+I/Cmd+Opt+I*).
2. Go to the "`Console`" tab. Look for any red error messages mentioning styles.css.
3. If no 404 errors appear for styles.css, this check passes.

Checking for CSS parse errors:

1. In DevTools, go to the "`Elements`" tab.
2. Select the `<head>` section of your document.
3. Find the `<link>` tag for styles.css.
4. Click the `styles.css` link to open it in the Sources panel.
5. Look for red underlines or error indicators in the CSS.
6. If no syntax errors are highlighted, this check passes.

Responsiveness testing:

1. Click the device toolbar (*Ctrl+Shift+M/Cmd+Shift+M*).
2. Test at 320px, 768px, and 1200px widths.
3. Check that layout adjusts properly.

You can run these validations checks directly in Chrome DevTools. Use the Device Toolbar for breakpoints, elements/accessibility for landmarks and headings, the console for errors, and the color contrast checker, no code changes required. We will dive into automated and a deeper manual check in the subsequent chapters.

Conclusion

In this chapter, we have built the foundation for effective prompt-based frontend development by setting up a clean, AI-friendly environment in VS Code. We started with essential installs, Node.js, Git, browsers, and carefully chosen extensions then scaffolded a minimal project structure that gives ChatGPT and GitHub Copilot consistent context to work from. We explored how ChatGPT works well with big moves like generating accessible, semantic UI, and how Copilot complements it with micro moves such as inline completions and pattern repetition. We introduced the spec-first prompt pattern to keep AI output lean, accessible, and performant, and discovered how file-scope intent comments keep Copilot suggestions on brand state. We practiced previewing and refining AI-generated HTML/CSS using live reload, and Chrome DevTools, and learned to trim bloat via the Coverage panel. Finally, we have tied everything together in a minimalist project, producing a Healthcare appointment page using a repeatable workflow.

In the next chapter, we will discuss with hands-on approach prompt engineering patterns and strategies to generate, refine, and maintain complex frontend user interfaces with absolute confidence.

Points to Remember

- ChatGPT shines at big moves, generating new components, doing audits, large refactors, or writing tests from scratch.
- GitHub Copilot does well at micro moves, inline completions, repetitive patterns, small variants, and quick edits inside your IDE.
- Always start with a spec-first prompt when using ChatGPT. Include role framing, constraints, and deliverables to keep code lean and accessible.
- Keep a minimal project scaffold ready. AI works better with consistent structure and file naming.
- Use file-scope intent comments in CSS and HTML to steer Copilot's output toward your naming conventions, variables, and accessibility standards.
- Live preview speeds iteration. Combine `npm run dev` with Chrome's Device Toolbar for quick checks at golden breakpoints (320/375/768/1024/1200px).
- The Coverage panel in Chrome DevTools is your friend for identifying unused CSS/JS and trimming bloat.

Multiple Choice Questions

1. Which task is best suited for ChatGPT in a prompt-based workflow?
    a. Completing repetitive hover styles inline.
    b. Generating a new responsive component with accessibility baked in.
    c. Renaming tags when editing HTML in VS Code.
    d. Applying Prettier formatting on save.
2. Which tool is recommended for real-time preview during AI-assisted frontend development?
    a. Axe DevTools
    b. Live Server
    c. GitLens
    d. HTMLHint

3. Which amongst these is the main benefit of adding an intent comment at the top of styles.css?
    a. Makes Prettier run faster.
    b. Tells Copilot your style and architectural rules.
    c. Enables container queries.
    d. Automatically fixes accessibility issues.
4. In the spec-first prompt, why is it important to set a maximum CSS line count?
    a. It ensures your file runs faster.
    b. It forces AI to avoid verbose, redundant styling.
    c. It prevents Prettier from breaking.
    d. It stops CSS from using container queries.
5. Which Chrome DevTools feature checks for unused CSS rules?
    a. Lighthouse
    b. Performance Tab
    c. Coverage
    d. Sources Panel
6. Which of these is not a recommended golden breakpoint for this chapter's workflow?
    a. 320px
    b. 375px
    c. 1024px
    d. 640px
7. Which VS Code extension automatically updates closing tags when you rename an opening tag?
    a. Auto Rename Tag
    b. CSS Peek
    c. Error Lens
    d. GitLens
8. Which of these is a common failure mode for AI-generated CSS mentioned in this chapter?
    a. Too many inline SVGs
    b. Overuse of BEM naming

   c. Bloated, generic selectors
   d. Excessive logical properties

9. Why should you avoid pasting secrets/PII into ChatGPT or Copilot Chat?
   a. It slows down Copilot.
   b. It could expose sensitive information to external systems.
   c. It prevents Prettier from running.
   d. It causes accessibility errors.
10. What is the purpose of using @media (prefers-reduced-motion) in CSS?
    a. Automatically compress assets.
    b. Honor users' OS-level reduced motion preferences.
    c. Disable animations in dark mode.
    d. Improve rendering speed in Chrome.
11. What is the advantage of using minimal diffs in AI prompts?
    a. Shorter loading times in the IDE.
    b. Keeps unrelated working code intact while applying fixes.
    c. Makes CSS files smaller automatically.
    d. Allows Git to ignore changes.
12. Which Prettier setting ensures that single quotes are used in generated code?
    a. `"quotes": "single"`
    b. `"useSingleQuotes": true`
    c. `"singleQuote": true`
    d. `"quoteStyle": "single"`

Answers

1. b
2. b
3. b
4. b
5. c
6. d
7. a
8. c

9. b
10. b
11. b
12. c

Key Terms

- **Spec-first prompt**: A structured AI request including role framing, constraints, and deliverables to guide high-quality output.
- **Minimal diff:** A request for only the exact lines needed to make a change, keeping the rest of the file untouched.
- **BEM naming:** CSS class naming convention: Block__Element--Modifier.
- **Container queries:** CSS feature that applies styles based on the size of the containing element, not the viewport.
- **Intent comment:** A top-of-file note stating coding conventions and goals to guide Copilot's suggestions.
- **Golden breakpoints:** Predefined viewport widths used for consistent responsive testing such as 320, 375, 768, 1024, 1200px.
- **Lighthouse:** Chrome DevTools tool for measuring performance, SEO, and accessibility.
- **Coverage tab:** Chrome DevTools feature showing unused CSS/JS.
- **prefers-reduced-motion:** CSS media query to detect and respect user settings for reduced animations.
- **Live Server:** Local dev server that auto-refreshes on file save.
- **Error Lens:** VS Code extension that highlights issues inline in the code editor.

CHAPTER 3
Prompt Engineering for HTML and CSS

Introduction

In Chapter 2: Tools and Setup for Prompt-Based Development, we had explored tools for prompt-based development; now, before we craft a single line of HTML and CSS, remember that true frontend engineering power begins with those tools including the AI systems. Modern frontend development is increasingly becoming a collaboration between humans and AI systems. When you ask an AI to build a pricing page or style a form, you are not just making a request, you are writing a specification that the system will execute. The quality of that specification, which is your prompt, determines your code quality in terms of semantic correctness, accessibility, responsiveness, maintainability, and performance. To simply put, good prompts lead to good HTML and CSS. You will learn to encode context like audience, brand, constraints, standards, and acceptance criteria directly into your prompts. You will design prompts that return cleanly formatted HTML and CSS, control verbosity, and prevent drift across iterations using unified diffs, a situation where prompt design is treated like code, versioned, reviewable, and precise. You will also learn to use few shot examples to imprint patterns, and to chain prompts so that results are predictable and auditable. In addition, you will be able to guide an AI like your reliable junior engineer: shaping structure first, styling second; keeping ARIA minimal; and proving success with a rubric. Whether you are generating a single component or an entire page, you will have the mental models, templates, and checklists to turn raw ideas into a production-ready code.

After reading this chapter, you will be able to treat prompts as mini-specs and apply the C.R.A.F.T.E.D. framework to generate semantic, accessible, and responsive HTML and CSS. You will learn to enforce strict formatting, design few-shot examples, and chain prompts for deterministic results. You will practice auditing outputs against WCAG 2.2 AA, scoping changes with unified diffs, and debugging prompts through reduction and questioning. On the CSS side, you will build token-first systems, enforce naming conventions, and refactor excessive use of div into clean, semantic, responsive layouts. Finally, you will leave with reusable prompt templates for components, pages, and audits to ensure consistency and speed.

Structure

In this chapter, we will cover the following topics:

- Prompt Engineering for HTML and CSS
- What Makes a Good Prompt
- Prompt Structure and Formatting
- Few Shots Prompting
- Prompt Chaining Techniques
- Avoiding Prompt Mistakes
- Debugging Prompts with AI

Prompt Engineering for HTML and CSS

Prompt engineering is the art and science of designing and refining prompts by setting context, intent, constraints, and examples to effectively guide Large Language Models (LLMs) toward outputs that are accurate, reliable, and safe, while aligning with user goals and broader system objectives. When you first learned HTML and CSS, there was something magical about typing a few lines of code, saving the file, and watching a plain browser window transform into a styled page. The simplicity of writing `<h1>Hello World</h1>` or `color: blue`; and seeing immediate results made programming feel accessible and rewarding. Remember Microsoft FrontPage? It was a game-changing WYSIWYG (What-You-See-Is-What-You-Get) HTML editor and website admin tool that let you whip up websites in no time. With its intuitive interface, you could rapidly build and deploy sites, seeing exactly how they would look without needing to code from scratch. Prompt engineering carries that same magic, but instead of styling pixels on a screen, you are shaping words, meanings, and outputs from the LLMs. At its core, prompt engineering is both an art and a science. The art comes from creativity: choosing the right words, tone, and context to elicit the kind of response you want. The science lies in the structure: testing, refining, and optimizing prompts in a methodological way that allows a web developer totest and refine code. The combination of prompt art and science is gradually forming the discipline that is rapidly becoming essential for anyone working with AI. Let us examine a simple ChatGPT prompt to write HTML for a login form and visually introduces the concept of prompt and output:

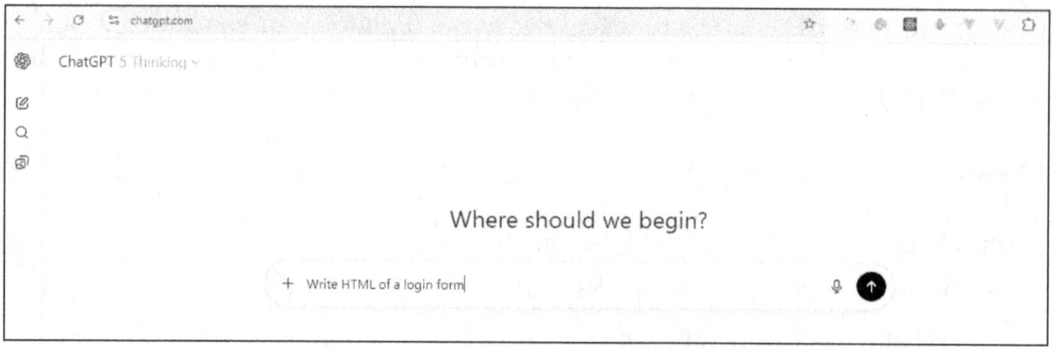

***Figure 3.1**: ChatGPT Console Showing Output of Login Form*

Shifting from Commands to Conversations

Prompt as a term, has its roots deep in computing history. In the early days, a prompt was just the command-line symbol, usually a blinking cursor waiting for your input. When you type mkdir in the computer terminal, the computer makes a folder. This is simple, direct, and literal. Today, prompts are no longer concise commands we used to know it with the terminal. A prompt can be a paragraph, a dialogue, or even a set of examples. Instead of rigid instructions like `cd ../`, we now say things like:

"*Generate a blog post about responsive design in CSS.*"

"*Write HTML and CSS for a centered login form with modern styling.*"

"*Explain the difference between <div> and <span> to a beginner.*"

This shift from commands to conversations marks a fundamental change in how we interact with machines. Prompt engineering emerged as the skill set to handle this change. This is enforcing the ability to guide complex systems through natural language while still being precise enough to get predictable results. In a nutshell, HTML and CSS empowered people to build websites without extensive programming knowledge. Prompt engineering enables users to effectively interact with AI models without needing to know the underlying complexities. Traditionally, HTML provides structure. It tells the browser what a heading is, what is a paragraph, what is a list. Prompts also provide structure as well; they set the stage, define the role, and frame the task for the AI. CSS provides style and controls appearance, mood, and responsiveness. Prompts provide style too – they can make outputs formal or casual, technical or beginner-friendly, concise or elaborate. Unfortunately, browsers make assumptions when markup is unclear. If you forget a closing tag, the browser guesses. Similarly, if a prompt is vague, the AI guesses and sometimes gets it wrong, or hallucinates. This is where the art of prompt engineering comes in. It is about choosing a language that nudges the model towards the voice, perspective, and style you want. You are not just asking for output, you are curating an experience.

Structure and Reliability

Prompt engineering is deeply technical. Think about how CSS has rules: specificity, inheritance, the cascade. If you misuse them, your styles will break. Prompts also obey patterns. Small changes in wording can drastically alter results. For instance, when you write HTML for a form in a ChatGPT console, it produces something minimal. And when you write semantic HTML5 for a form with ARIA labels and accessibility best practices, you get something richer and more reliable. Let us examine the output from a second prompt:

ChatGPT prompt: *Write semantic HTML5 for a form with* ARIA *labels and accessibility best practices.*

```
<!-- Accessible, semantic HTML5 form example -->
<form action="/submit" method="post" aria-labelledby="contact-form-
title">
<h1 id="contact-form-title">Contact us</h1>
<p id="required-hint">Fields marked with * are required.</p>

<!-- Error summary (shown after validation); focus this on error -->
<div id="error-summary" role="alert" aria-labelledby="error-summary-
title" hidden tabindex="-1">
<h2 id="error-summary-title">Please fix the following</h2>
<ul>
<!-- Example items; populate dynamically on validation -->
<li><a href="#email">Enter a valid email address</a></li>
<li><a href="#terms">You must accept the terms</a></li>
</ul>
</div>

<fieldset>
<legend>Personal information</legend>

<div class="field">
<label for="given-name">First name <span aria-hidden="true">*</span></
label>
<input
        id="given-name"
        name="given-name"
        type="text"
        required
        autocomplete="given-name"
        aria-describedby="required-hint given-name-hint"
        />
```

```
<p id="given-name-hint" class="hint">As shown on your ID.</p>
<p id="given-name-error" class="error" role="alert" hidden>First name is
required.</p>
</div>

<div class="field">
<label for="family-name">Last name <span aria-hidden="true">*</span></
label>
<input
        id="family-name"
        name="family-name"
        type="text"
        required
        autocomplete="family-name"
        aria-describedby="required-hint family-name-hint"
        />
<p id="family-name-hint" class="hint">As shown on your ID.</p>
<p id="family-name-error" class="error" role="alert" hidden>Last name is
required.</p>
</div>

<div class="field">
<label for="email">Email <span aria-hidden="true">*</span></label>
<input
        id="email"
        name="email"
        type="email"
inputmode="email"
        autocomplete="email"
        required
        aria-describedby="required-hint email-hint email-error"
        />
<p id="email-hint" class="hint">We'll only use this to contact you about
your request.</p>
<p id="email-error" class="error" role="alert" hidden>Please enter a
valid email address.</p>
</div>

<div class="field">
<label for="tel">Phone (optional)</label>
<input
        id="tel"
        name="tel"
        type="tel"
```

```
inputmode="tel"
        autocomplete="tel"
        aria-describedby="tel-hint"
        />
<p id="tel-hint" class="hint">Include country code if outside your
region.</p>
</div>

<div class="field">
<label for="country">Country/Region</label>
<select id="country" name="country" autocomplete="country-name" aria-
describedby="country-hint">
<option value="">Select a country/region</option>
<option value="CA">Canada</option>
<option value="US">United States</option>
<option value="GB">United Kingdom</option>
<!-- Add more as needed -->
</select>
<p id="country-hint" class="hint">Choose the country where you currently
reside.</p>
</div>
</fieldset>

<fieldset aria-describedby="contact-pref-hint">
<legend>Preferred contact method</legend>
<p id="contact-pref-hint" class="hint">Choose one option.</p>

<div class="field">
<input id="pref-email" name="contact-preference" type="radio"
value="email" required />
<label for="pref-email">Email</label>
</div>
<div class="field">
<input id="pref-phone" name="contact-preference" type="radio"
value="phone" />
<label for="pref-phone">Phone</label>
</div>
</fieldset>

<fieldset>
<legend>Your message</legend>

<div class="field">
<label for="subject">Subject <span aria-hidden="true">*</span></label>
```

```
<input
        id="subject"
        name="subject"
        type="text"
        required
        aria-describedby="required-hint subject-hint subject-error"
        />
<p id="subject-hint" class="hint">A short summary of your request.</p>
<p id="subject-error" class="error" role="alert" hidden>Subject is
required.</p>
</div>

<div class="field">
<label for="message">Message <span aria-hidden="true">*</span></label>
<textarea
        id="message"
        name="message"
        rows="6"
        required
        aria-describedby="required-hint message-hint message-error"
></textarea>
<p id="message-hint" class="hint">Provide as much detail as possible.</
p>
<p id="message-error" class="error" role="alert" hidden>Message is
required.</p>
</div>
</fieldset>

<div class="field">
<input id="terms" name="terms" type="checkbox" required aria-
describedby="terms-hint terms-error" />
<label for="terms">I agree to the Terms and Privacy Policy <span aria-
hidden="true">*</span></label>
<p id="terms-hint" class="hint">You must agree before submitting.</p>
<p id="terms-error" class="error" role="alert" hidden>You must accept
the terms to continue.</p>
</div>

<!-- Live region for async messages (e.g., "Saving…", "Submitted!") -->
<div id="form-status" role="status" aria-live="polite"></div>

<button type="submit">Submit</button>
<button type="reset">Reset</button>
</form>
```

The preceding code shows a semantic HTML5 contact form designed with accessibility best practices, including proper use of **<label>, <fieldset>,** and **<legend>** elements, as well as ARIA attributes for hints, error messages, and live updates. It ensures that screen reader users and keyboard users can navigate, understand, and interact with all inputs and error feedback clearly.

Understanding these mechanics, what the model prioritizes, how it interprets context, and how it responds to examples is the science of prompt engineering. It is systematic, testable and repeatable.

Note: *If a human junior dev would need more details, your AI likely does, too.*

What Makes a Good Prompt

Now that we have explored the fundamentals of prompt engineering, we can now focus on crafting prompts that unlock the full potential of AI systems. Mastering these fundamentals is crucial for obtaining reliable, reproducible, and insightful results. It is essential to recognize the characteristics of well-crafted prompts for a more reliable result. By understanding what makes a good prompt, you will be able to elicit better answers, faster, and more tailored to your specific needs. Interestingly, frontend development provides a great lens to understand prompting: it is visual, highly structured, and sensitive to ambiguity. When you write a prompt for generating HTML and CSS code, you are essentially writing instructions that combine creativity designand precision syntax. This duality makes it a perfect environment to dissect what separates a weak prompt from a strong one.

Let us break down the key elements of effective prompts as follows:

Clarity in Prompts

You need to be explicit, not implicit. What do I mean? Imagine you want LLM model to generate a simple webpage. Here is a vague prompt: "*Make me a webpage with some text and colors.*" This leaves enormous ambiguity: what text? Which colors? Should it follow accessibility guidelines? Should it be responsive? Now, take a look at a stronger prompt:

"*Create an HTML page with a centered headline that says 'Welcome to My Portfolio', styled with CSS. Use a dark background (#121212), white text, and a modern sans-serif font. Add a button styled in teal (#00bfa5) that changes color when hovered.*"

Can you notice the difference? The second example reduces uncertainty by specifying the content, structure, style, and interaction. This makes the AI model more likely to generate usable HTML and CSS on the first try.

Note: *Clarity in prompts reduces guesswork. In HTML and CSS, every detail matters, from color codes to layout instructions.*

Contextualizing Prompts with Information

Crafting effective prompts requires more than just clarity; context is crucial. A well-structured prompt provides the AI with essential details, eliminating ambiguity and guesswork. For instance, instead of a vague request like "*Add a navigation bar*," a more informative prompt would specify the nav bar's location, design, and behavior. By adding context, such as the type of website, layout requirements, and desired interactions, you enable the AI to generate accurate and relevant results that meet your needs. Let us examine this bad and good prompts:

> Bad prompt:
>
> *"Add a navigation bar."*
>
> Good prompt:
>
> *"Add a horizontal navigation bar to the top of the existing portfolio webpage. It should contain links to 'Home', 'Projects', and 'Contact'. Use flexbox for layout and ensure the links change color on hover."*

The second prompt adds context: we are working on a *portfolio site*, the nav bar belongs at the *top*, and *flexbox* is the layout method. With context, AI does not need to guess your intent.

Note: *Context often means specifying where in the page an element should appear, what role it serves, and how it should behave.*

Adding Constraints

Constraints in prompt engineering refer to the specific guidelines or limitations that shape the LLM's output. This ensures that the AI stays focused and aligned with the desired outcome. By defining clear constraints, you can prevent the AI from producing generic or misaligned results. For instance, without constraints, a prompt like "*Make a landing page with* CSS" might yield a wide range of unpredictable outcomes. However, with constraints, a more directed prompt like "Build a landing page for a mobile app with a specific hero section, layout, and color palette" guides the AI to generate a more precise and relevant result. By applying constraints, you can effectively control the design language, layout system, and overall aesthetic of the output, much like CSS rules constrain element behavior. HTML and CSS are languages of constraints; you declare rules that limit how elements behave. Likewise, prompts should constrain what the AI produces.

Testing and Iteration

Testing and iteration are the essential components of crafting effective prompts. Due to the complexities of AI models, it is rare to nail the perfect prompt on the first try. Instead, prompt engineering requires an iterative approach, where you test your prompt, evaluate the output, and refine it accordingly. This process is like debugging code or fine-tuning a website's layout. It involves identifying areas for improvement and adjusting until you achieve the desired result. By embracing testing and iteration, you can incrementally refine your prompts to produce more accurate and relevant outputs, ultimately unlocking the full potential of AI models. A more useful mindset is seeing prompting as closer to debugging than ordering for pizza. For instance, it will be a bad assumption to think if you write a prompt once, you will get the exact output you need. Rather have this mindset of testing prompts, see what output you get, and refine accordingly. In HTML and CSS, you would not expect your first attempt at a structuring and styling layout to look perfect across all browsers. You would test, debug, and tweak until it feels right. Prompts behave the same way.

Abstraction Levels in Prompt Engineering

Abstraction in prompts refers to the level of detail and specificity provided. Prompts can range from high-level, which give the AI creative freedom, to low-level, which dictate precise specifications. High-level prompts, such as "*Create a modern blog layout with a header, sidebar, and article content*", allow the AI to take the lead in designing the overall structure and aesthetic. In contrast, low-level prompts, like "Use CSS *grid to divide the page into a header (full-width), a sidebar* (25%), *and main content* (75%) *with specific padding and typography*," provide exact instructions for the AI to follow. This dichotomy mirrors the frontend development workflow, where the high-level wireframes sketch out concepts and low-level adjustments fine-tune details. With the understanding of the level of abstraction required in prompting designs, you can tailor your prompts to achieve the desired balance between creative freedom and precision, ultimately leading to more effective collaboration with AI models.

Prompt Structure and Formatting

When working with AI models, especially in domains like HTML and CSS, it is necessary to shape prompts that are scannable, consistent, and machine friendly. Unstructured prompts can lead to easily broken and ambiguous results, much like un-semantic HTML. In contrast, structured prompts provide predictability and extensibility, like a well-scoped CSS and semantic HTML.

To achieve this structure in prompting, we can use these 7-part prompt(R–G–C–S–A–O–V) scaffold as follows:

- **Role:** This defines the assistant's role or persona.
- **Goal:** It clearly articulates what success looks like.
- **Context:** This provides relevant constraints, prior work, assets, and audience information.
- **Specs:** It outlines exact requirements and acceptance criteria.

- **Accessibility:** It specifies non-negotiables for inclusivity and performance.
- **Output:** This defines the desired file format, structure, naming, and length.
- **Verification:** It establishes checks, tests, or a self-review rubric.

This scaffold serves as a backbone for composing very good prompts. While you can adapt it to your needs by dropping irrelevant sections, maintaining the order helps reduce ambiguity and ensures more accurate results. You need to understand how to shape prompts, so they are scannable, consistent, and machine-friendly, especially when working with HTML and CSS. Let us implement this scaffold in the ChatGPT in composing HTML and CSS for a price card for a Software as a Service (SaaS) landing page:

```
ROLE: You are a senior front-end engineer.

GOAL: Produce a responsive, accessible "pricing cards" section
for a SaaS landing page.

CONTEXT:
- Continuation of the portfolio starter we built (dark slate
palette, system-ui font).
- Audience: B2B teams; tone: professional, minimal.
- Assets: none; use placeholder copy.

SPECS:
- 3 cards on desktop, 2 on tablet (≤ 900px), 1 on mobile (≤ 600px).
- Each card: plan name, price, features list, CTA button.
- Use CSS Grid for layout; max-width: 1100px; gap: 1rem; radius:
.75rem.
- Hover: elevate card slightly; focus-visible styles for links
and buttons.

ACCESSIBILITY:
- Semantic HTML (<section>, <article>, <h3>, <ul>, <li>, <button>).
- WCAG AA contrast; 44px tap targets; readable focus outlines.
- "Skip to content" remains functional; no motion if prefers-
reduced-motion.

OUTPUT:
- One self-contained HTML file with embedded <style>.
- No external libs; tiny JS only if necessary.

VERIFICATION:
- Confirm columns change at 900px and 600px via CSS only.
- Confirm all interactive elements reachable via keyboard and have
visible focus.
- Briefly explain layout decisions (Grid vs Flex) in 3 bullet points.
```

In the preceding prompt specifications, you can see the role being expected to be a senior front-end engineer, the goal is to create a responsive and accessible pricing cards section for a SaaS landing page. The section should feature three cards on desktop, scaling down two on tablet and one on mobile, with each card including a plan name, price, features list, and CTA button. The design is expected to adhere to a dark slate palette and system-ui font, with a focus on accessibility, semantic HTML, and WCAG AA contrast standards. The output should be a single, self-contained HTML file with embedded CSS, and the solution should be verified through specific checks, including responsive design, keyboard navigation, and layout decisions.

Hit your ChatGPT and let us see what you can come with your prompt tweaking!

Few-Shot Prompting

In AI-driven development, few-shot prompting is a technique where you provide the model with examples of inputs and outputs before asking it to perform a new task. Reasonable, right? By showing the model examples, you can anchor its style and ensure consistent code output. This is particularly important in frontend development where subjective decisions abound. In the frontend development, there are numerous choices that can impact the quality and consistency of the code, such as naming conventions, layout strategies, and accessibility practices. Without clear guidance, AI models may produce inconsistent results, including inconsistent class naming conventions **`.btn-primary vs .cta vs .button`**, different layout strategies (flexbox versus grid), mismatched accessibility practices. With a clear example, you can define the voice of the code, effectively creating a living design system that guides the AI's output. This approach enables you to establish a consistent coding style, ensure adherence to specific design principles and patterns, reduce errors and inconsistencies, and improve overall code quality. The structure of a few-shot prompt recipe is designed to effectively guide the LLM to learn from examples and apply the pattern to a new task.

Here is a breakdown of the components of a few-shot approach:

- **Instruction:** This section provides an overall description of what you want the AI model to achieve. It sets the context and defines the task's objective.

- **Examples:** This section includes at least 1-3 concrete *input* → *output*pairs that demonstrate the desired pattern or behavior. These examples serve as training data for the AI model, allowing it to learn from specific instances and generalize to new cases.

- **Task:** This section presents the new input that the AI model should apply the learned pattern to. The task is the actual problem you want the AI model to solve, using the knowledge gained from the examples.

By structuring a few-shot prompt this way, you provide the AI model with clear guidance on the task's objective (Instruction), concrete examples to learn from

(Examples), and a specific problem to apply the learned pattern to (Task). This structure enables the AI model to learn from examples and generate outputs that are consistent with the demonstrated pattern. On the other hand, we have zero-shot prompting, where you provide a direct instruction like "Generate a responsive card component with a title, text, and button." However, this approach risks inconsistent coding styles and overlooked accessibility features. Few-shot prompting mitigates these risks by providing examples that demonstrate the desired coding style and patterns. Here is a general format to handle few-shot prompting:

Instruction: You are a front-end assistant. Follow the style in the examples.

Example 1: (input → output)

Example 2: (input → output)

Now, this simply translates for this new input, so generate the output in the same style!

Few-shot prompt

Prompt:

```
You are a senior front-end engineer. Follow the coding style in
the examples.

EXAMPLE 1 (input → output):
Input: "Make a button"
Output:
<button class="btn">Click me</button>
<style>
.btn {
display:inline-block; padding:.75rem 1.25rem;
    border-radius:.5rem; font-weight:600;
background:var(--accent); color:#001018;
text-decoration:none; transition:transform .2s ease;
  }
.btn:hover { transform:translateY(-2px); }
.btn:focus-visible { outline:2px solid #fff; outline-offset:2px; }
</style>

EXAMPLE 2 (input → output):
Input: "Make a hero section"
Output:
<section class="hero">
<h1>Welcome</h1>
<p>Your tagline here.</p>
<a href="#start" class="btn">Get Started</a>
</section>
```

```
<style>
.hero { min-height:100vh; display:grid; place-items:center; text-
align:center; }
.hero h1 { font-size:clamp(2rem,5vw,3rem); margin:0; }
.hero p { color:var(--muted); }
</style>

TASK:
Input: "Make a responsive card component with a title, text, and
button"
Output:
```

To craft effective few-shot prompts, focus on the following strategies:

- **Keep examples short:** Don does not overwhelm with full-page templates; show small, targeted components. Example: one button, one hero, one form field.
- **Show naming conventions:** If your system uses **`.btn`**, **`.card`**, **`.nav-link`**, show those in examples. Avoid mixing **`.primary-btn`** in one and **`.cta`** in another.
- **Break in accessibility:** Demonstrate ARIA attributes — focus-visible, semantic tags. The model will replicate them across outputs.
- **Format consistently:** Always use the same spacing, indentation, code fences. Models mimic formatting habits too.
- **Mix inputs:** Use both descriptive inputs like "Make a card component" and functional ones like "Form field with label and error message". This teaches the AI flexibility in mapping different prompt types to the same coding style.

Prompt Chaining Techniques

When you work with AI models, especially in HTML and CSS development, prompt chaining is a valuable technique that can supercharge your workflow. Prompt chaining involves breaking down complex requests into multiple connected prompts. This approach allows for a more structured and accurate output. This mirrors the way web developers typically work, scaffolding first, styling second, and refining last. In HTML and CSS tasks, competing goals often arise, such as achieving semantic correctness, responsive layout, design language, and accessibility. Asking for all these aspects at once can lead to omissions and inaccuracies. Prompt chaining ensures that each goal gets its own stage, improving accuracy and readability.

One common prompt chaining pattern is the Scaffold - Style - Interact approach. This involves first creating the semantic HTML skeleton, then adding layout CSS for structure, and finally layering in interactions such as hover, focus, and responsive behavior. For example, when building a pricing section in a website, you would start by creating the HTML structure with semantic tags, followed by adding CSS Grid layout for responsiveness, and finally applying design tokens and theming. Another pattern is the Generate - Critique - Refine approach, where the model critiques its own output and then refines it. This involves generating a code, reviewing it for accessibility or performance issues, and then fixing those issues while maintaining the same design style. This chaining pattern turns the AI into both an author and a reviewer, ensuring a more robust and reliable output. Also, there is Explain - Generate pattern, which is also useful, where you ask the model to explain its approach before generating a code. This ensures that the solution is intentional. and not arbitrary. By combining few-shot prompting with chaining, you can teach the model a specific style and then build complex structures step by step. Finally, branching chains allow you to experiment with variations and integrate them later. This involves breaking down tasks into parallel subtasks and merging the outputs into a final file. By using prompt chaining techniques, you can achieve more accurate and reliable outputs and improve the overall quality of your HTML and CSS development projects. In practice, prompt chaining can be applied to various tasks like building a responsive website, creating a login form, or designing a gallery. By breaking down these tasks into smaller, manageable chunks, you can ensure that each aspect of the project is given the attention it deserves, resulting in a more polished and professional output.

Let us dive into implementing a prompt chaining technique with this example:

Instead of:

"Build me a complete responsive website with navigation, hero, gallery, form, and footer."

We chain prompts as follows:

1. Generate the semantic HTML skeleton.
2. Add layout CSS for structure.
3. Apply design tokens and theming.
4. Layer in interactions (hover, focus, responsive behavior).
5. Finally, review + document limitations.

This mirrors how web developers work in real life: scaffold first, style second, refine last. Asking for all at once risks omissions. Prompt chaining ensures that each goal gets its own stage, improving accuracy and readability.

Now, let us explore some of the patterns in prompt chaining starting with the Scaffold→ Style → Interact approach to prompt chaining as follows:

Scaffold - Style - Interact Approach

This approach is like building a house: frame first, paint later, and appliances last.

Step 1: Scaffold HTML

TASK 1: Create semantic HTML for a pricing section with 3 plans.

Include `<section>`, `<article>`, headings, paragraphs, and CTA links.

Do NOT include any CSS.

Output: Pure HTML with `<article>` for each plan.

Step 2: Layout CSS

TASK 2: Add CSS Grid layout for the pricing section created above.

Requirements:

- 3 columns desktop, 2 at ≤900px, 1 at ≤600px
- Gap: 1rem
- Container max-width: 1100px

Output: Responsive grid CSS.

Step 3: Style & Interactions

TASK 3: Add tokens, colors, hover/focus states, and radius to the pricing cards.

Reuse the tokens from earlier examples.

Output: Themed, accessible cards with hover elevation and focus-visible outlines.

Generate Critique and Refine Approach

Let us examine the *Generate Critique* and Refine approach; the model critiques its own output, and then refines it:

Step 1: Generate

TASK 1: Create a login form with labels, inputs, and a submit button. Include CSS.

Step 2: Critique

TASK 2: Review the login form code above. List 3 accessibility or performance issues.

Step 3: Refine

TASK 3: Fix those issues while keeping the same design style. Return the improved code.

This chaining turns the AI into both, an author and a reviewer.

Explain – Generate Prompt Chaining Approach

Then finally, the *Explain – Generate* prompt chaining approach, ask for an cxplanation of an approach before code:

Step 1: Explain

TASK 1: Explain in 3 bullets how you would build a responsive gallery with CSS Grid.

Include breakpoints, object-fit handling, and hover states.

Step 2: Generate

TASK 2: Now generate the HTML/CSS code for the gallery you just described.

This ensures that the solution is intentional, not arbitrary.

Few-Shot + Chain

This combines a few-shot prompting with chaining. It starts by giving examples, then chain progressive tasks.

An Example Workflow:

1. Provide few-shot examples of button + card.
2. Ask the AI to scaffold gallery HTML.
3. Next, style gallery with CSS tokens.
4. Finally, refine for accessibility.

This hybrid approach teaches style first, then builds complex structures step by step.

Branching Chains

When working on complex projects, you might encounter tasks that can be broken down into smaller, independent subtasks. This is where branching chains come in handy. Instead of following a linear workflow, you can branch out into parallel subtasks and then merge the results later. Let us take the example of creating a modal dialog for a website. Here is how you can apply branching chains:

Step 1: Generate Semantic HTML

Create the basic structure of the modal dialog using semantic HTML. This will provide a solid foundation for your component.

Step 2(a): Generate CSS for Layout

In this branch, focus on creating the CSS for the modal layout. This might include styles for:

- Centering the modal on the page
- Creating an overlay to dim the background
- Adding a radius to the modal corners

Step 2(b): Generate CSS for Theming

In this parallel branch, work on creating the CSS for the modal theming. This might include styles for:

- Dark tokens (including backgrounds, text colors, and so on).
- Button styles (colors, hover effects, and the like).

Step 3: Merge Layout and Theming Outputs

Once you have completed the layout and theming CSS, then merge the two outputs into a single, final CSS file. This will give you a complete and visually appealing modal dialog.

By applying branching chains to your workflow, you can work more efficiently, try out new ideas, and create more complex and sophisticated projects. Overall, prompt chaining is a powerful technique that can help you achieve better results in HTML and CSS development. With the structuring of your prompts in a logical and step-by-step manner, you can ensure that your AI model produces high-quality outputs that meet your specific needs and requirements.

Avoiding Prompt Mistakes

When composing prompts for AI models, it is easy and common to fall into pitfalls that can lead to unpleasant results. Like coding errors, prompt mistakes can be avoided by approaching prompting systematically. In this section, we will explore some prompt pitfalls and discuss conflicting requirements. Let us start with prompt vagueness.

Vagueness

When you fail to provide concrete constraints or outputs, your prompt can lead to ambiguous results. Ensure that you clearly define what you are looking for. For instance, do not say; "Make a portfolio webpage in HTML." When you issue a vague prompt, you are likely to have results that add CSS/JS, unclear sections, generic copy, missing meta tags and accessibility, plus unnecessary surrounding explanation text. What if we rewrite this way?

Prompt:

You are generating a single HTML5 document. Return ONLY one code block with valid HTML—no explanations, no CSS, no JavaScript, no external assets.

Goal: *A simple personal portfolio landing page that introduces <Your Name> and drives contact.*

Requirements:

- Use semantic structure: <header>, <main>, <footer>.

- In <header>: site title "<Your Name> – Portfolio" and a nav with anchors to #about, #projects, #contact.

- In <main>:

- <section id="about"> brief bio (2–3 sentences).

- <section id="projects"> list 3 projects; each as <article> with <h3>, 1–2 sentence summary, and a placeholder link (href="#").

- <section id="contact"> email link (mailto:you@example.com) and a short note on response time.

- Accessibility:

- One <h1> (site title), logical heading order, alt text for any images (use placeholders), landmark roles via semantic tags.

- SEO and mobile:

- <title> up to 60 chars, meta description ~155 chars.

- <meta name="viewport" content="width=device-width, initial-scale=1">.

- Constraints:

- Pure HTML only. No <style>, no <script>, no inline styles, no comments.

- English, concise, no lorem ipsum.

- Output Rules:

- Return exactly one fenced code block containing the complete HTML document and nothing else.

The preceding prompt result is expected to be intentionally minimal, and to show structure, not design. To create an effective prompt, set a clear scope and goal, specify tech constraints and structure, and include details like accessibility features and SEO elements.

Conflicts

Conflicts are a part of the mistake to avoid in prompt composition. When a prompt contains incompatible asks, the model has to guess which rule to break, often producing messy or self-contradictory code. These are some of the conflict patterns:

Tech Bans versus Features

- HTML-only, no CSS/JS **versus** responsive grid, modal, accordion (needs CSS/JS).

- No frameworks **versus** use Tailwind classes (Tailwind is a framework).
- No external assets **versus** load Google Fonts / CDN icons.

Format versus Narration

- Return only the HTML file **versus** explain your choices and add comments.
- Structure **versus** Semantics.
- Exactly one **`<h1>`** **versus** each section should have an <h1>.

Now, let us examine the full fledge of a conflicted prompt:

Prompt:

Build a single-file, HTML-only landing page. No CSS or JavaScript. Make it responsive with a Tailwind grid and include a modal. Use Google Fonts. Return the HTML plus an explanation.

The problem with the preceding prompt is that it contains contradictory requirements, such as banning CSS/JS while requesting features that need them.

Let us look at a better prompt design.

Prompt:

You are generating ONE valid HTML5 document. Output exactly one fenced code block with the complete HTML. No explanations, no comments, no external assets.

Priorities (highest → lowest):

1) *Output format (single code block, HTML only)*
2) *Tech constraints (no CSS, no JavaScript, no frameworks, no external assets)*
3) *Structure and semantics*
4) *Content and copy*
5) *Aesthetics*

Conflict rules:

- If a requested feature requires banned tech, implement the closest HTML-only alternative.

- If two rules still conflict, follow the higher priority above or the stricter constraint.

Requirements:

- Use semantic tags: <header>, <main>, <footer>.

- Make navigation and sections accessible.

- For "accordion"/"modal"-style content, use <details>/<summary>; do NOT add JS.

- Exactly one <h1> in the document; use <h2>/<h3> for subsections.

- Include <title>, meta description (~155 chars), and viewport meta.

- No frameworks (for example, Tailwind), no inline styles, no external fonts/icons.

Deliverable:

- Return one fenced code block containing only the HTML document.

This preceding approach works because it sets clear priorities, uses fallbacks to meet intent within constraints, establishes hard bans, and specifies a tight deliverable format that effectively guide the model to make necessary trade-offs.

Overreach

The overreach mistake occurs when prompts ask too much at once, forcing the model to juggle multiple aspects like design, copy, and accessibility This often result in bloated and error-prone output; instead, break down large requests into smaller, manageable steps.

Let us explore the scenario where we have too many goals, mixed deliverables, and contradictory tech needs.

An Overreach Prompt:

"Build a complete portfolio site in one HTML file. Make it responsive, add a modal, write compelling copy, ensure WCAG AA, great SEO, and explain decisions."

Preferred Prompt:

Step 1 — Lock the spec (JSON only)

You are defining requirements, not writing code.

Goal: *Single-file HTML5 portfolio (HTML only; no CSS/JS/external assets).*

Output: *JSON with keys: title, meta_description (≤155 chars), sections (array of ids & headings: about, projects, contact), nav_order (array of ids), accessibility_rules (array), seo_rules (array), constraints (array).*

Rules: *Return valid JSON only. No prose.*

Step 2 — Draft the content (concise copy)

Using the previous JSON spec, write microcopy for each section.

Output: *JSON with keys matching section ids; each has headings and 2–3 sentence body. Include 3 project entries (name, 1–2 sentence summary, "#" link).*

Rules: *JSON only. No HTML, no prose.*

Step 3 — Wireframe the HTML (structure only)

Generate ONE complete HTML5 document using the spec and copy JSON.

Constraints: HTML *only*. No *<style>, no <script>, no external assets, no comments.*

Structure:*<header>/<main>/<footer>,* one *<h1>, logical <h2>/<h3>, nav to #about #projects #contact, <details>/<summary> allowed for collapsibles.*

Accessibility: *landmarks via semantic tags, aria-labels for nav, alt="" on placeholders.*

Output: *Return exactly one fenced code block containing the full* HTML *and nothing else.*

Step 4 – A11y & SEO checklist (diff, not code)

Audit the HTML *against* WCAG *quick checks and basic* SEO.

Output: A *markdown checklist of findings with explicit* "Fix:" *actions* (no *code*). *Keep it* ≤12 *items.*

Step 5 – Final HTML pass (apply fixes)

Regenerate the single-file HTML *applying* ONLY *the approved fixes.*

Constraints unchanged: HTML *only; no* CSS/JS/*external assets.*

Output: *Exactly one fenced code block with the complete, valid* HTML *document.*

Step 6 – Acceptance gate (yes/no)

Validate the final HTML against these gates:

- *Single fenced code block, no prose*

- One *<h1>; proper heading order*

- *Required sections/anchors present*

- *Meta title + description + viewport present*

- No *style/script/external assets*

Output: "PASS" *or* "FAIL" *with a* 3–5 *item reason list.* No *code.*

This preceding six-step chain defines a JSON spec, writes section copy in JSON, generates a single-file HTML wireframe from it, audits accessibility/SEO via a checklist, regenerates the HTML with only approved fixes, and finishes with a strict pass/fail acceptance check.

Hidden State

Chat history bias can influence the current output. Prior messages can bias the model, causing drift from current constraints. To neutralize chat history, reset the scope with phrases like "*Treat this as a new task*" and restate constraints verbatim. Adding a priority ladder and using an echo check, where the model restates constraints in a small JSON, can also help. This ensures predictable outputs and adherence to constraints.

For instance, the following shows how to prevent inherent bias due to chat history:

Treat this as a new, independent task. Use only the instructions in THIS message.

Artifact: *ONE complete HTML5 document.*

Output contract: Return exactly one fenced code block with the full HTML. No explanations, no comments, no CSS/JS, no external assets.

Constraints (repeat back before coding):

- Pure HTML only (no <style>, no <script>, no inline styles, no external fonts/icons/ CDNs)

- Structure: <header>, <main>, <footer>

- Nav anchors: #about #projects #contact

- Headings: exactly one <h1>; use <h2>/<h3> for subsections

- SEO: <title> ≤60 chars, meta description ≤155 chars, viewport meta

- Accessibility: semantic landmarks, aria-label on nav, alt text on placeholders

Step A – Constraint echo (JSON only):

Output a single JSON object with keys: html_only, structure, nav, headings, seo, a11y, deliverable. Values are short confirmations. No prose.

Step B – HTML (only if Step A is correct):

Return exactly one fenced code block containing the complete HTML document and nothing else.

It is a good practice to start fresh with a new conversation, and begin with the standard reset, constraints, and contract block to prevent any hidden state or past context from influencing the model's output.

No Verifiability

When you fail to provide a checklist or tests along with your prompt can make it difficult to verify the output. To ensure that the HTML output meets specific requirements and constraints, include a detailed acceptance checklist and a strict *pass/fail* gate in the prompt. The checklist should cover key aspects such as:

- Output format and structure
- Doctype, head, and meta tags
- Mobile and SEO optimization
- Tech bans (no CSS, JS, or external assets)
- Accessibility basics (semantic landmarks, aria-label, alt text)
- Link and reference integrity

The pass/fail gate should verify that all requirements are met, like ingle fenced code block with only HTML, required sections and nav anchors, title and description length limits, no CSS/JS/external assets and the accessibility basics. To make verification easy, include grep/search-style micro-tests: scan for banned tech (CSS, JS, external assets like `<style>`, `<script>`, `inline style=`, `http(s)://`), confirm exactly one `<h1>`, ensure required IDs exist with matching nav targets, for example `#about`, `#projects`, `#contact`, and measure `<title>` (≤60 chars) and meta description (≤155 chars); if any gate item fails, mark the document FAIL with a brief reason list, otherwise PASS, ensuring the output meets all specified requirements and constraints.

With common mistakes with prompt composition highlighted, and best practice discussed, let us explore debugging prompts with AI, where we will explore techniques for identifying and resolving issues that arise when working with AI models.

Debugging Prompts with AI

Debugging prompts is important when working with AI models to achieve the desired output. By treating the prompt like code, we can use a systematic approach to reproduce, isolate, fix, and prevent issues. This section explores the steps to debug prompts with AI, starting with minimal reproduction.

Step 1: Minimal reproduction

To start debugging, ask the AI model to produce the smallest HTML/CSS snippet that still shows the problem. This is known as a minimal reproduction. By isolating the issue, you can iterate on just that snippet and avoid unnecessary complexity. For example, let us say, we are experiencing an issue with a card component overflowing at 360px. We can prompt the AI model to create a minimal reproduction:

"Create a minimal reproduction of the card overflow at 360px. No icons, no animations. Return only the HTML/CSS required to reproduce the bug."

This will give you a simplified version of the code, allowing you to focus on the specific issue.

Step 2: Isolation and ablation

To further isolate the issue, you can use ablation prompts to remove classes or rules and see what changes. This helps you to understand the impact of each component on the output.

For example, we can prompt the AI model to remove transforms and transitions:

"Show a diff that removes all transforms/transitions; keep layout and spacing only."

By removing these elements, you can see if the issue persists and you can focus on the layout and spacing.

Step 3: Constraint re-statement

When working with AI models, chats can drift, and constraints can be forgotten. To avoid this, restate constraints or start a fresh thread with the exact spec.

For example, we can prompt the AI model to start fresh with "*Let us start fresh. Create a card component with the following constraints:*

Width: 300px
Padding: 20px
Border: 1px solid #ddd
Font size: 16px
Responsive: yes
Breakpoint: 360px"

By restating the constraints, you can ensure that the AI model understands the requirements and produces the desired output.

Step 4: Add a verification layer

It is one of the best practices to have the AI model generate a short checklist that verifies that the output meets the requirements. For example, prompt the AI model with: "*Create a short checklist to verify the card component meets the requirements.*"

This will produce a list of items to verify, including:

- Width is 300px on desktop.
- Padding is 20px.
- Border is 1px solid #ddd.
- Font size is 16px.

Component is responsive and adapts to 360px breakpoint. By adding a verification layer, you can ensure that the output meets the requirements and catch any issues early on. Debugging prompts with AI requires a systematic approach to reproduce, isolate, fix, and prevent issues. By using minimal reproductions, ablation prompts, constraint re-statement, and verification layers, you can ensure your outputs meet the requirements and achieve the desired results.

Conclusion

Prompt engineering for HTML and CSS is about transforming intent into verifiable code by encoding context, role, standards, and acceptance criteria. Through iterative critique and targeted fixes, AI becomes a reliable partner, not a creative variable. By prioritizing semantics and accessibility, utilizing tokens for styling, and leveraging diffs for controlled changes, you can achieve consistent results. Mastering prompt engineering involves avoiding common prompt mistakes, debugging prompts effectively with AI, and applying best practices to ensure high-quality outputs. With these skills, you will spend less time rewriting and more time shipping accessible, resilient interfaces. Key aspects to focus on include avoiding prompt mistakes that lead to bloated or error-prone code, debugging prompts with techniques like minimal reproduction, isolation, and verification layers, and applying these habits to generate high-quality core HTML code that meets specific requirements and best practices.

In the next chapter, we will explore workflow for building the core structure of web pages with semantic HTML while using ChatGPT, an AI system.

Points to Remember

- Prompts are specifications; clarity beats cleverness.
- Use C.R.A.F.T.E.D.: Context, Role, Acceptance, Format, Tone/Tactics, Examples, Done-definition.
- Designing with semantics and WCAG 2.2 AA; keep ARIA minimal.
- Control output with code fences, section order, and explicit file blocks.
- For responsiveness, specify breakpoints and mobile-first behavior.
- Enforce CSS hygiene: tokens, no inline styles, predictable naming.
- Use few-shots sparingly to imprint patterns without copying.
- Chain prompts: spec -code -critique -fix -finalize.
- Prevent drift with unified diffs and scoped edits.
- Add self-checks and rubrics to verify success.

Multiple Choice Questions

1. Which part of a prompt most directly ensures verifiable success?
    a. Tone of voice
    b. Acceptance criteria
    c. Brand adjectives
    d. Example color palette
2. Which instruction best prevents uncontrolled rewrites during iteration?
    a. Be creative
    b. Return verbose commentary
    c. Apply only these changes as a unified diff
    d. Regenerate from scratch

3. Which is the most semantic way to mark up the main content region?
    a. `<div id="content">`
    b. `<section>`
    c. `<main>`
    d. `<article>`
4. A fewshot example should be:
    a. Long and comprehensive
    b. Short and pattern focused
    c. Stylistically unrelated
    d. Pure prose with no code
5. Which is an appropriate antipattern to forbid in HTML/CSS prompts?
    a. CSS variables
    b. Code fences
    c. Inline styles
    d. Mobilefirst CSS
6. When should ARIA roles be added to native semantic elements?
    a. Always
    b. Only when necessary to convey semantics that HTML cannot express
    c. Never
    d. Whenever styling requires it
7. Which acceptance criterion best supports accessibility?
    a. Use lots of colors
    b. Focus states must be visible and noncoloronly
    c. Use three cards
    d. Center the headline
8. Which chaining step comes immediately after generating a first draft?
    a. Finalize
    b. Critique/Audit
    c. Spec
    d. Deploy

9. Which prompt clause controls output structure and verbosity?
    a. Role
    b. Format
    c. Context
    d. Examples
10. To reduce prompt failure, which technique isolates the problematic instruction?
    a. Prompt bisection
    b. Color theming
    c. Increasing font size
    d. Adding more images
11. Which breakpoint set communicates mobilefirst expectations clearly?
    a. 1280, 1024, 768, 375
    b. 320, 375 only
    c. 640, 800, 900
    d. 500, 700, 900
12. Which instruction best enforces maintainable CSS?
    a. Prefer id selectors
    b. Use CSS variables for color and spacing tokens
    c. Inline all critical CSS in HTML
    d. Avoid comments

Answers

1. b
2. c
3. c
4. b
5. c
6. b
7. b
8. b
9. b
10. a

11. a
12. b

Key Terms

- **Prompt Engineering:** The practice of specifying context, constraints, standards, and success checks so that AI can generate a reliable code.
- **C.R.A.F.T.E.D.:** A prompt framework: Context, Role, Acceptance criteria, Format, Tone/Tactics, Examples, Donedefinition.
- **FewShot Prompting:** Guiding outputs with a few small examples that imprint structure/style patterns.
- **Prompt Chaining:** Sequencing tasks such as spec -code -critique -fix -finalizeto control quality and drift.
- **Acceptance Criteria:** Verifiable checks that define "done" for instance landmarks present, contrast ≥ 4.5:1.
- **Semantic HTML:** Using meaningbearing elements (header, main, nav, section, article, footer) instead of generic divs.
- **WCAG 2.2 AA:** Accessibility guidelines defining perceivable, operable, understandable, robust criteria at the AA conformance level.
- **ARIA:** Accessible Rich Internet Applications; use minimally and only when native semantics are insufficient.
- **Output Control:** Techniques (code fences, file blocks, section order) that enforce clean, predictable results.
- **Unified Diff:** A compact patch format that scopes changes and prevents full rewrites.
- **TokenFirst CSS:** Styling with design tokens (variables) for color, spacing, radius, etc., to ensure consistency.
- **Landmarks:** Page regions that assist navigation (header, nav, main, aside, footer).
- **FocusVisible:** A CSS pseudoclass and principle ensuring keyboard users can see their focus location.
- **MobileFirst:** Designing from small to large viewports with progressive enhancement.
- **AntiPattern:** A commonly seen but harmful approach like inline styles, unnecessary ARIA, fixed heights for layout.

CHAPTER 4
Core HTML with AI Assistance

Introduction

In *Chapter 3, Prompt Engineering for* HTML *and* CSS, we discussed prompt strategies and best practices. In this chapter, we will develop a practical workflow for building the core structure of web pages with semantic HTML while using AI systems as reliable collaborators. You will learn how to turn requirements and outlines into verifiable HTML scaffolds that respect accessibility, search engine discoverability, and team collaboration.

We will use prompt patterns to generate headers, navigation, main content regions, and footers, then we will improve on the results with accessibility reviews and checklists. By the end of this chapter, you will be able to produce a production-ready, accessible web page skeleton, efficiently and consistently.

After reading this chapter, you will be able to choose the correct semantic element for each section of a webpage, map content into a clear H1–H2–H3 outline, and scaffold a standards-compliant homepage. You will write precise AI prompts that compose semantic Hypertext Markup Language (HTML) structure with headings, and alt text, enforce a one-page level H1; and distinguish multiple navs with aria-labels. You will generate form with a label and validate form controls, add a visible skip link, and separate semantics from layout using Grid/Flexbox. You will test keyboard flow and contrast, run basic accessibility audits, and refactor div-heavy pages into meaningful sections and articles that improve maintainability, SEO, and assistive technology navigation.

Structure

In this chapter, we will cover the following topics:

- Understanding Semantic HTML and Layout Structure
- Prompting for Core Page Elements
- Creating a Logical Content Outline

- Scaffolding a Semantic Homepage with AI
- Making Semantic Structure Accessible

Understanding Semantic HTML and Layout Structure

Semantic HTML is simply the practice of writing HTML markup that follows the intended meaning and structure of content, rather than its visual presentation (*https://en.wikipedia.org/wiki/Semantic_Web*). The semantic HTML communicates with intent to browsers, assistive technologies, and search engines. It improves accessibility by making the structure of a page programmatically obvious, so that the assistive technologies screen readers, voice control, switch devices, browsers, and bots can understand and navigate it quickly. With the semantic HTML, you can enhance SEO through meaningful structure and accelerate team collaboration by making pages purposefully self-evident. The core layout of a web page typically includes a site-wide header, a primary navigation, a single main region for the page's unique content, optional asides, and a footer.

Let us examine the core elements of a web page and their typical use starting with the `<header>`.

`<header>`:*Branding, global actions, top-of-page intro.*

This is a top area for a page or a section. You can place the logo, site name, search, and account/cart links here. You may have a site header at the top of the page and smaller headers inside sections or articles. Let us briefly explore an example:

```
<header>
<a href="/"><imgsrc="logo.svg" alt="Oupex" /></a>
<form role="search"><input aria-label="Search" /></form>
</header>
```

The preceding code displays a page header that displays the Oupex logo linking to the homepage and includes an accessible site search form identified by the search role.

`<nav>`: Navigation menus.

This is a container for the major sets of links that move around the site or within a page. If you have more than one, give each an `aria-label` like Primary or Footer. Let us briefly explore an example:

```
<nav aria-label="Primary">
<ul><li><a href="/products">Products</a></li></ul>
</nav>
```

The preceding code creates a semantic navigation for the site's primary menu, the **`aria-label="Primary"`** gives the nav an accessible name so that the screen readers can distinguish it from other navs, the **<ul>** groups menu items, and each <li> contains a link like products link.

<main>: Unique page content, ideally one per page.

This represents the primary content of a page. It is used exactly one per page. You can also use it as the target of a skip link for keyboard users. Let us briefly explore an example:

```
<a class="skip-link" href="#main">Skip to content</a>
<main id="main">…page-specific content…</main>
```

The code above shows a visible "*Skip to content*" link that lets keyboard and assistive technology users bypass repeated navigation and jump directly to the page's **<main>** region identified by **id="main"**.

<section>: Thematic grouping of related content with a heading.

This groups related content under a clear heading. You can use it to structure the page, not as a generic wrapper. Each section should have a visible heading. Let us briefly explore an example:

```
<section aria-labelledby="features">
<h2 id="features">Features</h2>
<p>Key capabilities…</p>
</section
```

The aforementioned code groups related content into a semantic section whose accessible name is provided by **aria-labelledby="features"** pointing to the<h2 **id="features">Features</h2>,** which serves as the section's visible heading for the accompanying description.

<article>: Self-contained, independently distributable content.

This represents the content that can stand on its own or be shared: a blog post, product card, news item, or forum post. It usually has its own heading and metadata. Let us briefly explore an example:

```
<article>
<h2>How we built the app</h2>
<p>Story and details…</p>
</article>
```

The preceding code shows a self-contained **<article>** that can be distributed independently, with its own heading such as "*How we built the app*" and supporting text content.

<aside>: Complementary content such as related links and info.

This is useful but not core to the main flow: related links, tips, promos, or a mini profile. Screen readers treat it as complementary. Let us briefly explore an example:

```
<aside aria-labelledby="related">
<h2 id="related">Related</h2>
<ul><li><a href="/guide">Getting started</a></li></ul>
</aside>
```

The former example shows a complementary **<aside>** landmark region, named "Related" via aria-labelled by pointing to **<h2 id="related">**, that presents a small list of related links such as "*Getting started.*"

<footer>: Site or section-level closing information

This represents the ending area for a page or a section. It allows you to display contact details, copyright, small print, or secondary navigation here.

You can also have a footer inside an article. Let us briefly explore an example:

```
<footer>
<nav aria-label="Footer">
<a href="/privacy">Privacy</a>
</nav>
<p>© 2025 Oupex Co.</p>
</footer>
```

This example defines a page footer containing a labeled navigation landmark (**aria-label="Footer"**) with a Privacy link and a copyright notice ("**© 2025 Oupex Co.**").

Next, let us explore how to use prompts to build the core page elements that form the foundation of a semantic HTML structure.

Prompting for Core Page Elements

Designers and developers often ask for a magic phrase that makes an AI produce great markup on the first try. Honestly, there is no magic phrase, but there is a clear structure that consistently leads to clean, semantic structure. In this section, we will focus on how to write those prompts for core page elements. You will learn what to include, what to exclude, and how to validate the output. Along the way you will see complete examples, acceptance checklists, and small variations for common site layouts. The goal is simple: speak to the AI as a frontend architect would, encode the intent and constraints, and receive a HTML that is production-ready, meaningful, accessible, and easy to extend.

Why Targeting Core Elements Matters

The core elements like the header, nav, main, section, article, aside, and footer are not mere placeholders. They create the document outline, define structure for assistive technologies, and reduce the amount of ARIA you need. When your prompt names these elements and explains how they relate, the AI is far less likely to invent nonstandard patterns or produce div soup that harms navigation and maintainability.

Note: *Div soup refers to the practice of using excessive and unnecessary div elements in HTML markup, resulting in a cluttered, non-semantic, and often inaccessible structure.*

Let us examine a simple mental model for strong prompts. As discussed previously, think of your prompt as a small specification. Each specification answers six questions as follows:

1. ***Role and goal***: Who is the AI in this task, and what is the exact deliverable?
2. ***Required landmarks***: Which regions must appear?
3. ***Content model***: How headings and sections are structured?
4. ***Accessibility constraints***: What rules ensure that the page is usable for everyone?
5. ***Non-requirements***: What is it that you do not want explicitly?
6. ***Validation***: How to verify that the output meets your standard?

The following sections unpack each part with examples you can paste into your own prompts:

Role and Goal

This tells the AI who it is and what outcome you expect. This anchors the tone and scope. An example of a good role and goal:

You are a front-end architect. Create a semantic HTML scaffold for a small business homepage.

The preceding defines the professional role. It names the deliverable as a template, not a full design or a CSS mock-up. It sets the context like a small business homepage rather than a generic page like "*Make a homepage*". When your prompt is vague like "Make a homepage", it often produces extraneous libraries, UI frameworks, or decorative markup. Being explicit is the key.

Required Landmarks

List the landmarks you want so the AI cannot skip or substitute them. You specify a clear requirement. These are required web page structure: header, nav[aria-label="Primary"], main, footer, one aside inside main, and a visible "Skip to content" link. The *skip link* is critical for keyboard users. You can use multiple navregions, but each needs a distinct accessible name like "Primary", "Footer", "Utility". You can also use at least one aside that is a complementary content; it exists without letting it dominate the layout.

Content Model

This describes the heading hierarchy and sectioning rules. Use one page-level h1 in main. The subsections use `h2` and every section has a visible heading. This is essential for screen reader users as they rely on the heading outline to navigate. A single h1 per page keeps the outline predictable. Every section needs a heading; otherwise, the region becomes anonymous and harder to scan.

Accessibility Constraints

This bakes accessibility into the prompt to prevent costly rework. When specifying accessibility constraints, consider including requirements such as visible focus styles for interactive elements, a logical tab order that follows the DOM order, reduced motion handling for animations, and using **`aria-describedby`** to tie input help and errors to fields, as well as aria-label for multiple nav regions and role="search" for site search forms.

Non-Requirements

When defining requirements, it is equally important to specify what not to include, as this helps remove ambiguity and prevent potential issues. Effective exclusions can include prohibiting inline styles, framework classes, and minimal placeholder text, as these can lead to maintainability problems, accidental styling, and bloated files that obscure the real structure. By excluding these elements, you can ensure a more robust and maintainable solution. Let us explore the breakdown of the reasons why these exclusions are valuable:

- Inline styles can hide specificity problems and are hard to maintain.
- Framework classes can be added later by choice, not by accident, allowing for more control over the styling.
- Placeholder text can bloat the file and hide the real structure, making it harder to work with.

All these helps to streamline the outcome to expectations with unnecessary surprises!

Validation

Validation is pivotal. Always ask the AI to help you check the result and consider adding HTML comments to explain why each element was chosen. This makes the scaffold self-documenting and helps spot potential issues, such as:

- Invented attributes
- Nonstandard ARIA
- Other hallucinations

By including comments, you can ensure that the code is not only functional, but also maintainable and understandable.

Copy and paste this example prompt into your ChatGPT and let us see what produces for you.

Create an HTML5 *scaffold for a marketing homepage. Include: skip link; header with logo and utility nav; nav (primary); main with hero (h1), features (section + h2), testimonials (section + h2), and a newsletter form. The newsletter form is a standard form; the site search is separate and should use <form role="search">. Include one complementary aside inside main, and a footer. Use meaningful headings, one page-level h1, and aria-label where appropriate.* No CSS *or JavaScript. No inline styles. No framework classes. Minimal placeholder text. Add* HTML *comments that explain why each element was chosen.*

Note: *Refer to GitHub for the semantic* HTML *generate for this section.*

Turning Structure into a Reusable Prompt Template

When working on multiple projects, it is efficient to have a reusable template that can be adapted to different requirements or projects. Here is a template for generating a reusable semantic HTML5 starting structure for a page:

Template

You are a front-end architect. Produce a semantic HTML5 *scaffold for [page type].*

Include landmarks:

- skip link targeting #main

- header with [branding] and nav[aria-label="Utility"]

- nav[aria-label="Primary"] for main site sections

- main with [sections list]

- one aside inside main for complementary content

- footer with secondary navigation and address

Content model:

- exactly one page-level h1 in main

- sections use h2; subsections may use h3

- every section has a visible heading

Accessibility:

- aria-label on multiple nav regions

- meaningful alt text

- site search as <form role="search">; newsletter as a standard form with labels

- labels and aria-describedby for forms

Non-requirements:

- no CSS, no JS, no inline styles, no framework classes

- minimal placeholder text

Validation:

- add HTML comments explaining each element choice

- ensure the structure passes the checklist

Replace [page type], [branding], and [sections list] for each project.

Let us apply this template to two different projects and you will explore the results on your ChatGPT console.

Variation A: Service Business Homepage

Header: logo, phone number link, search

Nav[aria-label="Primary"]: Services, Pricing, Reviews, Contact

Main: hero, services grid, testimonials, FAQ section with disclosure controls, newsletter form

Aside: operating hours and a callback link

Footer: address, legal, social links

Variation B: Conference Website Homepage

Header: logo, date, location, search

Nav[aria-label="Primary"]: Speakers, Schedule, Tickets, Venue

Main: hero with h1, featured speakers as article cards, schedule snapshot, call for papers, newsletter

Aside: travel tips and hotel discounts

Footer: code of conduct, accessibility statement, sponsor list

Both share the same backbone, but adjust headings and sections for the audience and content. A strong prompt does more than list elements. It sets a role, defines the landmarks, shapes the heading outline, and requires accessible relationships. It rules out inline styles and frameworks so the bare-bones semantic HTML5 layout remains portable. It asks for comments that justify each choice and provides a checklist for verification. This combination consistently produces clean, semantic HTML that is ready for styling, content, and behavior.

When you treat prompts as small specifications, your AI partner stops guessing and starts delivering. You spend less time deleting invented attributes or untangling div soup, and more time polishing the experience that users actually feel. You can use the templates and examples in this section as a starting point, refine them for your team's conventions, and keep them versioned so improvements compound over time.

Now, let us translate strategy into structure by building a content outline that captures scope, hierarchy, and logical progression.

Creating a Logical Content Outline

When creating a website, it is important to have a solid architectural information. This involves organizing content in a logical and accessible way. Let us break down the process of mapping information architecture to headings and sections using a simple example. For instance, let us consider a homepage for a fictional bike company, Oupex Bikes. The main sections of the page are:

- *Introduction to Oupex Bikes*
- *Featured bike models*
- *Benefits of choosing Acme Bikes*
- *Testimonials from riders*
- *Latest news and insights*
- *Newsletter signup*
- *Complementary information like store hours, support links, phone number, and so on.*
- *Secondary navigation and small print in the footer*
- *Mapping to Headings and Sections*

Using the information architecture outlined above, we can map each section to a corresponding HTML element:

- **H1: OupexBikes — Ride Further**

  This will be the main heading for the page, containing the value proposition and a Call-to-Action (CTA).

- **H2: Featured Models**

  This section will contain a list of featured bike models, each represented as an `<article>` element with a name, price, and spec summary.

- **H2: Why Choose Oupex**

  This section will highlight the benefits of choosing Oupex Bikes, presented in a bulleted list.

- **H2: Stories From Riders**

  This section will feature testimonials from satisfied riders, represented as `<article>` elements or `<figure>` elements with quotes.

- **H2: Latest Insights**

  This section will contain a list of latest blog posts or news articles.

- **H2: Stay in the Loop**

  This section will contain a newsletter signup form.

- **Complementary Information (Aside)**

  This section will contain store hours, support links, and a phone number, presented in an **<aside>** element.

- **Footer**

  The footer will contain secondary navigation, address, social media links, and small print.

Let us explore an example of how the HTML structure for the homepage might look:

```
<!-- Main heading -->
<h1>Oupex Bikes – Ride Further</h1>
<!-- Value proposition and CTA -->

<!-- Featured models section -->
<section>
<h2>Featured Models</h2>
<article>
<h3>Bike Model 1</h3>
<p>Price: $1000</p>
<p>Spec summary...</p>
</article>
<article>
<h3>Bike Model 2</h3>
<p>Price: $1200</p>
<p>Spec summary...</p>
</article>
<article>
<h3>Bike Model 3</h3>
<p>Price: $1500</p>
<p>Spec summary...</p>
</article>
</section>

<!-- Why choose Oupex section -->
<section>
<h2>Why Choose Oupex</h2>
<ul>
<li>Benefit 1</li>
```

```
<li>Benefit 2</li>
<li>Benefit 3</li>
</ul>
</section>

<!-- Stories from riders section -->
<section>
<h2>Stories From Riders</h2>
<article>
<blockquote>Testimonial 1</blockquote>
<cite>Rider 1</cite>
</article>
<article>
<blockquote>Testimonial 2</blockquote>
<cite>Rider 2</cite>
</article>
</section>

<!-- Latest insights section -->
<section>
<h2>Latest Insights</h2>
<ul>
<li><a href="#">Article 1</a></li>
<li><a href="#">Article 2</a></li>
<li><a href="#">Article 3</a></li>
</ul>
</section>

<!-- Newsletter signup section -->
<section>
<h2>Stay in the Loop</h2>
<form>
<label for="email">Email:</label>
<input type="email" id="email" name="email">
<button type="submit">Subscribe</button>
</form>
</section>

<!-- Complementary information -->
<aside>
<h2>Store Hours</h2>
<p>Monday to Friday: 9am to 5pm</p>
<h2>Support</h2>
<ul>
<li><a href="#">Contact Us</a></li>
```

```
<li><a href="#">FAQs</a></li>
</ul>
<p>Phone: 123-456-7890</p>
</aside>

<!-- Footer -->
<footer>
<nav>
<ul>
<li><a href="#">About Us</a></li>
<li><a href="#">Contact Us</a></li>
</ul>
</nav>
<address>
    345 Main St, Anytown, Canada 12345
</address>
<ul>
<li><a href="#" aria-label="Facebook">Facebook</a></li>
<li><a href="#" aria-label="Twitter">Twitter</a></li>
</ul>
<small>&copy; 2026 Oupex Bikes</small>
</footer>
```

When building a semantic HTML structure, keep the following rules of thumb in mind:

- Use one page-level **<h1>** element and descend with **<h2>** elements for each major section.
- Every section needs a heading, as screen readers use these to build their own tables of contents.
- Use **<article>** elements for units of content that make sense on their own, such as cards, posts, or products.

By following these rules and using semantic HTML elements, you can create a website that is accessible and easy to navigate for all users.

In the next section, we will bring the power of the AI to explore how to map this content outline to semantic HTML elements and create a basic website structure.

Scaffolding a Semantic Homepage with AI

Scaffolding a semantic homepage with AI ensures that the website's structure and content are accessible, user-friendly, and optimized for search engines. AI systems excel in tasks that follow well-defined rules, and semantic HTML markup is a prime example where AI can deliver precise and consistent results. This approach uses AI to automate the process, improving consistency and reducing errors, while also enhancing accessibility for users with disabilities. With AI assisting with semantic HTML composition, you can create a solid foundation for a website that is both functional and adaptable to future technologies. Let us create a semantic homepage for a fictional bike riding business, Oupex & Co., using a prompt.

Prompt:

1) ***Header + Primary Navigation***

   You are a senior frontend engineer. Generate semantic HTML for a site header with brand title "Oupex" and a primary navigation with links: Home, About, Services, Blog, Contact. Use only HTML (no CSS/JS). Include an aria-label on the <nav>. Ensure there will be exactly one <h1> in the page and it will live in <main>, not the header.

2) ***Outline → Semantic Scaffold***

   Convert this outline into semantic HTML with one <main>, correct heading hierarchy, and explicit landmarks:

   - Header with logo + primary nav

   - Hero with page title and call-to-action

   - Services (3 items)

   - Testimonials (2 quotes)

   - Footer with contact and social links

   Constraints: HTML only. Add aria-labels if multiple <nav> are present.

3) ***Accessibility Audit***

   Audit the following HTML for accessibility:

   - Confirm a single <main>, proper heading order, link purpose clarity, and alt text coverage.

   - Return a bullet list of issues and a minimal diff showing only corrected lines.

   Use only HTML (no CSS/JS). Include an aria-label on the <nav>. Ensure there will be exactly one <h1> in the page and it will live in <main>, not the header.

Explore the output from ChatGPT and see how it works. A copy of the code generated is uploaded to the GitHub for this book.

The deliverable from the preceding prompt will be that the header prompt produces a semantic `<header>` with a properly labeled primary <nav> and guarantees the single `<h1>` appears inside `<main>`. The outline prompt yields a complete, accessible page scaffold that maps sections to correct landmarks and enforces a logical heading hierarchy. And the audit prompt returns a concise issue list and a minimal diff that fixes common problems such as duplicate **<main>**, misplaced **<h1>**, ambiguous links, missing alt text, and unclear aria-labels.

Note: *A diff is a textual summary of changes between two versions of a file or sets of files, showing what was removed and what was added.*

In the next section, making semantic structure accessible, we will examine the crucial role of semantic HTML in creating websites that are usable by everyone, including individuals with disabilities, and discuss best practices for ensuring accessibility in semantic web development.

Making Semantic Structure Accessible

Creating an accessible website is essential to ensure that all users, including those with disabilities, can navigate and understand the content of your website. A semantic structure plays a vital role in achieving accessibility by providing a clear and consistent framework for content. Let us briefly discuss some key considerations for making your semantic structure truly accessible, starting with the headings:

Headings

Always use one page-level **<h1>** element to define the main heading of the page. Use heading levels in a logical order like **<h2>**, **<h3>**, **<h4>** without skipping levels. Avoid using headings solely for styling purposes; instead, use them to define the structure and hierarchy of content. Let us see an example:

```
<h1>Main Heading</h1>
<section>
<h2>Subheading</h2>
<p>Content...</p>
<h3>Sub-subheading</h3>
<p>More content...</p>
</section>
```

Landmarks

For landmarks, use elements like **<header>**, **<nav>**, **<main>**, **<footer>** to define the main landmark regions of the page. Always include a **<main>** element to define the primary content area. It is essential to use aria-label to distinguish between multiple navigation elements like "**Primary Navigation**" and "**Footer Navigation**". Let us see an example:

```
<nav aria-label="Primary Navigation">
<ul>
```

```
<li><a href="#">Home</a></li>
<li><a href="#">About</a></li>
<li><a href="#">Contact</a></li>
</ul>
</nav>
<main>
<!-- Primary content area -->
</main>
<footer>
<nav aria-label="Footer Navigation">
<ul>
<li><a href="#">Terms and Conditions</a></li>
<li><a href="#">Privacy Policy</a></li>
</ul>
</nav>
</footer>
```

Provide a skip link as the first focusable element on the page, linking to the #main content area like this example:

```
<a href="#main" class="skip-link">Skip to main content</a>
<!-- Navigation and other content -->
<main id="main">
<!-- Primary content area -->
</main>
```

This allows users to bypass repetitive navigation and jump directly to the main content.

Images

In images on you web page, use the alt attribute to provide a concise description of informative images. But you can use an empty alt attribute (**`alt=""`**) for decorative images that do not convey important information. Let us look at this example:

```
<imgsrc="logo.png" alt="Company Logo">
<imgsrc="decorative-image.jpg" alt="">
```

Forms

In working with forms, use **`<label for>`** or **`aria-labelledby`** to associate labels with form fields. It is important to mark required inputs and provide helpful error messages tied to fields using **`aria-describedby`**. Let us look at this example:

```
<label for="name">Full Name:</label>
<input type="text" id="name" name="name" required aria-
describedby="name-error">
```

```
<span id="name-error" class="error-message">Please enter your
full name.</span>
```

ARIA

When it comes to creating accessible web content, ARIA (Accessible Rich Internet Applications) roles and states can be a powerful tool. However, it is essential to use them judiciously and follow best practices. The thumb rule is to prefer native HTML elements over ARIA roles and states whenever possible. Native HTML elements, such as **`<nav>`**, **`<header>`**, and **`<footer>`**, provide built-in accessibility features that make it easier for the screen readers, and other assistive technologies to understand the structure and content of a web page. ARIA roles and states should only be used when there is no native HTML element that can achieve the desired accessibility outcome. This is because ARIA roles and states can be complex and may require additional maintenance and testing to ensure that they are working correctly.

For instance, you can use ARIA roles and states only when no semantic HTML element exists like **`role="search"`** on a sitewide search form as follows:

```
<form role="search">
<label for="search">Search:</label>
<input type="search" id="search" name="search">
</form>
```

Keyboard Navigation

Keyboard navigation is an essential aspect of web accessibility, allowing users to interact with a website using only their keyboard. To ensure a smooth and intuitive keyboard navigation experience, follow these best practices:

- **Logical DOM Order:** The order of elements in the Document Object Model (DOM) determines the order in which elements receive focus when navigating with a keyboard. Ensure that the DOM order is logical and follows the visual order of elements on the page. For example, if you have a navigation menu followed by a main content area, ensure that the navigation menu elements come first in the DOM order, followed by the main content area elements.

- **Visible `:focus` Styles:** When an element receives focus, it is essential to provide a visible indication of focus to help users understand where they are on the page. You can achieve this by styling the **`:focus`** *pseudo-class*. For example:

  ```
  :focus {
    outline: 2px solid #007bff;
  }
  ```

  This CSS rule adds a 2-pixel solid outline with a blue color (**`#007bff`**) to any element that receives focus.

- **Avoid Using `tabindex> 0`:** The `tabindex` attribute allows you to specify the order in which elements receive focus when navigating with a keyboard. However, using `tabindex> 0` can disrupt the natural tab order and cause confusion for keyboard users. Instead of using `tabindex> 0`, ensure that elements are in a logical order in the DOM, and use CSS to style the layout as needed. When you use `tabindex>0`, you are telling the browser to focus on that element before others with a lower `tabindex` value. This can cause an unexpected behavior, such as elements receiving focus out of order, keyboard users getting lost in the navigation flow, and screen readers announcing elements in an incorrect order.

Color and Contrast

When designing a website, it is important to consider the accessibility of color and contrast. Color can be a powerful way to convey information, but it is not enough to rely solely on color to communicate important information. Some users may have visual impairments, such as color blindness or low vision, which makes it difficult to distinguish between different colors. For instance, using red and green to indicate errors and successes without providing additional contextcan be problematic for users with color vision deficiency or visual impairments.With the provision of additional context, such as text labels or icons, can help ensure that all users understand the information being conveyed. Furthermore, sufficient contrast between text and background colors is crucial for readability. When the contrast is too low, the text can be difficult to read, especially for users with visual impairments. The Web Content Accessibility Guidelines (WCAG 2.1) recommend a minimum contrast ratio of 4.5:1 for normal text and 3:1 for large text (18pt or larger). Leverage the use of a color contrast analyzer tool to ensure that your text and background colors meet the recommended contrast ratio. You can also use online tools to generate accessible color palettes to improve overall user experience

By following these guidelines and best practices, you can create a website that is accessible to all users, including those with disabilities. By ensuring that your color and contrast choices are accessible, you can provide a better experience for everyone.

Conclusion

Semantic HTML is your applications backbone. Building a robust and accessible web application starts with a solid understanding of semantic HTML and layout structure. By grasping the fundamentals of semantic HTML, you can create a logical content outline that enhances user experience and accessibility. With the ability to prompt for core page elements and create a well-structured layout, you can leverage AI-powered tools to scaffold semantic web pages efficiently. With these skills with best practices for making semantic structure accessible, you can create web applications that are both functional and inclusive, providing a better experience for all users.

With a solid foundation in semantic HTML and accessibility, in the next chapter, we will explore how to leverage AI to generate content-specific HTML that meets the unique needs of various web applications. This will allow you to create a more tailored and effective user experiences.

Points to Remember

- Semantics first, CSS later.
- Landmarks like header, nav, main, footer, aside define regions; section groups topics; article is self-contained.
- Every section deserves a heading.
- Include a skip link and a single page-level h1.
- Prefer native elements over ARIA; use ARIA to fill semantic gaps, not to replace HTML.
- Label every form control; keep keyboard order logical.
- Use exactly one <main> per page and make the skip link the first focusable element, targeting #main.
- If you have multiple navigations, distinguish each with an aria-label like "Primary", "Footer", or "Utility".
- Keep a single page-level **`<h1>`** inside **`<main>`**; structure the rest with **`<h2>`** for major sections and **`<h3>`** for subsections—no level skipping.
- Prefer native elements over ARIA; only add ARIA when no semantic element exists (for instance, **`role="search"`** on the sitewide search form).
- Label every form control with <label for> and connect help/error text via aria-described by; mark required inputs.
- Ensure smooth keyboard use: logical DOM/tab order, visible :focus styles, and avoid **`tabindex> 0`**.
- Meet contrast targets: at least 4.5:1 for body text and 3:1 for large text. Don't rely on color alone to convey meaning.
- In prompts, be explicit about "non-requirements": no CSS/JS, no inline styles, no framework classes, minimal placeholder text.
- Validate AI output: ask for HTML comments explaining choices; watch for invented attributes, nonstandard ARIA, and other hallucinations.
- Use **`<article>`** for self-contained units (blog card, product card, news item) that make sense out of context.
- **`<aside>`** is for complementary/tangential content (related links, promos); screen readers treat it as a complementary region.

- Headers/footers can appear at page or section/article level; a page can have a site footer plus article-scoped footers.
- Give sections accessible names with visible headings and, when helpful, aria-labelled by. Every section deserves a heading.
- Separate semantics from layout—use semantic elements for meaning and Grid/Flexbox later for placement.
- Avoid "`div soup`": refactor generic `<div>` wrappers into meaningful landmarks and sectioning elements to improve SEO and AT navigation.
- Treat prompts as mini-specs: set role/goal, required landmarks, content model, accessibility constraints, non-requirements, and validation.
- Site search should be a dedicated `<form role="search">` separate from newsletter/other forms.

Multiple Choice Questions

1. Which element represents the main, unique content of a page?
   a. section
   b. main
   c. article
   d. div
2. Which element is the best for site-wide navigation menus?
   a. nav
   b. menu
   c. ul
   d. aside
3. Which statement about headings is the recommended practice?
   a. Use multiple h1s for every card
   b. One page-level h1, then descend (h2, h3...)
   c. Skip heading levels to match visual size
   d. Use only h3–h5 for flexibility
4. The most appropriate element for a blog post preview that can stand alone is:
   a. article
   b. section

   c. div
   d. aside

5. Which of the following is the correct use of ARIA?
   a. Add roles to everything for better SEO
   b. Use ARIA only when no suitable native element exists
   c. Replace button with **`role="button"`** on links
   d. Always add **`role="main"`** to main

6. Where should a "`Skip to content`" link point?
   a. `#header`
   b. `#footer`
   c. `#main`
   d. `#top`

7. Which element is intended for content tangentially related to the main flow?
   a. aside
   b. article
   c. footer
   d. figure

8. If you have multiple navigation regions, how should you distinguish them for screen readers?
   a. Give each a unique id and nothing else
   b. Add aria-label like "**`Primary`**" or "**`Footer`**"
   c. Use **`role="navigation"`** on divs
   d. Place them all inside header

9. Which is the best way to label a sitewide search landmark?
   a. `<search>`
   b. `<form role="search">…</form>`
   c. `<input role="search">`
   d. `<form aria-role="search">`

10. Which element should contain the site's contact details?
   a. address
   b. footer only

   c. section
   d. article

11. Which choice best separates *layout* from *semantics*?
   a. Use div for meaning; CSS for layout.
   b. Use semantic elements for meaning; CSS Grid/Flexbox for layout.
   c. Inline styles define both.
   d. Use ARIA roles for layout.

12. You need a sidebar of related links next to an article. The most appropriate structure is:
   a. main > section + section
   b. main > article + aside
   c. main > div + footer
   d. header > aside + article

Answers

1. b
2. a
3. b
4. a
5. b
6. c
7. a
8. b
9. b
10. a
11. b
12. b

Key Terms

- **Semantic HTML:** Markup that reflects the meaning or structure of content not its visual look, improving accessibility, SEO, and collaboration.
- **Landmarks:** High-level regions <header>, <nav>, <main>, <footer>, <aside> that define the page's structure for assistive tech.

- **Section:** Thematic grouping of related content that must have a visible heading; use for structuring, not as a generic wrapper.
- **Article:** Self-contained content that stands alone (post, card, news item) and usually carries its own heading/metadata.
- **Aside (Complementary region):** Tangential content related to the main flow (related links, promos, tips), announced as complementary.
- **Skip link:** A visible "`Skip to content`" anchor that lets keyboard users jump directly to `<main id="main">`.
- **Heading hierarchy:** One page-level `<h1>` followed by `<h2>`, `<h3>`... in order, forming a navigable outline for screen readers.
- **ARIA:** Accessible Rich Internet Applications attributes; use sparingly to fill semantic gaps like aria-label, aria-labelledby, and aria-describedby.
- **`role="search"`:** ARIA role placed on the sitewide search <form> to expose a dedicated search landmark.
- **Div soup:** Overuse of generic `<div>` elements, leading to non-semantic, hard-to-navigate, and less accessible markup.
- **Content model:** The planned mapping of headings/sections/articles that defines how page information is organized.
- **Accessibility audit:** A review checking single `<main>`, heading order, link purpose clarity, alt text, labels, and ARIA usage.
- **Contrast ratio:** Numeric measure of text/background contrast; targets: 4.5:1 (normal text) and 3:1 (large text).
- **Logical DOM order:** The source order users tab through; should match visual reading order for predictable keyboard navigation.
- **`:focus` styles:** Visible styling applied when elements receive keyboard focus, crucial for discoverability of interactive controls.
- **`Tabindex`:** Avoid positive values; rely on natural DOM order and only use `tabindex="0"/-1` where appropriate.
- **Information Architecture (IA):** Organizing content into a clear hierarchy that maps directly to headings and sectioning elements.
- **Prompt as specification:** A structured prompt that defines role/goal, required landmarks, content model, accessibility constraints, exclusions, and validation steps.
- **Diff:** A minimal textual summary of changes between two versions, used here to present accessibility fixes succinctly.

CHAPTER 5
Content-Specific HTML with AI

Introduction

In *Chapter 4: Core HTML with AI Assistance*, we discussed prompt engineering, as it applies to the core elements of HTML. In this chapter, we will explore content-specific HTML with AI. Modern user interfaces are beyond aesthetics—semantics, accessibility, and performance are built into the markup. With AI in the workflow, the difference between a design that looks good in a screenshot and one ready for production lies in how prompts are written and outputs validated. This chapter explores processes for three high-impact content types: *forms*, *data tables*, *media*, and *external embeds*. The foundation of native HTML is explored while we prioritize accessibility, performance, and security from the outset.

During the chapter, you will build three essential components that demonstrate content specific principles in action. You will create an accessible contact form featuring real validation patterns, keyboard support, autocomplete tokens, and inline error messages. Additionally, you will develop a sortable and CSV-exportable data table with proper semantic structure, including caption, **`thead`**, **`tbody`**, **`tfoot`**, and **`th scope`** elements. We will be hands-on on media embedding, crafting a responsive image using the picture element with **`srcset`** and sizes attributes, and accessible video with track captions and a transcript. This chapter will guide you through the process of leveraging AI-powered tools to streamline form creation, organizing data into clear and concise tables, and enriching content with multimedia elements. By mastering these skills, you will be equipped to design engaging, user-friendly, and accessible digital experiences that cater to diverse needs and preferences, ultimately elevating the quality of your online presence and interactions.

After reading this chapter, you will be able to generate forms with AI, create structured tables for effective data presentation, embed various media, including images and videos, incorporate external content seamlessly, and enhance accessibility features through intuitive prompting.

Structure

In this chapter, we will cover the following topics:

- Generating Forms with AI
- Creating Structured Tables for Data Presentation
- Embedding Media
- Embedding Images, Videos, and External
- Adding Accessibility Features via *Prompting*

Generating Forms with AI

Artificial Intelligence (AI) is revolutionizing the process of generating forms across various industries, providing pre-built templates, automating the coding process, and promoting accessibility compliance. This transformation is evident in industries such as healthcare, where AI-generated forms streamline patient intake and medical history forms, and finance, where they automate compliance and regulatory forms. Additionally, AI-generated forms are being used in customer service to generate feedback and survey forms; in education to create enrollment and assessment forms; and, in manufacturing, to streamline inventory and supply chain management forms. By leveraging AI-generated forms, businesses can improve efficiency, accuracy, and accessibility while reducing costs, and accordingly enhancing customer experiences. Overall, AI-generated forms are transforming the way industries operate more efficiently and effectively. In this section, we will explore how to leverage the power of AI to create accessible forms that cater to diverse user needs. Let us startby creating a prompt that generates accessible forms with AI and discuss relevant best practices.

Understanding the Minimum Viable Structure

Forms are a pivotal touchpoint where the web users can interact with your services, sharing sensitive information, or requesting assistance. However, this is also where accessibility and validation flaws can have the most significant impact, potentially excluding some users or compromising data integrity. With an AI system, you can compose targeted prompts that enforce robust semantics and implement reusable production patterns for form generation. This allows for consistency, accessibility, and reliability across your digital services. Let us explore this prompt for accessible form generation.

Prompt

Build an accessible, semantic contact form in pure HTML5 with minimal inline CSS, following these requirements:

Structure and Semantics

- *Organize controls using <fieldset> and <legend> for logical grouping.*
- *Use explicit <label for> attributes for every form control.*
- *Apply semantic input types (email, tel, number, date, and so on).*
- *Include <main> and a proper heading hierarchy with one <h1>.*

Accessibility

- *Provide helpful hints using <small> elements linked with id + aria-describedby.*
- *Mark required fields with required and visually indicate them with *.*
- *Ensure all buttons have accessible names and visible focus indicators.*
- *Keep logical tab order and ensure full keyboard operability.*

Form Controls and Validation

- *Use native HTML validation only (no JavaScript).*
- *Apply required, min, max, pattern, inputmode, and autocomplete attributes appropriately.*
- *Include explicit Submit and Reset buttons.*

Usability

- *Ensure consistent styling for inputs, errors, focus, and active controls.*
- *Minimal CSS is enough to demonstrate progressive enhancement (rounded borders, focus outlines, spacing).*
- *Do not include any JavaScript.*

Output:

A complete, standalone HTML file containing the form and inline <style> block for minimal styling. The form should include sections for:

- *Contact information (name, email, phone).*
- *Inquiry details (reason, team size, preferred date).*
- *Message field.*
- *Preferred contact method (radio).*
- *Consent (checkbox).*

The aforementioned generated prompt is detailed and well-structured. It clearly specifies the structure, accessibility, validation, and usability requirements. The prompt ensures that the model outputs a complete, standalone HTML file with inline CSS and no JavaScript. This level of precision is excellent for prompting, because it reduces ambiguity, and aligns the output with accessibility best practices. However, prompts for code generation can often become overly detailed or inflexible. A good balance is often needed: enough detail to ensure compliance, such as semantic HTML, ARIA attributes, and required attributes, while leaving flexibility for the model to optimize. Let us improve the preceding AI form with a prompt and the best practices as follows:

- **Be explicit about output format:**
  - Always state: Output a single HTML5 file with `<html>, <head>, <body>,` and inline `<style>.`
  - This avoids cases where the model outputs only a fragment.
- **Enforce accessibility requirements:**
  - Include explicit WCAG references: Follow WCAG 2.1 AA guidelines for form fields, labels, focus indicators, and color contrast.
  - Require `aria-describedby` for hints and error placeholders.
- **Guide error handling**
  - Even if no JavaScript is requested, mention "*include inline <p class='error-text'>* placeholders next to fields for progressive enhancement."
  - This makes the form future-proof for when JS is added later.
- **Encourage progressive enhancement**
  - Add: "*Form must remain functional and accessible if CSS fails or is disabled.*"
  - This reinforces robustness across environments.
- **Keep prompts modular**
  - Split requirements into bullet categories (Structure, Accessibility, Validation, Usability, Output).
  - This helps the model avoid missing important sections.
- **Request self-explanation**
  - Add: "*Briefly explain how accessibility is achieved in your output.*"
  - This encourages the model to generate more thoughtful and auditable results.

Let us put all this together and generate an improved prompt with best practices implemented.

Prompt

Build a complete, standalone HTML5 contact form with inline CSS only (no JavaScript).

Requirements

1. *Structure and Semantics*

   Wrap the form in <main> with one <h1> heading.

   Use <fieldset> and <legend> to group related inputs.

   Provide explicit <label for> for every control.

   Use semantic input types (email, tel, number, date, etc.).

2. *Accessibility*

   Ensure WCAG 2.1 AA compliance.

   Provide hints with <small> elements linked using id + aria-describedby.

   *Mark required fields with required and visually indicate with *.*

   Ensure keyboard operability and logical tab order.

   Provide visible focus indicators on all controls.

   Ensure buttons have accessible names.

3. *Validation*

   Use only native HTML validation (no JavaScript).

   Apply required, min, max, pattern, inputmode, and autocomplete attributes.

   Include error message placeholders (<p class="error-text">) next to each field for progressive enhancement.

4. *Usability*

   Style inputs, buttons, and focus states consistently with minimal inline CSS.

   Ensure the form is still functional and accessible if CSS or JavaScript is disabled.

5. *Output*

   Return a single HTML file including <html>, <head>, <body>, and an inline <style> block.

   At the end, provide a short explanation (3–4 sentences) of how accessibility is achieved in the form.

The preceding prompt structure makes the prompt modular, testable, and reusable. Next, we shall discuss how to create a structured table for data presentation.

Creating Structured Tables for Data Presentation

A table is one of the most effective and versatile tools when it comes to presenting data on the web. Despite the rise of data visualization libraries, dashboards, and interactive charts, there are many cases where a table is still the clearest way to communicate structured information. Tables can organize large amounts of data, provide clear relationships between rows and columns, and offer a familiar, grid-like format that users know how to navigate. That said, tables are also easy to misuse. A poorly structured table can quickly become overwhelming, inaccessible, and unfriendly to users on smaller screens. For instance, simply pasting a spreadsheet into a <div> without considering semantic HTML or responsive behavior often results in a clumsy experience, particularly for people using assistive technologies. To leverage the full potential of tables, you need to think of them not just as visual grids, but as data with relationships. In this section, we explore how to create structured tables that are visually appealing, semantically correct, responsive across devices, and, most importantly, accessible to everyone. Whether you are presenting a simple dataset, or a multi-level, complex table, these principles will help you to ensure that your tables are useful, future-proof, and user-friendly.

The Impact of Structure on Usability

The purpose of a table is to communicate relationships between different pieces of data in a clear and concise manner. Tables are designed to organize and present complex information in a way that is easy to understand and analyze. Each header should describe a row or column of data, and every cell should be understood in that context. If a table lacks proper structure, assistive technologies like screen readers will struggle to announce the content meaningfully. Even sighted users can struggle to understand a table if the visual layout does not clearly associate headers with their corresponding values, making it difficult to interpret the data.

With a well-structured table, screen readers can announce the right headers for each cell, making the table understandable to non-visual users. Proper scaffolding allows the tables to adapt gracefully to small screens instead of breaking layouts. Also, a semantic approach makes your HTML easier to extend or modify later. Finally, using conventions such as `<thead>`, `<tbody>`, and `<tfoot>` ensures that your data presentation follows predictable patterns across projects.

Now, let us start with a reusable prompt to generate tables programmatically through AI prompts. The following baseline ensures correct table scaffolding and responsiveness:

Prompt:

Create a semantic, responsive, and accessible HTML5 data table with the following requirements:

Caption and Summary

Include a <caption> that clearly describes the dataset.

Add a short summary paragraph before the table for context, referenced with aria-describedby.

Structure

Use <thead>, <tbody>, and <tfoot> for organization.

Include both single-level and one multi-level header row (e.g., grouped headers with scope="colgroup").

Mark column headers with scope="col" and row headers with scope="row".

Accessibility

Use id on <th> elements and reference them with headers attributes on <td> where necessary.

Wrap the table in a container (.table-wrap) with overflow-x: auto for small screens, ensuring relationships are preserved.

Ensure good color contrast and focus outlines.

Numeric Data

Right-align numeric values with a .num class.

Show units only in the header cells, not repeated in each row.

CSV Export (No JavaScript)

Provide a "Download CSV" button or link above the table using an <a> element with download and a data:text/csv URI.

Ensure the CSV matches the DOM table data.

Styling

Add minimal CSS for borders, spacing, background for headers, and responsive scroll.

Use neutral, professional colors (gray, white, light background), and rounded corners on the table wrapper.

Dataset Example

Projects:

API Gateway Revamp – Platform – Production – 84,500 USD – 112 ms – 99.95% SLA

Data Lake Ingestion – Data – Staging – 57,200 USD – 265 ms – 99.90% SLA

Realtime ML Inference – AI/ML – Production – 121,000 USD – 78 ms – 99.99% SLA

Totals/Averages row in <tfoot> with cost = 262,700, latency = 152, SLA = 99.95%.

Return the complete HTML document (<!doctype html> ... </html>) with inline <style> in <head>. No external CSS or JavaScript.

The former prompt instructs the model to generate a fully semantic, responsive, and accessible HTML5 data table with a caption, summary, and a proper use of the **`<thead>`, `<tbody>`, `<tfoot>`,** and `scope` attributes. Numeric data should be right-aligned with units only in headers, and the table must be wrapped for horizontal scrolling on small screens. A pure HTML **`data:text/csv`** download link should allow CSV export without JavaScript, styled minimally with professional neutral colors.

Embedding Media

Media embedding refers to adding multimedia elements such as images, videos, and audio to digital content. Creating engaging content today goes beyond text alone. Images, videos, and audio files bring depth and context to digital experiences, but they must be accessible to all users, including those with disabilities. Embedding media with AI systems can make this process both more efficient and more inclusive. In HTML, this can be done with tags such as:

- **`<img>`** for images
- **`<video>`** for videos
- **`<audio>`** for audio files

However, simply embedding media is not enough without proper accessibility features. This approach may exclude people using assistive technologies. Let us consider an image included in content like **`<img src="image.jpg" alt="A description of the image">`.** The `alt` attribute provides alternative text, a concise description that screen readers can announce for users with visual impairments. A well-written alternative text is essential for accessibility.AI systems can augment accessibility efforts by automating tasks that are otherwise time-consuming, such as AI-powered image recognition, which can suggest or auto-generate alternative text for images. You can use AI-based video analysis to produce captions and transcripts, making video content more accessible for people with hearing impairments. In addition, Natural Language Processing (NLP) can refine descriptions to make them more relevant and human-like. These tools save time, but they should complement, and not replace, human oversight. In a nutshell, embedding media with AI systems empowers developers and designers to produce HTML content that is both engaging and inclusive.

Embedding Images, Videos, and External Media

Media is at the heart of user engagement and effective communication. Images, videos, and audio elements not only make content more dynamic but also help convey meaning in ways that plain text cannot. However, when adding media to websites or web applications, accessibility must come first to ensure that everyone, including people with disabilities, can perceive and interact with the content. Modern HTML5 provides semantic tags such as `<img>`, `<video>`, `<audio>`, and `<iframe>` for embedding media, while best practices and accessibility techniques such as alternative text, captions, transcripts, and descriptive titles make these elements inclusive. In this section, we will explore a step-by-step how to embed different types of media, such as images, videos, audio, and external content, while adhering to accessibility standards and user-friendly design. Let us start with the implementation of accessible image embedding.

Accessible Image Embedding

Working with images is a daily staple in frontend development, and making sure they are accessible to all users is essential. Whether you are adding a logo, a product photo, or a background image, accessibility should always be top of mind to create an inclusive user experience. Let us examine this image embedded in the following example:

```
<img src="team-photo.jpg" alt="The development team smiling together in
front of a conference booth">
```

In the preceding code, the **`src:`** specifies the path to the image,and **`alt:`** provides a text description used by screen readers if the image cannot be displayed. As a best practice, if the image is decorative only, use `alt=""`to indicate that it is not essential for understanding the content. Prevent layout shifts by providing width and height attributes to reserve space for the image and prevent layout shifts.

For complex images such as charts or diagrams, link to a longer description using **`aria-describedby`** as follows:

```
<img src="infographic.png" alt="Infographic summarizing company growth"
aria-describedby="infographic-desc">

<p id="infographic-desc" hidden>The infographic shows a breakdown of
company growth over the past year, including revenue increases and
expansion into new markets. </p>
```

With these best practices and the provision of alternative text, you can ensure that your images are accessible to everyone, regardless of their abilities.

Accessible Video Embedding

Videos are a powerful way to engage users and clearly convey complex information. However, when embedding videos on your website, it is essential to prioritize accessibility to ensure that everyone can enjoy and understand the content. By following the best practices for video embedding, you can create a more inclusive and human-centered experience. Let us look at this example:

```
<video controls width="640" height="360">
<source src="promo.mp4" type="video/mp4">
<track src="promo-captions.vtt" kind="subtitles" srclang="en"
label="English">  Your browser does not support the video tag.
</video>
```

In the preceding snippet, the controls show play, pause, and volume buttons, allowing users to control the video playback. The **`<source>`** allows multiple formats (mp4, webm, ogg) to ensure compatibility with different browsers. The <track> adds captions or subtitles to the video using **`.vtt`** files, making it more accessible to users with hearing impairments. Finally, the fallback text provides a message for the older browsers which do not support the video tag. To enforce the best practice, you may add captions **`<track kind="subtitles">`** to provide one or, subtitles for users with hearing impairments. Include a transcript of the video below the player for screen readers, and those who prefer to read the content. Also, avoid autoplay with sound from auto playing videos with sound, as it can be distracting and harm accessibility.

Embedding videos can be a great way to improve user engagement, but it is important to prioritize accessibility, so that everyone can enjoy and understand your content.

Accessible Audio Embedding

Audio content such as podcasts and audiobooks can be a great way to engage users and provide valuable information. However, it is vital to make sure that audio content is accessible to everyone, including users with hearing impairments or those who prefer to read content. By providing transcripts and using best practices for audio embedding, you can create a more inclusive and user-friendly experience. Let us examine this implementation example:

```
<audio controls>
<source src="podcast.mp3" type="audio/mpeg">
<source src="podcast.ogg" type="audio/ogg">
  Your browser does not support the audio element.
</audio>
```

The controls provide play/pause, seek bar, and volume control, allowing users to manage their listening experience. The multiple formats, MP3and OGG, ensure compatibility with different browsers and devices.

To implement the best practice, include a transcript of spoken content below the audio player for users who prefer to read or need assistance with understanding the content. It is advisable to provide a clear and descriptive title for the audio content to help users understand what it is all about. Make sure you use audio players that are accessible to screen readers and other assistive technologies. Let us implement these best practices as follows:

```
<audio controls>
<source src="podcast.mp3" type="audio/mpeg">
<source src="podcast.ogg" type="audio/ogg">
  Your browser does not support the audio element.
</audio>
<p>Transcript:</p>
<p>Lorem ipsum dolor sit amet, consectetur adipiscing elit. Sed sit amet nulla auctor, vestibulum magna sed, convallis ex.</p>
```

With these best practices, you can create a more inclusive and accessible experience for users with audio content.

Embedding External Media

Embedding external media like YouTube videos can enhance user engagement and provide valuable content. However, you need to embed content that is accessible and responsive. Let us see this example:

```
<div class="video-container">
<iframe width="560" height="315"
         src="https://www.youtube.com/embed/ScMzIvxBSi4"
         title="YouTube video player"
         frameborder="0"
         allow="accelerometer; autoplay; clipboard-write; encrypted-media; gyroscope; picture-in-picture"
         allowfullscreen>
</iframe>
</div>
```

The iframe loads the video from YouTube, allowing users to view the content without leaving your website. The title attribute provides a description of the iframe content for screen readers, essential for accessibility, and the **`allowfullscreen`** enables users to expand the video to full screen. How can you make external videos responsive? Let us look at this example of the updated CSS as follows:

```
.video-container {
  position: relative;
  padding-bottom: 56.25%; /* 16:9 ratio */
```

```
  height: 0;
  overflow: hidden;
  max-width: 100%;
}
.video-container iframe {
  position: absolute;
  top: 0; left: 0;
  width: 100%; height: 100%;
}
```

The aforementioned CSS code creates a responsive container for the iframe, allowing the video to scale properly on different screen sizes without breaking the layout. To enforce best practices with external media embedding, use a responsive container to ensure that the iframe is wrapped in a responsive container to adapt to different screen sizes. Also, provide a title attribute that includes a descriptive title for the iframe to improve accessibility. Finally, verify that the embedded video is accessible and usable for users with disabilities.

By following these best practices and using responsive design, you can create a seamless and accessible experience for users while embedding external media in your website project. Next, add accessibility features via prompting to leverage the AI system and ensure that digital products are usable by everyone using the websites we developed.

Adding Accessibility Features via Prompting

As discussed previously in this chapter, embedding media such as images, videos, and audio makes digital content more engaging, but without accessibility features, it can exclude people with special needs. AI systems and intentional prompts can be used to automatically generate or guide the creation of accessibility features. This ensures that everyone can consume and interact with digital content. Prompting in this context refers to instructing AI tools or systems to add cues, descriptions, captions, or structures that make multimedia content inclusive and usable.The followingare the key types of accessibility features that can be implemented through AI prompting, along with example prompts that illustrate how you can put these tools into practice.

- **Alternative text for images:** AI image recognition models like ChatGPT can be prompted to generate descriptive alt text. For example, you can prompt ChatGPT as follows: "*Generate a concise alt text for an image that describes the main subject without interpretation.*"
- **Captions and subtitles for video and audio:** Speech-to-text AI can automatically transcribe spoken content. For example, you can prompt ChatGPT as follows:

"Provide accurate closed captions for this video in WebVTT format, maintaining speaker changes and timing."

- **Audio descriptions for videos:** AI narration systems can generate audio descriptions for key visual details. For example, you can prompt ChatGPT as follows: "*Describe the visual elements of this video in one to two sentences per scene.*"
- **Transcripts for podcasts or audio clips:** Transcripts provide hearing-impaired users equal access. For example, you can prompt ChatGPT as follows: "*Transcribe this podcast episode into a readable, timestamped transcript.*"
- **Screen reader compatibility and structure:** An AI system can help ensure that a semantic HTML is applied. For example, you can prompt ChatGPT as follows: "*Generate semantic HTML markup for this video player with appropriate* ARIA *roles and labels for accessibility.*"

AI-powered prompting provides a powerful way to embed accessibility into media-rich content. With the use of a well-structured prompt, you can generate alternative text for images, captions, and transcripts for videos and audio, and semantic markup that supports screen readers. However, AI is not a replacement for human oversight, as stated earlier. The combination of AI efficiency and human judgment ensures that embedded media is not only engaging, but equally accessible to all categories of digital users.

Conclusion

In this chapter, we have discussed content-specific HTML with AI, starting with accessible form generation, structured data tables, and media embedding. We explored how AI-powered prompting can enforce best practices in semantics, accessibility, validation, and usability. The chapter emphasized accessibility-first design, responsive layouts, and progressive enhancement across forms, tables, and multimedia content. Finally, we highlighted how AI can support accessibility features such as alternative text, captions, transcripts, and ARIA roles, while noting that human oversight remains essential for inclusivity and quality. In the next chapter, we will explore how AI can support and accelerate the styling process using CSS, both traditional and utility-first frameworks.

Points to Remember

- AI can generate accessible and semantic HTML5 forms with proper validation and keyboard support.
- Forms must use `<fieldset>`, `<legend>`, `<label for>`, semantic input types, and proper validation attributes.

- Tables should be semantic, structured with **`<thead>`**, **`<tbody>`**, **`<tfoot>`**, and **`<caption>`**, and responsive for small screens.
- CSV export can be enabled in pure HTML without JavaScript using **`data:text/csv`** links.
- Media embedding images, video, audio, and external content must prioritize accessibility with alt, track, transcripts, and descriptive titles.
- AI prompts can generate accessibility features such as captions, transcripts, and alternative text.
- Always enforce WCAG 2.1 AA compliance when generating or embedding content.
- Progressive enhancement ensures that forms, tables, and media remain functional even without CSS or JavaScript.
- Human oversight is required to review AI-generated content for clarity, accuracy, and inclusiveness.

Multiple Choice Questions

1. Which attribute best links help text to a form control?
   a. `aria-label`
   b. `aria-describedby`
   c. `tabindex`
   d. `role`
2. Which amongst these is the minimum semantic requirement for a data table?
   a. `<tbody>` only
   b. `<table>` with `<caption>` and correct `<th>` headers
   c. A bordered `<div>` grid
   d. `<table>` with inline styles
3. Which is the preferred first step for video accessibility?
   a. Autoplay with sound
   b. Provide a `<track kind="captions">` and a transcript
   c. Rely on platform auto-captions
   d. Mute the audio

4. Which image technique improves responsiveness without JavaScript?
    a. srcset and sizes
    b. aria-busy
    c. defer
    d. translate
5. Which association is correct for complex tables?
    a. headers on `<th>` referencing `<td>` ids
    b. id on `<th>` and headers on `<td>`
    c. `scope="all"` on every `<th>`
    d. No association is needed
6. Which input attribute improves numeric entry on mobile?
    a. `inputmode="numeric"`
    b. `autocapitalize="on"`
    c. `spellcheck="true"`
    d. `wrap="soft"`
7. Which is the safest way to embed external content?
    a. `<iframe>` with sandbox and descriptive title
    b. `<object>` without attributes
    c. `<iframe>` with `allow="*"`, no title
    d. Inline the external site with <embed>
8. Which table header marking is correct for a column header?
    a. `<th scope="col">`
    b. `<td role="columnheader">`
    c. `<th scope="row">`
    d. `<td>`
9. Which is the best default for video loading?
    a. `preload="auto"`
    b. `preload="metadata"`
    c. `preload="none"` and autoplay
    d. No preload defined and autoplay

10. Which ensures keyboard discoverability?
    a. Remove focus outlines for aesthetics
    b. Use `tabindex="5"` to jump ahead
    c. Provide visible focus styles and logical DOM order
    d. Trap focus inside every section
11. Which statement about ARIA is most accurate?
    a. Use ARIA on every element for clarity
    b. ARIA replaces native semantics
    c. Use ARIA only when a suitable native element does not exist
    d. ARIA improves performance automatically
12. Which is an appropriate autocomplete token for a street address field?
    a. `autocomplete="line"`
    b. `autocomplete="street-address"`
    c. `autocomplete="address1"`
    d. `autocomplete="addr"`

Answers

1. b
2. b
3. b
4. a
5. b
6. a
7. a
8. a
9. b
10. c
11. c
12. b

Key Terms

- **AI-Powered Prompting**: This is instructing AI systems to generate structured and accessible HTML.
- **Semantic HTML**: This is the use of correct HTML elements (`<form>, <table>`, `<caption>`, `<th>`) to convey meaning.
- **Accessibility (a11y)**: Designing digital content usable by people with disabilities (for example, via screen readers).
- **Accessible Rich Internet Applications (ARIA)**: Attributes that improve accessibility when native HTML is insufficient.
- **WCAG 2.1 AA**: Web Content Accessibility Guidelines that define accessibility standards.
- **Progressive Enhancement**: This ensures core functionality works without CSS or JavaScript.
- **Alternative Text (alt)**: Descriptions of images for screen readers.
- **Captions and Transcripts**: Text alternatives for video and audio content.
- **Responsive Design**: Content that adapts across different devices and screen sizes.
- **CSV Export**: Exporting table data in CSV format using pure HTML.

CHAPTER 6
Styling with Prompt-Based CSS

Introduction

In the preceding *Chapter 5, Content-Specific HTML with AI*, we had focused on how to generate an interactive, media-rich, and accessible web content using AI assistance. In this chapter, we will explore how Artificial Intelligence can accelerate the styling process in modern web development. We will start with CSS fundamentals, covering the cascade, inheritance, and specificity, and then dive into layout systems like Flexbox and Grid. You will learn how to compose AI prompts that generate reliable CSS for real-world projects. In the course of the chapter, you will discover how utility-first frameworks, like Tailwind CSS is used in responsive design strategies, including mobile-first development and authoring media queries.

Throughout, you will discover how to encode constraints, naming conventions, tokens, and acceptance criteria into your prompts, ensuring that the AI-generated CSS is maintainable, standards-compliant, and aligned with your design system. With practical exercises and AI-assisted styling, you will be able to turn the design intent into a clean and responsive CSS. By combining technical expertise with AI assistance, you will rev up your delivery while maintaining semantic HTML and accessible patterns. Let us get started leveraging full potential of AI-assisted CSS development.

After reading this chapter, you will be able to understand the foundational principles of CSS styling, including selectors, properties, and the box model. You will gain practical skills in constructing layouts with Flexbox and CSS Grid through prompt-driven approaches. You will also be able to apply utility-first frameworks such as Tailwind CSS to accelerate interface development. Additionally, you will learn how to generate responsive designs using media queries and AI assistance, ensuring that layouts adapt effectively to multiple screen sizes. These objectives prepare you to balance readability, maintainability, and performance in modern styling workflows.

Structure

In this chapter, we will cover the following topics:

- Styling Basics
- Understanding the Box Model
- Creating Layouts with Flexbox and Grid Using Prompts
- Accelerating Development with Tailwind CSS
- Responsive Design and Media Queries Powered by AI

Styling Basics

Styling in Cascading Style Sheets (CSS) is a simple process of controlling the visual appearance and layout of HTML elements on a web page. Before diving into advanced layout systems and frameworks, it is vital to understand how CSS applies styles to HTML elements. Styling basics covers the syntax of selectors, properties, values, and cascading rules. These fundamentals are quite significant because all the modern frameworks and AI-driven approaches rely on them. In this section, the building blocks of CSS will be explored, including selectors, properties, cascading, and specificity. At the end, you will prompt CSS with ChatGPT to generate a CSS code or a web page. Let us start with CSS selectors and properties.

CSS Selectors and Properties

CSS selectors target specific elements in an HTML document, while properties define how those elements appear. So, what are these elements in HTML? HTML elements define the structure and content of a web page, and can be categorized into various types, including structural elements like **`header, nav, main`**, content elements such as `p, img, a,`and interactive elements like `details, summary`. Other key elements are headings (**`h1-h6`**), lists **`(ul, ol, li)`**, tables (**`table, tr, th, td`**), forms (**`form, input, textarea`**), and media elements **`(audio, video)`**. Semantic elements like **`time, mark, cite`** provide additional meaning to content, while generic elements like `div` and `span` are used for layout and styling purposes. Selectors can be based on element types, classes, IDs, attributes, or a combination of these. Properties, on the other hand, are the styles applied to the selected elements. Let us see an example where selectors and properties are used in the code as follows:

```
p {
  color: navy;
  font-size: 16px;
}
```

In the aforementioned example, `p` is the selector, targeting all paragraph elements. Color and font-size are properties, defining the text color and font size, respectively. The **`navy`** and **`16px`** are values, specifying the color and font size. As stated above, CSS selectors target elements using methods like element type, class, ID, attributes, and combinators, symbols used to combine multiple selectors to target specific elements based on their relationships, while properties control the styling. Common properties in CSS include text, box, background, and border styles. Together, the selectors and properties act as a glue to precise web page layout and design. Next, we shall discuss cascading and specificity to examine what happens when multiple styles are applied to the same element, and which of the styles get to be applied to HTML elements.

Cascading and Specificity

The cascade determines which style is applied when multiple rules affect the same element. Specificity is calculated based on selector type. Understanding the cascade and specificity is essential to writing efficient and effective CSS. Let us examine some of the cascading rules, starting with the origin rule.

> **Origin rule:** Styles can come from three sources, browser defaults, user-defined CSS (someone who is viewing your website), and author CSS (website creator). Author CSS overrides user CSS, which overrides browser defaults. To simply put, whatever style rule you as a developer or designer apply to HTML takes precedence regardless of browser's default or user defined CSS.
>
> For example, a **`p`** HTML element with *hello world* as text: `<p>Hello World! </p>`
>
> The browser default CSS to **`p`** element, which is the built-in style that comes with the browser and are applied to **`p`** element by default as font-size with 16px value as follows:

`Browser default CSS`

```
p {
  font-size: 16px;
  color: black;
}
```

`User defined CSS, it is set by someone tweaking web page to their preference, either background color or font-size either directly or through the use of browser' extension software.`

```
p {
  color: blue;
}
```

`Author CSS, developer's stylesheet`

```
p {
```

```
  color: red;
}
```

The origin rule for the preceding p element states that the text will appear red because author CSS overrides user CSS, which in turn overrides browser defaults.

Specificity rule: The more specific selectors override less specific ones. Inline styles have the highest specificity, followed by ID selectors, class selectors, and element selectors. For example: `<p id="greeting" class="highlight">Hello World! </p>`

This is the element selector with lowest specificity.

```
p {
  color: green;
}
```

This is the Class selector stronger than element.

```
.highlight {
  color: blue;
}
```

This is the ID selector stronger than class.

```
#greeting {
  color: purple;
}
```

And finally, the Inline style, the strongest of all. `<p id="greeting" class="highlight" style="color: red;">Hello World!</p>`

The text will appear red, because inline styles (`style="color: red;">`) override IDs, which override classes, which override elements.

Order: When two selectors have the same specificity, the one that appears later in the CSS code wins. For example:

```
p {
  color: blue;
}

p {
  color: red;
}
```

In the preceding CSS code above, the paragraph text will be red, because the second rule appears later in the CSS code and has the same specificity as the first rule.

It is noteworthy to state that specificity is calculated based on the selector type. A higher specificity value means the selector is more specific. For instance:

- Inline styles: 1000
- ID selectors: 100
- Class selectors: 10
- Element selectors: 1

Let us take a look at an example of how specificity is calculated:

```
#header
  background-color: blue;
}

.header {
  background-color: red;
}

div
  background-color: green;
}
```

The values for their specificity are 100, 10 and 1 for **`#header`**, **`.header`** and **`div`** respectively. In the preceding example, the #header selector has the highest specificity, so its styles will be applied.

Now, let us use AI to generate a CSS code for a simple styling task. Fire up ChatGPT interface and enter this prompt:

"Create a single CSS stylesheet that:

Targets headings (h1–h6) and sets their color using a custom property --heading-color: #1e40af, with a dark-mode override that ensures WCAG AA contrast.

Styles paragraphs (p) with text-align: justify, hyphens: auto (include -webkit-hyphens for broader support), and overflow-wrap: break-word for readability.

Styles links (a) with a visible underline by default, and enhances the underline thickness/offset on :hover and :focus-visible. Preserve default focus outlines.

Includes a smooth transition for link decoration, but disables transitions when prefers-reduced-motion: reduce is set.

Uses low-specificity selectors (or :where() for zero specificity) and avoids utility classes, resets, and !important.

Optionally include styles for :visited and :active states for usability.

Provide only the CSS code in a single fenced code block."

The former prompt outputs a stylesheet that is accessible, and of readable text, by providing consistent heading colors with dark-mode support, justified paragraphs with better hyphenation, and links that remain visibly underlined while offering smooth, motion-sensitive interaction effects. It balances usability, accessibility, and low-specificity maintainability. Next, we aim to discuss box model, a fundamental concept in understanding how CSS styles are applied to elements on web pages.

Understanding the Box Model

The CSS box model is one of the most fundamental concepts in web design and development. Box model serves as the foundation for understanding how elements are rendered on a webpage and how spacing, alignment, and layout are calculated. Whether you are building a simple blog, a responsive web app, or a complex design system, the box model forms the basis of every pixel of the layout. Understanding it ensures that your designs behave predictably across different devices and browsers, and it reduces frustration when elements do not align as expected.

At its core, the box model treats every HTML element as a rectangular box. Even elements that seem simple, like a `<p>` tag or a `<button>`, are represented as boxes. Each box has four key components: *content*, *padding*, *border*, and *margin*. These layers determine how much space an element occupies and how it interacts with neighboring elements. Let us start exploring box model with the understanding of box model structure.

Structure of the Box Model

It is helpful to break down box model parts individually to fully understand it. In this section, we break the box model parts as follows:

- **Content:** The content area is the innermost part of the box. This is where text, images, or other child elements are displayed. The size of the content area is determined by the width and height properties in CSS. Let us take a look at this example `.my-content {width: 200px;height: 100px;}`. In this example, the content area of the element `.my-content` will be 200 pixels wide and 100 pixels high.

- **Padding:** Padding is the space between the content and the border. It provides a cushion around the content, preventing it from touching the border directly. The padding property in CSS controls the amount of padding.. `my-content{padding: 20px;}`. This will add a 20-pixel padding on all sides of the content. You can also specify different padding values for each side:

  ```
  .my-content {
  padding-top: 10px;
  padding-right: 20px;
  ```

```
padding-bottom: 10px;
padding-left: 20px;
}
```

Alternatively, you can use the shorthand property:

```
.my-content {
 padding: 10px 20px; /* top/bottom | left/right */}

.my-content {
 padding: 10px 20px 30px; /* top | left/right | bottom */
}
.my-content {
 padding: 10px 20px 30px 40px; /* top | right | bottom | left */
}
```

- **Border:** Border is a line that surrounds the padding and content. Borders can be styled with colors, thicknesses, and patterns. They can be solid, dashed, dotted, or even have rounded corners with border-radius. Borders contribute to the total size of the box unless you modify the box sizing behavior. The border property in CSS controls the appearance of the border as follows:

```
.my-content {
border: 2px solid black;
}
```

This will add a 2-pixel solid black border around the element. You can also specify different border styles for each side as follows:

```
.my-content {
  border-top: 1px dashed red;
 border-right: 3px dotted blue;
  border-bottom: 1px dashed red;
  border-left: 3px dotted blue;
}
```

Alternatively, you can use the shorthand property:

```
.my-content {
border-width: 1px 3px; /* top/bottom | left/right */
border-style: dashed dotted; /* top/bottom | left/right */
border-color: red blue; /* top/bottom | left/right */
}

.my-content {
 border-width: 1px 3px 1px; /* top | left/right | bottom */
 border-style: dashed dotted dashed; /* top | left/right | bottom
```

```
*/
  border-color: red blue red; /* top | left/right | bottom */
}

.my-content {
  border-width: 1px 3px 1px 3px; /* top | right | bottom | left
*/
  border-style: dashed dotted dashed dotted; /* top | right |
bottom | left */
  border-color: red blue red blue; /* top | right | bottom | left
*/
}
```

- **Margin:** Margin is the space outside the border, separating the element from other elements. It provides a buffer around the element, preventing it from touching other elements directly. The `margin` property in CSS controls the amount of margin as follows:

```
.my-content {
  margin: 30px;
}
```

This will add a 30-pixel margin on all sides of the element. You can also specify different margin values for each side as follows:

```
.my-content {
margin-top: 15px;
margin-right: 30px;
margin-bottom: 15px;
margin-left: 30px;
}
```

Alternatively, you can use the shorthand property:

```
.my-content {
  margin: 15px 30px; /* top/bottom | left/right */
}
.my-content {
margin: 15px 30px 45px; /* top | left/right | bottom */
}
.my-content {
 margin: 15px 30px 45px 60px; /* top | right | bottom | left */
}
```

Let us examine this visual representation of a box model. Think of the box model as a set of concentric layers as follows:

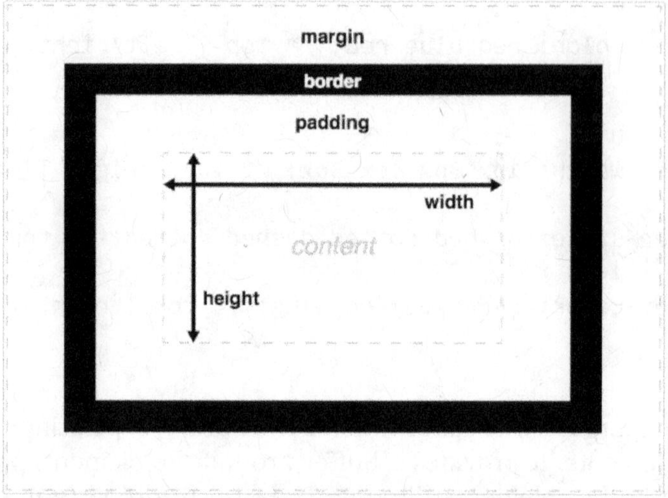

Figure 6.1: *Screenshot Showing the Box Model in CSS*
(Source: https://developer.mozilla.org/en-US/docs/Web/CSS/CSS_box_model)

This model makes it clear why an understanding each layer is so important. Every pixel of margin, padding, or border adds to the way elements are positioned and how much space they consume.

Box Sizing

As discussed earlier, the width and height properties apply only to the content area by default. This means that if you add padding or borders, they will increase the overall size of the element. When you use box-sizing property, for instance, **the `box-sizing: border-box;`** changes this default behavior, making the padding and border part of the total dimension. This means that the width and height properties will include the padding and border. This approach makes it easier to predict the size of elements. For example:

```
.box { width: 200px;  padding: 20px;  border: 1px solid black;  box-
sizing: border-box;}
```

The box-sizing in the preceding includes padding and border in width calculation. In your fun time, use ChatGPT to generate an example that demonstrates the box model in action with the prompt as follows:

"Generate a complete HTML file with inline CSS that shows three stacked boxes (divs) labeled Box 1, Box 2, and Box 3. Each box should have different margins, paddings, borders, and background colors for clarity. Use box-sizing: border-box; globally so that padding and borders are included in the element's total size. The boxes should be easy to distinguish visually."

The `box-sizing: border-box;` is applied globally. Each box with the declared width would include the content, padding, and border together. That means padding and border do not add extra size beyond the defined width; they are calculated inside it. In this example, because no widths are set, the boxes naturally expand to fit their content, but the border-box rule ensures consistent sizing behavior if widths were applied. Margins remain outside and are not affected by box-sizing.

In a nutshell, the CSS box model is much more than a technical detail; it is the core language of layout. By understanding its components like content, padding, border, margin and mastering how properties like box-sizing influence sizing behavior, you gain fine-grained control over the presentation of your web page elements. This control translates into predictable, consistent, and accessible designs. Whenever you encounter layout issues, returning to the box model often reveals the root cause. With practice, you will begin to anticipate how changes to padding, margin, or border will affect the final rendering, saving time and reducing frustration, even with the use of AI systems like ChatGPT.

Note: *The box model is the foundation of CSS layout mastery. Learn it deeply, and everything else like flexbox, grid, responsive design becomes far easier to understand.*

Next, we shall explore creating layouts with Flexbox and Grid using specific prompts to explore their capabilities and best use cases. What kind of layout would you like to create? A simple navigation bar, a complex dashboard, or something else?

Creating Layouts with Flexbox and Grid Using Prompts

Designing layouts is one of the most daunting fundamental tasks in web development. If not implemented rightly, this is where frontend development frustrations peak. Traditionally, developers had relied on floats, tables, or inline-block techniques to arrange elements, but those approaches were often cumbersome and difficult to maintain. Today, Flexbox and CSS Grid provide powerful, modern layout systems that make it easier to build responsive, scalable, and visually consistent interfaces. Flexbox is ideal for one-dimensional layouts where elements need to align in either a row or column. It excels at distributing space, handling alignment, and making components flexible across different screen sizes. CSS Grid, on the other hand, is designed for two-dimensional layouts, allowing you to define both rows and columns with precise control. It simplifies the creation of complex layouts such as dashboards, landing pages, or application shells. By combining both systems, you can create designs that are not only functional, but also adaptable to any device. In this age, AI can further assist by generating boilerplate CSS and HTML structures, reducing repetitive work, and helping you focus on design and customization. Let us get started with the discussion on flexbox essentials in layout design.

Understanding Flexbox Essentials

Flexbox is a powerful layout system for creating flexible and responsive one-dimensional layouts. These are some essential properties to get you started with Flexbox implementation.

Container Properties

Container properties define the layout structure, and dictate how child elements are arranged and sized, making them crucial for building responsive and flexible layouts. These properties control the layout behavior as follows:

- `display:` flex; This enables Flexbox for the container.
- `justify-content:` This aligns items horizontally, for example, center, space-between, space-around.
- `align-items:` This aligns items vertically for example, center, flex-start, flex-end.

The one-dimensional layouts are typically managed using Flexbox, which excels at handling single-axis layouts.

Item Properties

Item properties in Flexbox control the behavior of individual flex items within a flex container. These properties allow you to fine-tune the layout and responsiveness of each item. The key item properties include:

- `flex-grow:` This specifies how much an item should grow relative to others.
- `flex-shrink:` This specifies how much an item should shrink relative to others.
- `flex-basis:` This specifies the initial width or height of an item.
- `align-self:` This allows an individual item to override the container's alignment.
- `order:` This specifies the order of the item within the flex container.

By using these properties, you can create complex and responsive layouts that adapt to different screen sizes and content requirements. Let us generate a prompt to create a horizontal navigation bar as follows:

"Create responsive CSS for a horizontal navigation bar using Flexbox. Ensure that menu items are evenly spaced, automatically adjust to fill the container's width, and maintain proper alignment across various screen sizes."

Run the aforementioned prompt in ChatGPT and examine the output. You can take a further step to generate an HTML code that implement the navigation prompt!

Next, we will dive into the Grid essentials to understand how a web page layout is designed with grid approach.

Understanding Grid Essentials

CSS Grid is a powerful layout system for building two-dimensional layouts with precise control over rows and columns. It is especially useful when creating page templates, dashboards, or any design that requires both horizontal and vertical structuring. Let us take a look at the container and items properties in a Grid system starting with the container properties.

Container Properties

In CSS Grid, container properties are applied to the parent element that contains the grid items. These properties define the structure and layout of the grid. Key container properties include:

- **`display: grid;`**: This enables Grid for the container.
- **`grid-template-columns`**: This defines the number and width of columns.
- **`grid-template-rows`**: This defines the number and height of rows.
- Other properties like **`grid-gap,`** **`grid-template-areas,`** and **`justify-items/align-items`** further customize the grid layout.

By defining columns, rows, and gaps, you can create intricate grid-based designs. Overall, CSS Grid container properties provide a powerful toolset for building robust, responsive, and maintainable layouts.

Item Properties

Item properties in Grid control the placement and behavior of individual grid items within the grid container. Key item properties include:

- **`grid-column:`** It specifies which column(s) an item should span.
- **`grid-row:`** It specifies which row(s) an item should span.
- Other properties like **`grid-area`** and **`justify-self/align-self`** allow for fine-grained control over item placement and alignment.

By combining container and item properties, you can create complex and responsive grid layouts that adapt to different screen sizes and content requirements. Let us implement this prompt in ChatGPT to explore an example as follows:

"*Generate semantic HTML and an external CSS file to build a responsive three-column layout using CSS Grid. The layout should include a header, main content area, aside section, and footer. Define named grid areas for each section, apply spacing between grid items, and ensure the layout adapts gracefully to smaller screen sizes.*"

The following screenshot shows the output when you run the prompt and the eventual CSS and HTML codes:

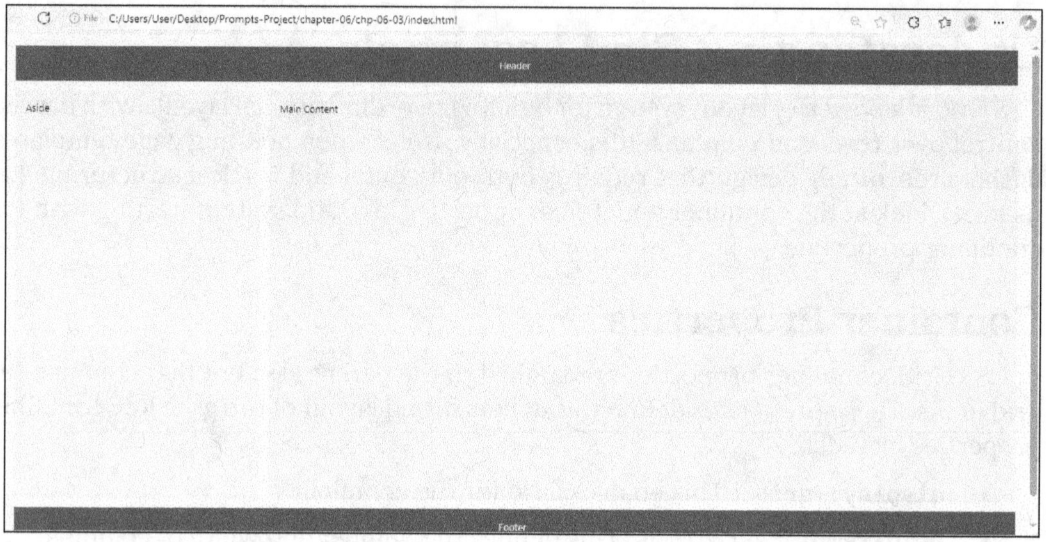

***Figure 6.2**: Screenshot Showing a Responsive Three-Column Layout Using CSS Grid*

The preceding screenshot shows layout structured with semantic elements like **`header`**, **`main`**, **`aside`**, **`footer`**, and use named **`grid areas`** for clarity, and includes a responsive media query so the layout collapses gracefully on smaller screens.

Combining Flexbox and Grid

In practice, developers rarely rely on just one design or layout system. A common approach is to use CSS Grid for the overall page structure and Flexbox for arranging elements within individual sections. This layered approach allows you to take advantage of each system's strengths. For an example:

```
.grid-container {
  display: grid;
  grid-template-columns: 1fr 3fr;
  gap: 10px;
}
.header {
  grid-column: 1 / -1;
  display: flex;
  justify-content: space-between;
  align-items: center;
  padding: 1em;
  background-color: #333;
```

```
  color: #fff;
}
.main {
  grid-column: 2;
  display: flex;
  flex-direction: column;
  padding: 1em;
}
```

In the preceding example, Grid defines a two-column layout for the page. Within the header and main sections, Flexbox provides precise alignment and distribution of child elements. By combining Flexbox and Grid, you can build layouts that are both flexible and robust, adapting seamlessly across different devices and screen sizes. With AI assistance, you can quickly generate these structures, experiment with variations, and focus more on refining your design.

Tip: *Come up with a prompt that combine the Grid and Flexible in a fictitious marketing page, using external styles and a semantic* HTML.

While understanding Flexbox and Grid provides a strong foundation for building responsive layouts, writing custom CSS for every project can still be time-consuming. This is where utility-first frameworks like Tailwind CSS come in. It offers prebuilt utility classes that let you rapidly prototype and style layouts without writing extensive custom CSS. Let us explore how Tailwind can accelerate development, and simplify the workflow.

Accelerating Development with Tailwind CSS

In modern frontend development, efficiency and maintainability are just as important as visual design. While traditional CSS and frameworks like Flexbox and Grid give developers fine-grained control, they often require writing and maintaining large amounts of custom CSS, which proves to be very tedious and time-consuming tasks in an enterprise projects. This can slow down projects and create challenges when scaling or collaborating on larger teams. Utility-first frameworks like Tailwind CSS have changed this dynamic. Instead of writing custom class selectors and managing long style sheets, developers can apply predefined utility classes directly in their HTML. It sounds magical right? This means you can build complex, responsive, and polished interfaces without constantly switching between HTML and CSS files. The utility-first approach aligns perfectly with AI-driven development, because prompts can directly generate ready-to-use HTML markup that already includes Tailwind classes for responsiveness, spacing, typography, and layout. This reduces the gap between the prototype and a production code, thereby, allowing the developers to build faster while maintaining design consistency. Let us discuss the principles of utility-first CSS approach.

Principles of Utility-First CSS

Utility-first CSS frameworks like Tailwind CSS replace traditional custom selectors with small, single-purpose classes. You can then compose entire designs by stacking these classes directly in HTML. This approach eliminates the need for naming conventions like BEM or custom class naming. It reduces CSS bloat by using only the classes you need, and improves maintainability, since styles are directly visible in the markup. For an example:

```
<button class="bg-blue-500 text-white px-4 py-2 rounded">
  Click Me
</button>
```

Here, instead of creating a **`.btn`** class in a separate CSS file, the button is styled entirely through Tailwind utilities: **`background color, text color, padding,`** and **`rounded`** corners.

AI-Driven Tailwind Prompts

When working with AI tools like ChatGPT, Tailwind CSS is especially more powerful. Since utility classes are predictable and composable, you can write prompts that generate fully functional, responsive components with minimal follow-up. Let us revisit the Flexbox navigation bar this time with Tailwind. The goal is to experience firsthand how much shorter and more readable a Tailwind-based code can be.

Prompts:

Create a responsive navigation bar using Tailwind CSS. The navigation bar should contain a logo on the left and navigation links on the right. On smaller screens, the links should stack vertically, while on medium and larger screens, they should align horizontally. Use utility classes like flex, justify-between, items-center, flex-col, and md:flex-row to handle layout and responsiveness. Apply background and text styling for clarity and include hover effects for the links.

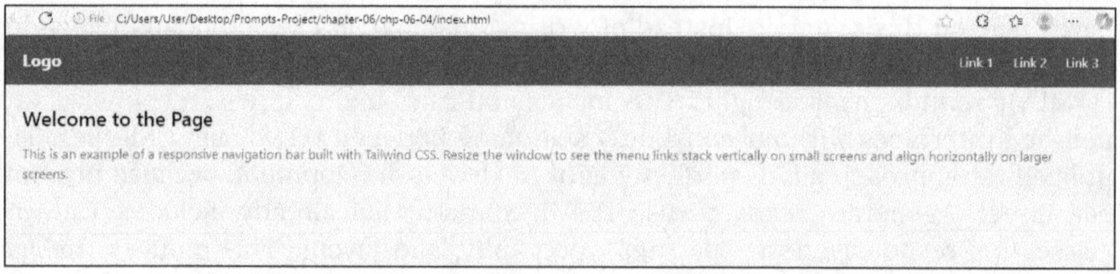

Figure 6.3: *Screenshot Showing a Responsive Navigation Bar Using Tailwind CSS*

With this approach, AI can output a code that is closer to production-ready, reducing the time developers spend refactoring.

The following table compares traditional and tailwind CSS:

Traditional CSS	Tailwind CSS
Manual naming of classes	Predefined utility classes
Write and manage CSS files	Compose directly in HTML markup
Longer CSS files	Shorter HTML with inline utility classes
Separation of structure and style	Styles visible alongside content

Table 6.1: *Table Showing Comparison between Traditional and Tailwind CSS*

This preceding table comparison shows how Tailwind shifts effort away from writing and maintaining large CSS files toward rapid, in-context styling within HTML. Now that you have seen how utility-first frameworks like Tailwind CSS accelerate development and simplify responsive layouts, the next step is to explore deeper into responsive design. By combining traditional media queries with AI-driven code generation, you can quickly create adaptive interfaces that adjust seamlessly across devices. Let us explore how responsive design principles and media queries can be enhanced with AI systems to streamline modern front-end workflows.

Responsive Design and Media Queries Powered by AI

Today, a responsive website that adapts to various devices is no longer optional. It is a fundamental requirement for delivering a seamless user experience. Websites must adapt fluidly to desktops, laptops, tablets, and smartphones of all shapes and sizes. A layout that looks perfect on a widescreen monitor should remain just as usable and visually appealing on a small mobile screen. The traditional way to achieve this adaptability is through CSS media queries, which allow you to conditionally apply styles based on the screen width, height, or even device orientation. Media queries form the backbone of responsive web design, but writing and maintaining them manually across large projects can become time-consuming and repetitive. This is where AI-driven development and utility-first frameworks like Tailwind CSS accelerate the process rapidly. With AI system like ChatGPT, you can generate responsive code snippets directly from prompts, reducing boilerplate work. Tailwind CSS takes responsiveness a step further by offering intuitive responsive prefixes like **`sm:, md:, lg:, xl:`** that let you compose adaptive layouts without writing raw media queries. Together, these approaches create a powerful workflow in a collaborative manner where the media queries provide fine-grained control, AI automates the generation of conditional styles and Tailwind CSS simplifies responsive patterns into composable classes. By combining media-query techniques, AI and Tailwind CSS, you can build adaptable, mobile-first designs faster, with cleaner code and fewer maintenance headaches. Let us start a deeper conversation in how media queries are implemented in a website design.

Understanding the Basics of Media Queries

Media queries apply styles conditionally based on screen width or other conditions. This enables different layouts for different devices. Take a look at this example:

```
@media (max-width: 768px) {
 nav {
    flex-direction: column;
  }}
```

The preceding media query applies a column layout to the navigation bar when the screen width is 768px or smaller. AI can generate responsive CSS on demand. By describing the desired layout in a prompt, you can quickly produce boilerplate media queries as follows:

Prompt:

"*Produce only a CSS snippet (no HTML, no resets) that implements a mobile-first responsive three-column layout using CSS Grid on a container with class .grid.*

Base (phones, <640px): 1 column.

Tablets (640px–1023px): 2 columns.

Desktops (≥1024px): 3 columns.

Use grid-template-columns with repeat() and gap: 1rem. Include brief comments explaining each breakpoint. Do not use JavaScript. Assume the HTML is like: <div class="grid"><div>...</div>...</div>."

The former prompt asks for a minimal, mobile-first CSS Grid snippet (CSS only) that makes a **`.grid`** container display 1 column on phones, 2 on tablets, and 3 on desktops using media queries—with gap: 1rem, brief comments, no JavaScript, and assuming simple **`<div class="grid">…</div>`** markup. This reduces the manual effort of writing repetitive breakpoints, making experimentation and prototyping much faster.

Integrating Tailwind Responsiveness

Tailwind CSS streamlines a responsive design using responsive prefixes. Instead of writing media queries, you attach classes that activate at specific breakpoints. For example:

```
<div class="grid grid-cols-3 md:grid-cols-2 sm:grid-cols-1">
```

```
<!-- Items -->
</div>
On large screens → grid-cols-3 (three columns)
On medium screens → md:grid-cols-2 (two columns)
On small screens → sm:grid-cols-1 (one column)
```

This declarative style makes responsiveness more readable, maintainable, and scalable. Let us build a responsive marketing page with a header, hero, services section, and footer. Then, implement two versions: one with traditional CSS media queries, and another with Tailwind CSS. Then compare the results for clarity, code length, and maintainability.

Prompt for index-traditional.html + styles.css (no JavaScript): *Create a small, responsive marketing page with semantic HTML and an external CSS file (no JavaScript). Files to output (as two separate full-file code blocks):*

1. *index-traditional.html*
2. *styles.css*

Requirements

- *Sections: header, hero, services, footer.*
- *Header: brand logo text "Brand" on the left; primary nav on the right with links: Features, Pricing, About, Contact. Use a semantic <nav aria-label="Primary">.*
- *Hero: two-column layout with headline "Build Responsive Sites Faster", a short paragraph, and a primary button "Get Started" on the left; on the right a decorative rectangle with rounded corners and subtle pattern; include role="img" and aria-label="Abstract placeholder illustration".*
- *Services: section title "What You Get"; 3 cards titled Performance, Accessibility, Scalability with short descriptive text.*
- *Footer: © 2025 Brand, Inc. All rights reserved. Footer nav with Privacy and Terms.*

Layout and Style (CSS)

- *Use a centered .container with width min(1100px, 92vw).*
- *Global box-sizing: border-box;, system UI font stack, light gray page background.*
- *Color tokens (CSS custom properties):*
    - *--surface: #ffffff;--section: #f8fafc;--ink: #0f172a;--muted: #475569;*
    - *--accent: #2563eb;--accent-ink: #ffffff;--ring: rgba(37,99,235,0.3);*
- *Header/footer: white surface with #e5e7eb borders.*
- *Buttons: rounded, subtle hover ring; primary uses --accent background and border, white text.*

- *Hero layout: grid with columns 1.2fr 1fr, gap 32px, vertical centering, generous padding. The art box has a soft blue/indigo gradient overlay and a repeating linear-gradient pattern, 12px radius, 1px light border.*
- *Services grid: 3 equal columns with 18px gap; cards have white background, 1px border #e5e7eb, 12px radius, soft shadow.*

Responsiveness (no JS)

- *Break at 900px: hero becomes a single column.*
- *Break at 700px: header stack (logo above nav), services grid becomes 2 columns.*
- *Break at 480px: services grid becomes 1 column; footer items stack.*

Accessibility & Semantics

- *Use <header>, <main>/sections, <footer>, <nav> with aria-label where appropriate.*
- *Link hover states have clear contrast.*

Output format

- *First code block: the complete index-traditional.html linking styles.css.*
- *Second code block: the complete styles.css.*
- *Do not include any commentary outside the two code blocks.*

Now, let us generate the `index-tailwind.html` prompt as follows:

Prompt to generate index-tailwind.html (Tailwind via CDN, no JavaScript):

Build the same marketing page as above using Tailwind CSS (no JavaScript), delivered as a single HTML file that includes Tailwind via CDN. File to output (one full-file code block):

index-tailwind.html
Requirements (match the traditional version's content)

- *Header: brand "Brand"; primary nav with Features, Pricing, About, Contact.*
- *Hero: headline "Build Responsive Sites Faster", supporting paragraph, primary button "Get Started", plus a decorative art box on the right (role="img" and appropriate aria-label).*
- *Services: section title "What You Get"; 3 cards (Performance, Accessibility, Scalability).*
- *Footer: © 2025 Brand, Inc. All rights reserved. Footer nav with Privacy and Terms.*

Tailwind specifics

- *Use a centered container width: w-[min(1100px,92vw)] with mx-auto.*

- *Header/footer: bg-white with border-slate-200.*
- Text colors: *base text-slate-900, muted text-slate-600.*
- Buttons: *rounded, primary button bg-blue-600 text-white with subtle hover:ring-4 hover:ring-blue-500/30.*
- *Hero layout: grid grid-cols-1 lg:grid-cols-[1.2fr,1fr] gap-8 items-center py-14.*
- *Decorative art box: rounded border, soft gradient (bg-gradient-to-br from-blue-500/15 to-indigo-500/15) plus a repeating pattern using an arbitrary background-image utility (CSS-in-Tailwind bracket syntax).*
- *Services grid: grid-cols-1 sm:grid-cols-2 lg:grid-cols-3 with card styling rounded-xl border border-slate-200 bg-white p-5 shadow-sm.*
- *Footer: flex layout that stacks on small screens (flex flex-col sm:flex-row) with spacing and hover states.*

Accessibility

- *Use aria-label on navs (Primary, Footer), and on the decorative art box.*

Output format

- *One code block containing the complete index-tailwind.html with the <script src="https://cdn.tailwindcss.com"></script> tag in <head>.*
- *No commentary outside the code block.*

By implementing the two aforementioned prompts, you will understand how media queries power traditional responsive design. Then, you will also understand how AI reduces the effort of writing boilerplate CSS and additionally, experience how Tailwind CSS makes responsiveness more intuitive. This approach ensures that you do not only grasp the theory of responsive design, but also practice applying it with modern tools and AI-driven techniques. Finally, open index-traditional.html and index-tailwind.html in separate tabs and resize the browser (≤900px, ≤700px, ≤480px) to observe grid/stack changes. You will examine how header stacks on narrow viewports. The hero turns from two columns to one and then, services grid collapses from 3 to 2 to 1 column.

Conclusion

This chapter has discussed extensively how AI system can level up CSS workflows from foundational styling like colors, typography, spacing to sophisticated responsive layouts. The AI approach turns clear prompts into production-ready codes that preserve performance and readability. Prompt-driven development allows teams to focus on high-level design decisions while offloading repetitive implementation, boosting productivity and freeing time for creative work. Looking ahead, AI will increasingly handle complex, bespoke components, integrate seamlessly with design systems to ensure cohesion, and analyze/optimize styles for performance and accessibility. As a next step, experiment with AI-generated CSS for your own design systems, use AI to audit and tighten stylesheets, and explore lightweight tools that assist with maintenance. Embracing these practices leads to faster, more consistent interfaces, and a more inventive, user-centered workflow. In the next chapter, we shall explore the advanced CSS techniques to style UI elements dynamically, giving them the ability to bring static components to life through AI-assisted CSS.

Points to Remember

- CSS applies styles to HTML elements using selectors, properties, and values. The cascade and specificity determine which rules take precedence.
- The box model (content, padding, border, and margin) governs how elements occupy space. Using box-sizing: border-box; ensures consistent sizing.
- Flexbox is a one-dimensional layout system ideal for aligning items along a row or column.
- CSS Grid is a two-dimensional layout system that provides precise control over rows and columns.
- Utility-first frameworks like Tailwind CSS accelerate development by applying predefined classes directly in HTML.
- Responsive design ensures layouts adapt across devices. Media queries in CSS or responsive prefixes in Tailwind (`sm:`, `md:`, `lg:`) achieve this.
- AI can generate styling code quickly, but developers should review and refine the output for readability, maintainability, and performance.
- Combining traditional CSS, modern layout systems, and utility-first frameworks gives flexibility and efficiency in building interfaces.
- Always prioritize semantic HTML and accessible design when applying styles, whether generated manually or through AI.
- Maintain a balance between rapid prototyping with AI-driven workflows and long-term maintainability of the stylesheet or utility classes.

Multiple Choice Questions

1. Which of the following best describes the CSS box model?
   a. A design framework for responsive layouts
   b. A structure consisting of content, padding, border, and margin
   c. A system of predefined utility classes
   d. A layout model limited to Flexbox

2. Which amongst the following does the CSS property box-sizing: border-box; do?
    a. Excludes padding from the element's total width and height.
    b. Includes padding and border in the element's total width and height.
    c. Resets all margins and paddings to zero.
    d. Forces all elements to be inline-block.
3. Which selector has the highest specificity in CSS?
    a. Class selector
    b. Element selector
    c. Inline style
    d. Universal selector
4. Which Flexbox property is used to align items horizontally within a container?
    a. align-items
    b. justify-content
    c. flex-direction
    d. align-content
5. In CSS Grid, what does the property grid-template-columns: repeat(3, 1fr); create?
    a. Three rows of equal height
    b. Three columns of equal width
    c. A nested grid with three tracks
    d. Three flexible items stacked vertically
6. Which CSS feature allows you to apply styles based on screen size or device type?
    a. Animations
    b. Media Queries
    c. Pseudo-classes
    d. Variables
7. Which of these is the main difference between Flexbox and CSS Grid?
    a. Flexbox is for two-dimensional layouts; Grid is for one-dimensional layouts.
    b. Grid is for two-dimensional layouts; Flexbox is for one-dimensional layouts.

   c. Both are only one-dimensional.
   d. Both are only two-dimensional.

8. Which Tailwind CSS class creates padding of 1rem on all sides?
   a. `p-4`
   b. `padding-4`
   c. `pt-4`
   d. `pad-4`

9. In Tailwind, what does the class md:grid-cols-2 mean?
   a. Always use two columns in a grid.
   b. Use two columns only on small screens.
   c. Use two columns starting from medium screen size.
   d. Use two columns only for large screens.

10. Which CSS property is used to change an element from block-level to inline-level?
    a. position
    b. display
    c. float
    d. visibility

11. Which of the following is a utility-first CSS framework?
    a. Bootstrap
    b. Foundation
    c. Tailwind CSS
    d. Materialize

12. What does flex-grow: 1; do to a Flexbox item?
    a. Makes it shrink when space is tight.
    b. Gives it equal space compared to other items with the same grow value.
    c. Aligns it to the right side of the container.
    d. Fixes its width to 100%.

13. Which of the following is an advantage of using AI-generated CSS prompts?
    a. Ensures that styles are always error-free.
    b. Automates repetitive styling tasks and speeds up workflow.

c. Removes the need to understand CSS fundamentals.

d. Guarantees compatibility with all browsers.

14. Which media query will apply styles to devices with a maximum width of 600px?

    a. `@media (max-width: 600px)`

    b. `@media screen and (min-width: 600px)`

    c. `@media (device-width: 600px)`

    d. `@media screen and (width: 600px)`

15. Why is readability important in AI-generated CSS?

    a. It ensures that styles load faster on browsers.

    b. It helps developers maintain, debug, and extend code efficiently.

    c. It reduces the file size automatically.

    d. It prevents inline styles from being overridden.

Answers

1. b
2. b
3. c
4. b
5. b
6. b
7. b
8. a
9. c
10. b
11. c
12. b
13. b
14. a
15. b

Key Terms

- **Cascading Style Sheets (CSS):** A stylesheet language used to control the presentation of HTML documents, including layout, colors, fonts, and spacing.
- **Selector:** A pattern used in CSS to target specific HTML elements for styling.
- **Property:** A characteristic of an element (such as color or margin) that can be modified using CSS.
- **Value:** The specific setting applied to a property, for example color: red;.
- **Cascade:** The process by which the browser determines which CSS rules to apply when multiple rules affect the same element.
- **Specificity:** A weighting system that decides which CSS rule overrides another when selectors conflict.
- **Box Model:** The conceptual structure of every element in CSS consisting of content, padding, border, and margin.
- **Flexbox (Flexible Box Layout):** A one-dimensional CSS layout system for aligning items horizontally or vertically within a container.
- **CSS Grid:** A two-dimensional layout system in CSS that arranges elements into rows and columns.
- **Utility-First CSS:** A design approach that uses small, predefined classes (which includes p-4, text-center) to style elements directly in the HTML.
- **Tailwind CSS:** A popular utility-first CSS framework that enables rapid styling with composable class names.
- **Media Query:** A CSS feature that applies styles conditionally based on device characteristics such as screen width or resolution.
- **Responsive Design:** The practice of creating layouts that adapt fluidly across various screen sizes and devices.
- **Box-sizing:** A CSS property that defines how width and height are calculated (content-box versus border-box).
- **AI-Assisted Styling:** The use of AI tools to generate or refine CSS, improving speed and reducing repetitive manual coding.

Chapter 7
Advanced CSS Techniques with AI Assistance

Introduction

Building on the foundational concepts from the previous chapter, where we explored how AI can support and accelerate the styling process using CSS, both traditional and utility-first frameworks; this chapter takes you further into the advanced techniques that enhance interactivity and visual appeal. We shall introduce advanced CSS techniques that will elevate user interfaces from static structures into visually dynamic experiences. While this chapter does not cover every advanced CSS technique, it does provide a solid foundation in the key areas that helps you enhance your UI design skills with AI system. With transitions, animations, gradients, shadows, filters and AI-assisted code generation, you can design more immersive and interactive web applications. Artificial intelligence tools such as ChatGPT and GitHub Copilot reduce the time spent writing repetitive style rules and instead allow focus on refining design intent through structured prompts. Each section demonstrates how to employ prompting strategies to generate a CSS code, validate its correctness, and apply it effectively to real components. You will gain both conceptual clarity and hands-on practice in applying advanced CSS features for professional-grade styling.

After reading this chapter, you will be able to apply advanced CSS techniques that improve interactivity and visual richness in web design. You will learn how to prompt and implement smooth transitions, and hover effects that elevate user feedback and usability. You will also gain the ability to generate and refine animations with keyframes, enabling you to create multi-stage, dynamic effects. In addition, you will understand how to use shadows to simulate depth, establish hierarchy, and highlight important elements. The chapter will guide you in designing engaging backgrounds and borders with gradients, as well as applying CSS filters to achieve creative visual effects such as blurring, brightness adjustments, and frosted glass styles. By understanding these skills, you will be equipped to transform static layouts into immersive, professional-grade user interfaces with the support of AI-assisted design tools.

Structure

In this chapter, we will cover the following topics:

- Prompting Transitions and Hover Effects
- Generating Animations with Keyframes
- Understanding Shadows and Depth Effect
- Using Gradients for Backgrounds and Borders
- CSS Filters and Visual Effects

Prompting Transitions and Hover Effects

Transitions and hover effects are essential for guiding user interaction and improving feedback in modern user interfaces. Transitions and hover effects are the feel of your interface. They communicate interactivity, confirm a change, and ensure that state changes to feel natural. Developers often add subtle animations to web page elements when a user hovers, clicks, or focuses on those elements. This usually creates a sense of responsiveness. Rather than writing repetitive rules manually, AI systems can generate scalable transition patterns that adapt to multiple components. This section explores how to compose prompts that yield semantic, accessible, and performant CSS transitions. We will be hands-on to illustrate the creation of hover effects for buttons, cards, and navigation links, all generated with the support of ChatGPT. Now, you will be guided through the AI assisted transitions and hover effects. Let us get started with defining transition properties with prompts.

Defining Transition Properties with Prompts

Generating effective transitions requires you to define the desired properties and behaviors. You need to specify transition duration, the length of time the transition takes to complete, transition timing function, the speed curve of the transition, such as linear, ease-in, or ease-out, transition delay, the time before the transition starts, and the specific CSS properties you want to animate, such as color, background-color, transform, or opacity. It is often one of the best practices to tell the AI system what to animate and how it should feel. As discussed in this book, clear prompts act like a tiny spec: *duration, timing, delay*, and the exact *properties to transition*. When you name these up front, you get a CSS that is consistent, accessible, and fast, without trial-and-error. Let us examine this example prompt and their expected CSS output.

Prompt: "*Add a hover transition to a primary button. Duration 200ms.*"

Output:

```
.button {
  transition: background-color 200ms ease-in-out, transform 200ms ease-
in-out;
}
.button:hover {
  background-color: #0959db;
  transform: scale(1.06);}
```

The preceding code shows AI-generated CSS snippet successfully adding a hover transition to the primary button with the duration of 200ms, smoothly changing the background color and scaling the button.

Note: *For optimal user experience, consider the following duration guidelines for animations: 120-180ms for micro interactions like icons, toggles, 180-240ms for buttons and links, and 240-320ms for cards and overlays.*

Hover States for Buttons and Links

A hover state is a visual change that occurs when a user's cursor moves over an interactive element, like a link or a button. It provides an immediate feedback that the element is clickable or actionable. ChatGPT as an interactive AI agent can generate hover effects for buttons and links, which are both visually appealing and accessible. Let us examine a composed prompt for this purpose as follows:

Prompt:

"Generate a complete HTML file that demonstrates hover states for both links and buttons.

Requirements:

Use a clean layout with a light background and simple typography.

Include two types of links:

A basic link that changes text color to #337ab7 and underlines smoothly on hover/focus with a 0.1s transition.

An animated underline link where a blue line (#337ab7) slides in from left to right when hovered/focused.

Include two types of buttons:

A basic button with a blue background (#337ab7) that darkens to #286090 and slightly lifts (translateY(-2px)) on hover/focus.

A gradient button with a left-to-right gradient (#337ab7 to #5bc0de) that reverses direction on hover/focus.

Ensure all hover effects are smooth with transition properties.

Add proper focus states so that keyboard users get the same feedback as hover users.

Organize the page with headings for Links and Buttons and include examples of each hover state in action."

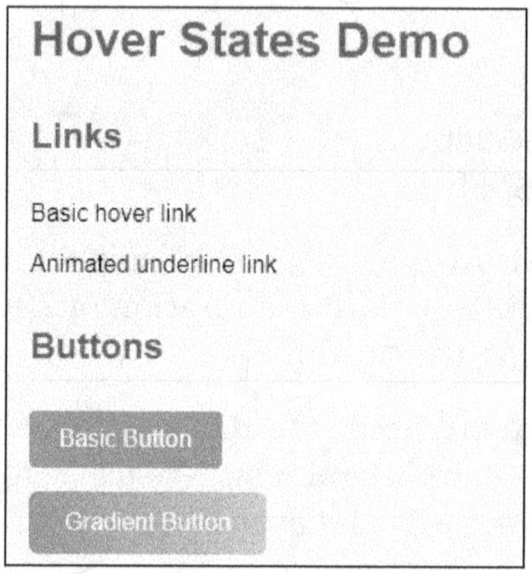

Figure 7.1: *Screenshot Showcasing Different Hover Effects for Links and Buttons*

The former prompt creates a complete HTML file that showcases different hover effects for links and buttons. Adding hover effects to your page element improves usability and discoverability of actions, improves web page element aesthetics and user engagement. All these factors contribute to your designed website accessibility when designed with clear contrast.

AI-Generated Micro-Interactions

AI-Generated Micro-Interactions are small, subtle animations or design responses created by the artificial intelligence to improve user experience. These micro-interactions happen when users perform simple actions, like hovering, clicking, or typing, and the interface reacts in a visually engaging way. AI can automatically generate these effects by analyzing best design practices, accessibility standards, and user behavior patterns, saving you time while ensuring consistency. For example, imagine a shopping app where a user hovers over the "*Add to Cart*" button. Instead of just changing color, AI could generate a smooth animation where the button slightly lifts, glows, and a tiny cart icon slides in. This not only confirms the action, but also delights the user. Such AI-powered improvements make digital experiences feel more intuitive, modern, and personalized without requiring you to manually code every interaction. Let us examine a prompt to generate the micro-interactions.

Prompt:

"Create a self-contained HTML file with internal CSS that centers a blue (#337ab7) 'Add to Cart' button on a light page; on hover/focus it darkens to #286090, lifts via translateY(-3px), gains a soft box-shadow, and reveals a left-aligned 🛒 icon that starts

hidden (shifted left and transparent) then slides in and fades in with smooth 0.2–0.3s ease transitions".

The preceding prompt asks an ChatGPT to generate a complete HTML page with a styled "Add to Cart" button that animates on hover/focus—changing color, lifting with a shadow, and smoothly revealing a sliding cart icon.

Note: *Try pasting the prompt into ChatGPT or any AI code generator to see how it produces a complete HTML file with an interactive "Add to Cart" button. Once generated, copy the code into a .html file and open it in your browser to experience the hover animation and cart icon effect in action.*

Next, we aim to explore CSS keyframes, a great way to move beyond simple hover effects. CSS keyframes let you create custom animations that unfold over time. With keyframes, you get a control over how an element changes at specific moments. This would open door to richer, more dynamic interactions in your web designs.

Generating Animations with Keyframes

Animations are no longer just cosmetic features in web design; they are central in creating interfaces that feel responsive, intuitive, and engaging. Subtle animations can guide user attention, provide feedback, and bring interfaces to life in ways that static elements never could. From loading indicators to hover effects, well-executed animations create a sense of continuity and polish that modern users expect. Among the most powerful techniques available to the front-end developers is CSS keyframe animation. Unlike transitions, which smoothly interpolate between two states, keyframes allow developers to define multiple stages of an animation sequence. This makes them ideal for more complex behaviors like bouncing elements, pulsing buttons, sliding panels, and even storytelling animations where elements appear in orchestrated sequences. A typical keyframe animation might manipulate properties such as:

- Position, moving an element across the screen.
- Opacity, fading content in or out.
- Transforms, scaling, rotating, skewing elements.
- Colors, gradually shifting backgrounds or text colors.

For instance, a loading spinner could rotate indefinitely using keyframes, while a card could flip to reveal a hidden content with a timed rotation sequence. These animations not only delight, but also serve functional purposes, providing visual feedback that something is happening behind the scenes.

What makes this topic especially exciting today is the intersection with AI prompting. As a developer or an enthusiast, you can now use plain language to describe animation behaviors, such as "pulse button on hover", and receive precise CSS output generated by AI system. This reduces the time spent tinkering with the syntax, and subsequently opens the door to faster experimentation. Instead of guessing at percentages or easing functions, developers can iterate ideas conversationally, leaving the AI to handle a boilerplate code. Let us now dive into understanding the mechanics of keyframes, and how AI model supercharges your workflow in working with animations.

Structuring Keyframes with AI

A CSS keyframe animation is defined with the `@keyframes` rule. Typically, developers specify a name for animation and then define stages often expressed as percentages that indicate how properties should change over time. For example, a simple fade-in animation might look like this:

```
@keyframesfadeIn {
  0% { opacity: 0; }
  100% { opacity: 1; }
}
```

In the aforementioned CSS code, the 0% block defines the start of the animation, and 100% defines the end. You can insert intermediate percentages to build more complex sequences. When applying this animation to an element, CSS uses the animation shorthand as follows:

```
.web-page-element {
  animation: fadeIn 1s ease-in-out forwards;
}
```

The **`fadeIn`** refers to the animation name as you can see in the former prompt with the **`@keyframefadeIn.1s`** defining the duration. The **`ease-in-out`** sets the timing function. The **`forwards`** ensures that the final style persists after the animation finishes. While the provided scenario is simple, real-world animations often involve multiple properties with delayed timings, or intricate transformations. Manually writing out 0%, 25%, 50%, 75%, and 100% blocks can be tedious. However, with AI prompting, you could instead describe the effect in natural language. Let us see an example of keyframe animation generated by AI system:

Prompts:

"Generate a keyframe animation that makes an image bounce three times vertically, each bounce slightly smaller than the last."

The output could then return code like:

```
@keyframes bounce {
  0%   { transform: translateY(0); }
  20%  { transform: translateY(-50px); }
  40%  { transform: translateY(0); }
```

```
  60%  { transform: translateY(-25px); }
  80%  { transform: translateY(0); }
  100% { transform: translateY(0); }
}
```

This workflow accelerates experimentation. Instead of fine-tuning numbers by hand, you can let the AI system generate a starting point, then refine the details as may be needed.

Applying Infinite and Finite Animations

As a developer or a designer, it is not all the time that we expect animations to run endlessly. Some animations serve as one-time introductions, while others provide ongoing feedback. CSS offers developers flexibility through properties like **`animation-iteration-count`** and **`animation-fill-mode`.** Finite animations either run once, or for a specified number of cycles. For instance, fading in a modal window only needs to happen when the modal is opened:

```
.modal {
  animation: fadeIn 0.5s ease forwards;
}
```

This preceding CSS code plays the fade-in once and then holds the final state. Finite animations are best for page-load effects such as introductory sequences, content reveals like accordions, modals, tooltips and micro-interactions that should not loop endlessly. With infinite animations, some animations like spinners, pulsing indicators, or background patterns are designed to repeat forever. To achieve this, you can use the infinite keyword in your CSS animation. Let us see an example of a spinner animation that rotates 360 degrees and repeats forever:

```
.spinner {  animation: spin 1s linear infinite;}
@keyframes spin {
  0%   { transform: rotate(0deg); }
  100% { transform: rotate(360deg); }
}
```

The aforementioned CSS code, the **`animation: spin 1s linear infinite;`**

- The **`spin`** is the name of the animation.
- **`1s`** is the duration of one animation cycle.
- **`linear`** specifies the timing function, in this case, a linear transition.
- **`infinite`** makes the animation repeat forever.
- **`@keyframesspin { ... }`** defines the animation sequence
- **`0%`** specifies the starting point 0 degrees rotation.
- **`100%`** specifies the ending point 360 degrees rotation.

By using infinite, the animation will repeat indefinitely, creating a seamless looping effect. Though, infinite animations are powerful, it should be used carefully. Overuse can distract your website users or degrade performance on low-powered devices. Designers should also consider accessibility. Users sensitive to motion may need reduced-motion alternatives, which can be handled via the prefers-reduced-motion media query.

Now, we will leverage ChatGPT to specify how AI can streamline your workflow to compose finite and infinite animations. Instead of recalling the exact CSS syntax, you might write compose prompts as follows:

Infinite animation prompt:

"Create a CSS animation that makes a loader spin indefinitely at 1 second per rotation."

Finite animation prompt:

"Generate a CSS animation where a card flips 180 degrees once and stays flipped."

AI system can provide CSS animation boilerplate while you focus on your intent. In the next section, we will discuss integrating animations with user events using pure CSS.

Integrating Animations with User Events

Animations become even more compelling when tied to user events. Hovering, clicking, or focusing elements can trigger animations that provide immediate feedback. Let us examine the hover Animations with CSS using pseudo-classes as follows:

```
.button:hover {
  animation: pulse 0.5s ease-in-out;
}

@keyframes pulse {
  0%, 100% { transform: scale(1); }
  50%      { transform: scale(1.1); }
}
```

The preceding CSS code ensures that the pulse plays only when a user hovers over the button. We can apply animations to focus and active states as well. Accessibility requires that keyboard users receive similar feedback. The same animation can be applied to **`:focus`**, or **`:active:`**.

```
.button:focus {
  animation: pulse 0.5s ease-in-out;
}
```

You can combine animation in such as way keyframes are layered for richer effects. For instance, a card could both pulse and fade simultaneously by applying multiple animations:

```
.card:hover {
  animation: pulse 1s ease-in-out infinite, fadeIn 2s ease forwards;
}
```

AI system simplifies keyframes animations by generating multi-step, combined animations when described in the natural language. You can use the following prompts to generate a single page HTML to explore all the animations discussed so far.

Prompt:

*"Generate a **single self-contained HTML file** (no external assets, no JS frameworks) that showcases a **gallery of pure CSS animations**.*

Requirements:

- *Dark theme with light fallback (prefers-color-scheme), CSS variables for colors, rounded cards, responsive grid.*
- *Sticky header with title, subtitle, and a **"Reduce motion"** toggle (CSS checkbox hack). When checked or if prefers-reduced-motion: reduce applies, all animations stop.*
- *Each card = demo of one animation, with title, description, and a small .badge. Cards lift slightly on hover.*

Animations to include:

- *Fade: fade-in, fade-up, fade-down*
- *Slide: slide-left, slide-right*
- *Zoom / Rotate: zoom-in, zoom-out, rotate-in*
- *Loader: spinner ring, indeterminate bar*
- *Micro: pulse, bounce, wobble, heartbeat*
- *Flip-in 3D chip (rotateY)*
- *Shimmer skeleton line*
- *Typing text with blinking caret*
- *Gradient morphing blob*
- *Ripple CTA button (hover)*
- *Swing (hover)*
- *Clip-path reveal*
- *Conic-gradient progress ring (data-label="72%")*
- *Sliding underline link (hover)*
- *Status pill with pulsing dot*
- *Sequenced entrances with .delay-N*
- *Sliding background sheen*

Others:

- *Use system-ui font stack.*
- *Header has dummy "Jump to Gallery" + disabled "No JS here 😄" button.*
- *Cards enter with staggered fade/slide.*
- *No JavaScript for animations.*

Output the full HTML file."

CSS keyframe animations unleash a world of creative possibilities for web developers. With multi-stage animation sequences, you can create immersive experiences that feel dynamic, responsive, and refined. AI-powered prompting has revolutionized animation creation. You can simply describe your design intent in natural language and receive a functional code in seconds. Building on our discussion of animations, we will now examine how to add a new layer of sophistication to our designs with the strategic use of shadows and depth effects.

Understanding Shadows and Depth Effect

With shadows, you can establish visual hierarchy, simulate depth, and add realism to flat layouts. Correct use of shadows improves user focus by distinguishing interactive from static components. AI-powered CSS can produce consistent shadow values and layered effects across design systems. In this section, we will explore how shadows can transform card components into visually distinct, layered elements that feel modern. By applying different shadow techniques, you simulate depth, hierarchy, and emphasis, making the content easier to scan and interact with. Let us get started with box-shadow for structural depth.

Box-Shadow for Structural Depth

The box-shadow property is one of the most effective tools for adding dimension and hierarchy to your designs. You only need to tweak just a few values like offset, blur, spread, and opacity. You can make an element appear flat, slightly raised, or dramatically elevated. Shadows guide the eye, separate layers, and make interfaces feel more tactile. Let us take a look at a card shadow as follows:

```
.card {
  background-color: #fff;
  padding: 20px;
  border-radius: 10px;
  box-shadow: 0 2px 4px rgba(0, 0, 0, 0.1);
}
```

The former CSS code shows a subtle shadow effect can be achieved with a horizontal *offset of 0, vertical offset of 2px, blur radius of 4px, spread radius of 0*, and a light gray color with 10% opacity *(box-shadow: 0 2px 4px rgba(0, 0, 0, 0.1))*. This creates a gentle lift, making elements appear as if they are floating above the background. To establish visual hierarchy, you can vary shadow intensities: light shadows *(box-shadow: 0 1px 2px rgba(0, 0, 0, 0.05))* for flat lists, medium shadows *(box-shadow: 0 4px 8px rgba(0, 0, 0.2))* for feature highlights, and dark shadows *(box-shadow: 0 8px 16px rgba(0, 0, 0, 0.5))* for dramatic emphasis. Let us examine a prompt to generate a box-shadow.

Prompt:

Create a simple HTML and CSS snippet for a card component that demonstrates a subtle box-shadow effect. The card should:

- *Have a white background, padding, and rounded corners.*
- *Use box-shadow: 0 2px 4px rgba(0, 0, 0, 0.1); to create a light, soft shadow.*
- *Contain a heading and some placeholder text to show how content looks inside.*
- *Be minimal and self-contained (no external CSS).*

Output only the complete HTML file with inline <style>.

Try to experiment with blur, spread, and opacity, you can design a whole range of depth effects from subtle cues to bold, layered interfaces.

Text-Shadow for Highlighted Typography

The text-shadow property is a versatile way to give typography depth, emphasis, and visual impact. When used creatively, shadows can make important text like headings or calls-to-action stand out while maintaining readability. The basic syntax is as follows:

```
.text { text-shadow: offset-x offset-y blur-radius color;}
```

Let us examine the implementation of text-shadow with this example:

```
.highlighted-text { text-shadow: 0 2px 4px rgba(0, 0, 0, 0.5);}
```

The highlights in the preceding CSS code are as follows:

- **Horizontal offset:** 0, shadow is centered under the text.
- **Vertical offset:** 2px, shadow sits slightly below the text.
- **Blur radius:** 4px, softens the edges of the shadow.
- **Color:** Semi-transparent black (rgba (0, 0, 0, 0.5)).

This creates a soft lift effect, and it gives the text a more contrast against the background. The text-shadow prompt is as follows:

Prompt:

Create a minimal HTML and CSS snippet that demonstrates the use of the ***text-shadow*** *property. The page should:*

- *Contain a heading with a subtle text shadow (for example, 0 2px 4px rgba(0, 0, 0, 0.5)).*
- *Show the CSS syntax and explain what each value (offset-x, offset-y, blur-radius, color) does.*
- *Use a clean, self-contained design (no external CSS).*
- *Output a complete HTML file with inline <style>.*

With text shadows, you can strategically draw attention, improve legibility, and add personality to highlighted text without overwhelming your design.

AI-Generated Shadow Presets

AI-generated shadow presets are transforming how designers and creators add depth and realism to images. Instead of manually adjusting layers or lighting in image shadow, AI can instantly generate natural-looking shadows that match the subject and its environment. This presents the images in a more professional way, and with a polished appearance. AI System like ChatGPT, eliminates the need for tedious manual editing, tweaking of CSS shadow metrics or costly reshoots and make professional results accessible in seconds. You can think of AI-generated shadow presets as a shortcut to designing reusable box-shadow and text-shadow styles in CSS. In CSS, shadows are defined with numeric values for offset, blur, spread, and color: `.card { box-shadow: 0 4px 8px rgba(0, 0, 0, 0.15);},` designers often hand-tune these numbers by trial and error. With prompt engineering, you can describe the style you want like soft neumorphic shadows, bold material UI shadows, or subtle floating card effect, and an AI system can output the corresponding CSS shadow presets. Let us explore an example of this concept with the following prompt:

Prompt:

"Generate three CSS shadow presets: light for subtle lists, medium for feature cards, and heavy for modals. Use rgba values with opacity under 0.3."

Output:

```
/* Light */
.shadow-light { box-shadow: 01px2pxrgba(0,0,0,0.08); }

/* Medium */
.shadow-medium { box-shadow: 04px8pxrgba(0,0,0,0.18); }

/* Heavy */
.shadow-heavy { box-shadow: 08px20pxrgba(0,0,0,0.25); }
```

These presets become reusable design tokens in your frontend development toolkit that you can apply consistently across components `.card`, `.button`, `.modal`, and ensure a consistent visual hierarchy and branding.

As shadows add depth and hierarchy to elements, gradients can enhance the visual richness of a design by introducing smooth color transitions. Next, we shall explore how gradients can be applied to backgrounds and borders to create vibrant interfaces.

Using Gradients for Backgrounds and Borders

Gradients allow you to create smooth color transitions that elevate visual richness of web page or elements. They can be applied to backgrounds, borders, and even text. Traditional manual configuration of gradient angles, stops, and blending modes is time-consuming. AI assistance simplifies this process by quickly generating variations based on descriptive prompts like *"a subtle diagonal blue-to-purple gradient for a hero section."* In this section, we will walk through linear and radial gradients, gradient overlays, and advanced cases prompts where gradients are combined with masks.

Let us take a look at this prompt as an example of visually striking and cohesive gradient palette.

Prompt:

"Create a visually striking and cohesive gradient palette (7–9 gradients) for use in web design, graphic design, and digital art. The gradients should work well together to establish a consistent visual brand identity.

Requirements

- ***Color Harmony**: Apply principles such as analogous, complementary, or triadic schemes to ensure gradients blend harmoniously.*
- ***Originality**: Generate a unique palette that avoids resembling popular, overused sets.*
- ***Contrast**: Provide enough variation between gradients to maintain visual interest and accessibility.*
- ***Versatility**: Ensure gradients adapt well to multiple use cases – backgrounds, buttons, overlays, or text highlights.*
- ***CSS Compatibility**: Deliver gradients in a format usable directly in CSS (hex, RGB, or HSL).*

Style Guidelines

- ***Modern and Trendy**: Reflect current design aesthetics.*
- ***Bold and Vibrant**: Include strong, energetic colors for emphasis.*

- ***Subtle and Pastel:*** *Balance bold tones with softer options for flexibility.*

Output Format

1. *Visual preview of the palette (image or graphic).*
2. *CSS-ready gradient codes (hex, RGB, or HSL).*
3. *A short explanation of the design inspiration and color decisions.*

Evaluation Criteria

- *Overall visual appeal and modern aesthetic.*
- *Harmony andbalance among gradients.*
- *Uniqueness compared to existing palettes.*
- *Practical adaptability across different design contexts.*
- *Technical accuracy of CSS gradient syntax.*

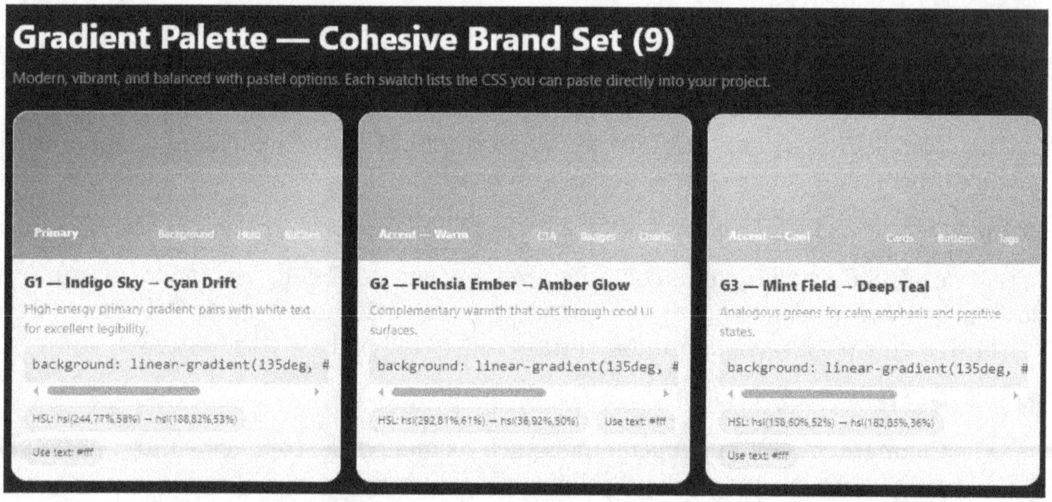

Figure 7.2: *Screenshot Displays a Cohesive Gradient Palette of 9 Styles*

The former prompt displays a cohesive gradient palette of 9 styles that can be applied across web and digital design projects to establish a consistent brand identity. It sets clear requirements: gradients should follow color harmony principles analogous, complementary, triadic, be unique (not generic), offer enough contrast for accessibility, and be versatile for use in *backgrounds, buttons, overlays, or text.* It also specifies CSS compatibility, requiring output in *hex,* RGB, *or* HSL. Stylistically, the gradients must balance modern trends with both *bold/vibrant* tones for emphasis and subtle/pastel tones for flexibility. The output format combines a visual preview, CSS-ready gradient codes, and a brief design rationale. This ensures that you are not only getting usable code but also understand the inspiration and purpose behind each gradient.

CSS Filters and Visual Effects

CSS filters extend the expressive capacity of web design by applying effects such as blur, brightness, contrast, and saturation. These effects allow developers to mimic image editing software directly in the browser without external assets. AI assistance plays a role in experimenting with filter chains by interpreting high-level requests like "make the background image resemble frosted glass." This section teaches how to layer filters, apply them conditionally, and test performance across browsers. Exercises help reinforce the correct application of filters in real-world interface scenarios.

Common Filter Functions

These are the building blocks of CSS filters. There are properties like **`blur()`**, **`brightness()`**, **`contrast()`**, **`grayscale()`**, **`saturate()`**, and **`hue-rotate()`**.By combining them, you can adjust visuals much like in photo-editing software, directly in the browser. They are often used to improve readability, tone down images, or create mood effects. Let us examine a prompt example.

Prompt:

"*Create a simple* HTML + CSS *example that demonstrates several common* CSS *filter functions (blur, brightness, contrast, saturate, grayscale, hue-rotate). Show an image and apply different filters side by side, each with a short label. Provide the full code in one file.*"

Frosted Glass and Backdrop Effects

By layering **`blur()`** with **`brightness()`**, or **`opacity()`**, and using the **`backdrop-filter`**, you can create the popular frosted glass look, like a translucent panel that blurs whatever is behind it. This effect adds depth, modern style, and visual hierarchy without heavy assets, commonly seen in dashboards, modals, and navigation bars. Let us examine a prompt example.

Prompt:

Write a self-contained HTML + CSS *snippet that creates a frosted glass card effect using backdrop-filter: blur() along with transparency and subtle shadows. Place the card over a colorful background image to make the effect visible. Ensure that the text inside the card remains clear and readable.*

AI-Generated Filter Chains

AI can help experiment with complex combinations of filters by translating natural-language prompts like "*make this button glow softly*" into CSS filter chains. This lowers the barrier for creativity, offering designers ready-to-use presets that can be refined for aesthetics and performance. It also accelerates prototyping by skipping manual trial-and-error. Let us examine a prompt example.

Prompt:

Simulate an AI-driven design workflow: given a high-level request like "make the background image look dreamy and soft", generate the corresponding CSS filter chain (e.g., blur + brightness + saturate adjustments). Provide a small HTML + CSS demo that applies the filter to an image. Include a brief explanation of how each filter contributes to the effect.

In a nutshell, CSS filters offer a powerful way to adjust visuals directly in the browser, using properties like blur, brightness, and hue-rotate to improve readability, tone down images, or create mood effects. AI can assist in generating complex filter combinations, accelerating prototyping and lowering the barrier for creativity by providing ready-to-use presets that can be refined for good looking digital projects, and for the best performance.

Conclusion

In this chapter, we explored how advanced CSS techniques, transitions, animations, shadows, gradients, and filters elevate web design from static layouts into dynamic, immersive experiences. During the chapter, you have learned how AI assistance simplifies repetitive coding tasks, generates reusable presets, and accelerates experimentation through natural-language prompts. By combining solid CSS fundamentals with prompt engineering, you can focus on creative intent while AI handles the syntax and boilerplate. This synergy enables modern, accessible, and scalable user interfaces.

Next, we shall explore the concept of UI components and focus on how AI can help you rapidly generate, customize, and scale interface elements through prompt-based workflows.

Points to Remember

- Transitions and hover effects guide user interaction, providing visual feedback and natural state changes.
- AI systems like ChatGPT can generate scalable transition patterns, saving time.
- Micro-interactions are small, subtle AI-generated animations that enhance usability.
- CSS keyframes allow multi-stage animations, unlike transitions which are limited to two states.
- Animations can be finite (one-time) or infinite (looping) depending on purpose.
- Shadows (box-shadow, text-shadow) add depth, hierarchy, and emphasis to designs.

- Gradients enhance visual richness and brand consistency when applied to backgrounds, borders, or text.
- CSS filters (blur, brightness, contrast, etc.) mimic image editing effects directly in the browser.
- AI assistance accelerates workflow by generating prompts, presets, and filter chains.

Multiple Choice Questions

1. Which CSS property is used to create hover transitions?
   a. Animation
   b. Transition
   c. Transform
   d. filter
2. Which AI tool can generate hover effects and animations quickly?
   a. Photoshop
   b. Illustrator
   c. ChatGPT
   d. Figma
3. What is the recommended duration for button hover animations?
   a. 120–180ms
   b. 180–240ms
   c. 240–320ms
   d. 400–500ms
4. Which CSS rule defines keyframe animations?
   a. `@media`
   b. `@transition`
   c. `@keyframes`
   d. `@animation`
5. Which property makes animations repeat forever?
   a. animation-delay
   b. animation-iteration-count: infinite

   c. animation-fill-mode: forwards
   d. animation-duration

6. Which shadow type is used for structural depth in cards?
   a. text-shadow
   b. box-shadow
   c. drop-shadow
   d. inset-shadow
7. Which property applies shadows to text?
   a. box-shadow
   b. font-shadow
   c. text-shadow
   d. glow-shadow
8. What do gradients in CSS create?
   a. Smooth color transitions
   b. Depth effects
   c. Hover interactions
   d. Infinite animations
9. Which gradient type spreads color from a center point outward?
   a. Linear gradient
   b. Conic gradient
   c. Radial gradient
   d. Angular gradient
10. Which CSS property creates effects like blur and brightness?
    a. Filter
    b. Shadow
    c. Transform
    d. transition
11. Which filter creates a frosted glass effect when combined with backdrop-filter?
    a. `grayscale()`
    b. `brightness()`

   c. `blur()`
   d. `contrast()`

12. Which AI feature helps generate reusable design tokens like shadow presets?
    a. AI-generated icons
    b. AI-generated filters
    c. AI-generated presets
    d. AI-generated animations

Answers

1. b
2. c
3. b
4. c
5. b
6. b
7. c
8. a
9. c
10. a
11. c
12. c

Key Terms

- **Transitions**: In CSS, transitions define how properties change smoothly over a specific duration when triggered by user interaction or state changes.
- **Hover Effects**: Hover effects are visual changes applied to elements when the user's cursor moves over them, providing feedback and improving interactivity.
- **Micro-interactions**: Micro-interactions are small, subtle animations or responses that occur when users perform simple actions, enhancing usability and engagement.
- **Keyframes**: Keyframes in CSS are rules that define multiple stages of an animation, allowing elements to change styles at specific points in time.

- **Finite Animations**: Finite animations are animations that run once or a set number of times and then stop, often used for introductions or content reveals.
- **Infinite Animations**: Infinite animations are CSS animations that loop endlessly, such as spinners or pulsing indicators, to provide ongoing visual feedback.
- **Box-shadow**: The CSS property box-shadow creates shadows around elements, adding depth and a sense of elevation to user interface components.
- **Text-shadow**: The CSS property text-shadow applies shadow effects to text, making it stand out and improving readability or visual impact.
- **Gradients**: Gradients in CSS are smooth transitions between two or more colors that can be applied to backgrounds, borders, or text for richer design aesthetics.
- **CSS Filters**: CSS filters are effects such as blur, brightness, contrast, and saturation that can be applied to elements to adjust their appearance directly in the browser.
- **Backdrop-filter**: The CSS property backdrop-filter applies effects like blur or brightness to the area behind an element, creating effects such as frosted glass panels.
- **AI-generated Presets**: AI-generated presets are predesigned CSS styles, such as shadows or gradients, created by artificial intelligence to ensure consistency and save time in design workflows.

CHAPTER 8
Building UI Components

Introduction

In the last chapter, we discussed advanced CSS styling features to enhance the visual richness and interactivity of web interfaces. This chapter introduces the concept of building User Interface (UI) components and how AI helps to rapidly generate, customize, and scale interface elements through prompt-based workflows. User interface refers to that part of a website or web application that users directly interact with in their browser. The UIs like forms, buttons, modals and dialogs, cards are built using HTML for structure, CSS for styling, and JavaScript for interactivity. In frontend development, UI is the bridge between users and your application. Here, you will learn how to create modular user interface components that are reusable, maintainable, and consistent.

With practical, prompt-driven examples, the chapter walks through the creation of navigation bars, footers, buttons, cards, and forms, along with more interactive elements like modals, accordions, and collapsible sections. You will also explore strategies for prompting AI to produce reusable patterns using consistent class naming, accessibility features, and responsive behaviors. Let us get started.

After reading this chapter, you will be able to decompose user interfaces into modular components, author high quality prompts that generate accessible and responsive UI code and systematize styling and interactivity as reusable patterns. You will practice building navigation bars, footers, buttons, cards, forms, modals, accordions, and collapsible sections. You will also learn how to design prompt templates that consistently produce components with stable class naming, theming hooks, and testing seams. Finally, you will apply prompt variations to derive multiple stylistic versions for A/B tests and brand themes while preserving an identical API surface.

Structure

In this chapter, we will cover the following topics:

- Designing with UI Components
- Creating Navigation Bars and Footers with AI Assistance
- Building of Buttons, Cards, and Forms
- Modals, Accordions, and Collapsible Sections
- Designing Reusable Component Patterns with Prompts

Designing with UI Components

User interface components are reusable building blocks that combine structure, styling, state, and behavior. They serve as explicit interfaces like buttons, cards, forms, and modals, that simplify the creation of complex applications. A well-designed component exposes only a small set of inputs and events while hiding its internal details, making it easier to assemble predictable and consistent interfaces. In practice, components align with semantic patterns like navigation, lists, forms, and dialogs. Strong component systems enforce standardized class naming, design tokens, and accessibility attributes, enabling teams to build scalable interfaces that remain consistent even under rapid iteration. In AI-assisted workflows, prompts act as specifications to repeatedly generate components with the same structure, reducing manual drift, improving testability, and accelerating delivery across applications and brands. In this section, we shall focus on UI components from structural and behavioral perspectives, while setting aside data flow, an essential topic, yet beyond the scope of this book. Let us begin by exploring the anatomy of a component.

Understanding UI Components Anatomy

A component's anatomy can be understood through two key dimensions: structure and behavior. Structure refers to the HTML markup and CSS hooks that define the component's layout and visual appearance. For instance, a `<button>` element with a class like `.btn-primary` establishes not only its semantic role, but also the styling rules that make it look distinctive. Behavior, on the other hand, is how the component responds to user input. A button may highlight when focused with the keyboard, submit a form when pressed, or toggle the visibility of a `<details>` element. Together, structure and behavior form the foundation of a reliable UI component. UI components also share certain key characteristics. They are self-contained, encapsulating structure and behavior into a single unit like a card that includes its heading, description, and action link. They are configurable, allowing you to adapt them without rewriting code. For instance, a `<select>` can switch from single to multiple selection by adjusting attributes. They also support composability, where smaller pieces combine into larger features like a grid of cards, or a sign-up form embedded within a modal making design, scalable and consistent. Although components often handle data, such as rendering items from an array or capturing user input, this aspect involves state management and data flow patterns that extend beyond the scope of this book. In modern applications, components not only render static markup, but also consume, display, and sometimes transform dynamic data. For instance, a list component may map over an array of items to generate `<li>`elements, while a form component might capture user input and pass it to a parent feature for processing. Similarly, interactive elements often rely on state like whether a dropdown is open or closed, driven by underlying data models. Handling data effectively involves patterns for passing information into componentsvia attributes or props, emitting events back out, and managing internal or shared state. These mechanisms are essential for connecting UI components to application logic, APIs, and user-driven workflows. However, exploring data flow, state management, and related architectural patterns requires a depth of discussion with popular frontend libraries like React and Vue framework, both are outside the scope of this book.

Categorizing UI Components

Structured web page is built from UI components. Each serves a distinct purpose in guiding users across a website and presenting information. Navigational components like breadcrumbs, tabs, or sidebars help users move smoothly through a site, while patterns such as accordions or hamburger menus conserve space and organize content. Input components like buttons, fields, dropdowns, checkboxes, and radio buttons capture user actions and choices, forming the interactive backbone of forms and workflows. To keep users informed, feedback components like progress bars, loaders, toast notifications, and modals provide status updates or request confirmation. Finally, displaying components such as cards, charts, icons, and feeds present information clearly. It makes content more engaging and scannable. When composing a web page, for instance, a marketing landing page for a business organization, these elements are not dropped in arbitrarily. They are combined into a logical hierarchy. A navigation bar might sit at the top, cards or feeds populate the main content area, and forms with buttons handle interaction. Feedback elements appear contextually, such as a loader during a search or a toast after a successful save. By layering navigation, input, feedback, and display components, frontend developers create pages that are modular, accessible, and scalable. This approach delivers a smooth user experience across digital devices. Let us examine an output a prompt that display the decomposition of a typical marketing landing page into various components as follows:

Prompt:

Break down a typical marketing landing page into its constituent UI components. For each component:

- *Clearly define its purpose (what role it plays on the page).*

- *List its props/attributes (configurable inputs).*
- *Describe its events (user interactions and expected responses).*
- *Provide variants (stylistic or structural alternatives, for example, primary vs. secondary buttons).*
- *Show the expected DOM outline (semantic HTML structure).*
- *Include relevant ARIA roles/attributes to ensure accessibility.*
- *Reference design tokens (colors, spacing, typography, radius, and so on.) that apply.*
- *Suggest meaningful CSS class names aligned with BEM or utility-first conventions.*

Assume a standard marketing landing page layout with the following sections:

1. *Hero section (headline, subheadline, CTA).*
2. *Features section (grid of feature cards).*
3. *Testimonial/social proof section (quotes, avatars, logos).*
4. *Call-to-action section (signup or contact prompt).*
5. *Footer section (navigation links, legal text).*

Provide a comprehensive specification for each component so it could be directly used in a design system or frontend implementation.

Let us explore a Hero section to explain the preceding prompt with a concrete example for the Hero in addition to a reusable subcomponent it depends on. This mirrors the structure your prompt will elicit for every component.

Hero Section

Purpose

To visually introduce the product/value proposition and drive a primary action "Start free".

Props / Attributes

Props is the short form for properties or attributes, the values of which are passed to a component that customize its behavior, appearance, or content, such as text, images, or styles.

- `title (string, required): Main headline text`
- `subtitle (string, optional): Supporting copy`
- `primaryCtaLabel (string, required)`
- `primaryCtaHref (string, required)`
- `secondaryCtaLabel (string, optional)`
- `secondaryCtaHref (string, optional)`

- **`mediaSrc (URL, optional): Illustration/screenshot`**
- **`mediaAlt (string, required if mediaSrc)`**
- **`tone (enum: default | minimal | contrast)`**
- **`align (enum: start | center | end)`**
- **`bg (token ref: surface/background option)`**

Events

Events refer to actions or occurrences that a component can respond to, like clicks, hover, focus, or form submissions, triggering specific behaviors or functions.

- **`onPrimaryClick (fires when primary CTA is activated).`**
- **`onSecondaryClick (optional).`**
- **`onInView (optional; when hero enters viewport—analytics).`**

Variants

Variants refer to the different versions or styles of a component, like different layouts, colors, sizes, or states (for example, primary/secondary button, success/error message), allowing for flexibility and reuse.

- **`Layout: text-only, text-left-media-right, text-center-media-below`**
- **`Emphasis: default, high-contrast (inverted), minimal (no media)`**

DOM Outline (Semantic)

```
<section class="hero hero--text-left-media-right hero--contrast" aria-
labelledby="hero-title">
<div class="hero__container">
<div class="hero__content">
<h1 id="hero-title">Grow faster with YourBrand</h1>
<p class="hero__subtitle">All-in-one platform to convert visitors into
customers.</p>
<div class="hero__actions">
<a class="btnbtn--primary" href="/signup">Start free</a>
<a class="btnbtn--ghost" href="#features">See how it works</a>
</div>
</div>
<figure class="hero__media">
<imgsrc="/img/hero.png" alt="Dashboard showing growth metrics">
<figcaption class="sr-only">Product dashboard with charts and metrics</
figcaption>
</figure>
</div>
</section>
```

ARIA/Accessibility

Accessible Rich Internet Applications (ARIA) attributes provide additional information to the screen readers and other assistive technologies. This enhances the accessibility of dynamic web content and interactive elements for users with disabilities.

- **Landmark:** `<section aria-labelledby="hero-title">`
- **Heading level:** *h1 appears once per page; demote to h2 if not the main heading.*
- **Images:** *alt required; use* `sr-onlyfigcaption` *for extra context if needed.*
- **Buttons as links:** *Ensure that* `<a>` *has clear labels; maintain visible focus (*`:focus-visible`*).*

Design Tokens

Design tokens are reusable, abstract values that represent design decisions, such as colors, typography, spacing, and more, used to maintain consistency and scalability in a design system.

- **Color:** *--brand, --brand-on, --surface-hero, --text, --muted*
- **Typography:** *--fs-hero (clamp), --fs-lead, --font-weight-bold*
- **Spacing:** *--space-4, --space-6, --section-pad*
- **Radius/Shadow:** *--radius-lg, --shadow-lg*

CSS Class Naming (BEM)

Block-Element-Modifier (BEM) is a CSS class naming convention that helps create clear, consistent, and maintainable class names.

- **Block:** *hero*
- **Elements:** `hero__container`, `hero__content`, `hero__subtitle`, `hero__actions`, `hero__media`
- **Modifiers:** `hero--contrast, hero--minimal, hero--text-only, hero--text-left-media-right, hero--center`

In frontend development, these discussed components can be combined to create a typical marketing landing page or any user interface based on business requirements.

With a solid understanding of UI components, how UI components are categorized, design tokens, and accessibility principles, let us move further to creating essential website elements like navigation bars and footers leveraging AI assistance for efficient and effective design and development.

Note: *UI means the collection of elements that create the interface a user sees and interacts with on a webpage.*

Creating Navigation Bars and Footers with AI Assistance

Navigation and footer components are foundational in any website. They represent your global information architecture, express brand identity, and satisfy legal requirements. Navigation and footer components must be fully responsive across viewports, operable by keyboard, logical tab order, visible focus, skip links, and friendly to screen readers with clear landmarks, labels, and accessible names. You need to design navigation and footer in such a manner that make their layouts to be resilient to content growth. The menu links need to gracefully wrap in a responsive way. Navigation and footer area of a website can be structured in a reusable pattern, predictable class names, scalable spacing, and tokenized colors/typography. Interestingly, AI system, especially ChatGPT, can translate these design principles actionable design and development checkpoints to ensure your navigation and footer remain usable, accessible, and maintainable as your site evolves. ChatGPT can accelerate scaffolding of your website projects by generating semantic markup, responsive layout rules, and interaction logic for disclosure menus. The key is to supply prompts that specify breakpoints, focused management, and aria attributes, plus constraints such as sticky behavior and reducedmotion preferences. You will guide the AI assistant to produce a consistent class structure, slot areas for dynamic links, and tokens for theming. Let us prompt this area of a website by following patterns that use semantic elements like <nav>, <header>, <footer> and ensure a correct tab order, visible focus, and escape paths on small screens. Let us start with the prompting of a navigation area.

Prompting a Responsive Navbar

Here, we aim to build a responsive navbar that adapts seamlessly to different screen sizes using ChatGPT prompt. We will create a design that prioritizes accessibility and user experience. The navigation structure is simple. It will be mobile-first, accessible navbar with the following features: brand at left, nav links, search input, and a hamburger that toggles a disclosure menu.

Prompt.

*Build a mobile-first, accessible **<header>** + **<nav>** with brand at left, nav links, and a search form—no JavaScript. On small screens, use a semantic disclosure pattern with <details>/<summary> (hamburger) to toggle the menu; on ≥768px, show horizontal links and hide the hamburger. Requirements:*

- **Semantics & ARIA:** *use <header>, <nav aria-label="Primary">, <form role="search">, and clear labels. Rely on native <details>/<summary> disclosure (no manual aria-expanded).*

- **CSS:** *expose custom properties --nav-height and --gap; include visible :focus-visible styles; respect prefers-reduced-motion; provide dark-mode colors via prefers-color-scheme.*
- **Layout:** *mobile-first; breakpoint at* **768px** *switches to a horizontal layout with the menu always visible and the disclosure control hidden.*
- **Progressive enhancement:** *page remains fully usable without JS or hover.*
- **Quality:** *high contrast, logical tab order, large tap targets."***

The following screenshot shows the result of the preceding prompt.

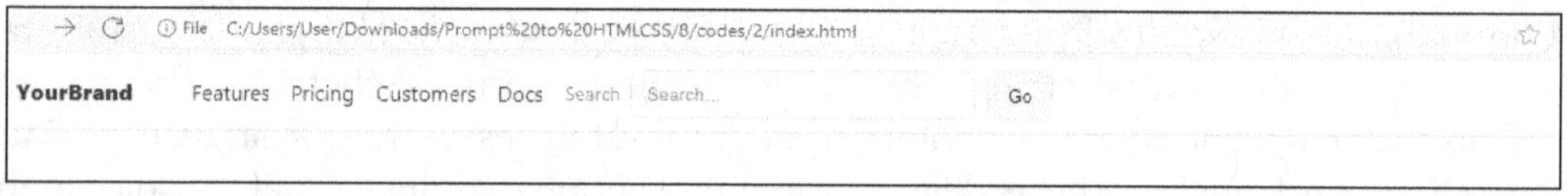

Figure 8.1: *Screenshot Showing Navigation Output from ChatGPT*

The mobile menu uses native **`<details>/<summary>`** for an accessible disclosure, screen readers announce its expanded/collapsed state. At min-width: 768px the mobile disclosure is hidden and a separate desktop nav is shown horizontally; duplication is acceptable because only one set is rendered/visible at a time. The custom properties **`--nav-height`** and **`--gap`** are defined and used; focus styles, reduced-motion, and dark mode are included.

Next, we shall discuss designing semantic footer with the assistance of AI.

Designing a Semantic Footer with Legal and Utility Sections

Footer provides the essential information and secondary navigation in a website. It boosts user experience and credibility. In designing a semantic footer, use a semantic structure like **`<footer>`** with clearly labeled regions that separates legal notices, copyright, terms, and privacy from utility links such as sitemap, contact, and FAQs. It is advisable you prioritize accessibility with clear headings, meaningful link text, and visible focus states. The approach ensures responsiveness, so links wrap seamlessly on small screens, and favor maintainability by using consistent class names and design tokens for spacing, type, and color. This approach yields a footer that is usable, scalable, and easy to update. Let us explore a prompt that generate a footer section.

Prompt:

Build an accessible, mobile-first <footer> with a four-column layout (stacking on small screens). Include: (1) a newsletter signup form with a visible label and required email field; (2) a language switcher (<label> + <select>); (3) two link columns for navigation; (4) legal notices (copyright, terms, privacy). Use semantic HTML with appropriate *landmarks (<footer>, <nav aria-label="Footer">), clear headings, and ARIA where helpful (e.g., aria-labelledby). Ensure full keyboard navigation and visible :focus-visible styles. No JavaScript. Use CSS custom properties for spacing and colors (e.g., --footer-bg, --footer-fg, --space-*) and set a blue background with high-contrast text. Include responsive grid at 768px+.*

The screenshot from the preceding shows the products, company, resources and a newsletter.

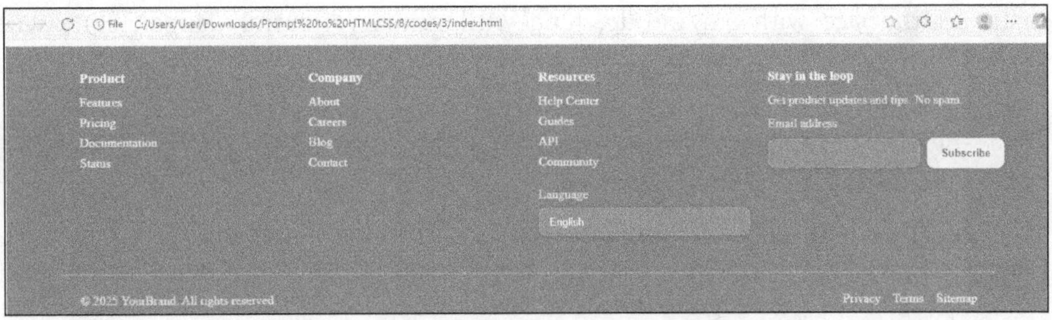

Figure 8.2: *Screenshot Showing Footer Output from ChatGPT*

The interactions like links, select, form submit work without JavaScript. The language switcher is a real <label> + <select and translated legal links fit, the grid and wrapping handle longer strings. The blue background meets in contrast with the white text; retain **`visible: focus-visible`** outlines for all links/controls to support keyboard and low-vision users. Next, we build buttons, cards and forms as reusable UI components of a website.

Building of Buttons, Cards, and Forms

Buttons, cards, and forms represent the most frequently reused components in frontend development. Robust implementations support multiple variants, sizes, and states, while exposing consistent class hooks and CSS variables. Buttons need to advertise intent through label, iconography, and accessible names. Cards handle media, metadata, and actions with responsive arrangement. Forms need to provide labelled controls, validation messaging, and keyboard navigation. With ChatGPT, we can synthesize the bulk of boilerplate if prompts enumerate tokens, states, and ARIA patterns and require a single source of truth for variants. The following patterns define design tokens, implement base components, and then extend them through composition to keep APIs small and predictable across projects.

Design System with Tokens and Variants

In frontend development, design tokens are named variables for visual decisions like spacing, color, type, radius, shadow. Let us examine this example:

```
:root { --space-3: 1rem; --brand-600: #2f6fed;  --text: #111;  --radius: 12px;}
```

Token help maintain consistency and scalability in a design system. It is advisable to develop design tokens, which capture your visual decisions like spacing, color, typography, radius, shadows as named variables that the whole product shares. This approach delivers consistency, easy theming, and low-risk refactors across platforms.

Variants are the controlled ways a component changes while still using token. For instance, the *size* with sm/md/lg, *tone* with primary/neutral/danger, *state* with default/hover/disabled. Let us examine an example CSS variant design.

```
.btn{ padding:.5rem 1rem; border-radius:var(--radius); }
.btn--primary{ background:var(--brand-600); color:#fff; }
.btn--sm{ padding:.375rem .75rem; }
```

The preceding CSS code defines a reusable button component with a base style (**.btn**) and variant styles (**.btn--primary** for primary buttons and **.btn--sm** for small buttons) that leverage design tokens for consistency. Let us take a look at how we can leverage AI assistance.

Prompt to create tokens:

Derive a token set (color, spacing, type, radius, shadow) from the palette below. Use semantic aliases (--surface, --text, --accent) mapped to brand scales. Output CSS variables plus a short usage guide.

Prompt to generate variants:

Using the tokens, produce button and card variants (sizes sm/md/lg, tones primary/neutral/danger, states default/hover/disabled). Output minimal CSS that references only tokens, no raw values, and a matrix describing behavior.

With a well composed prompt, you can speed up creation, refactoring, and governance of tokens and variants. This style guide, propose token names/values grouped by color/spacing/typography; follow 4/8px spacing and WCAG AA contrast. Replace raw hex/px in this CSS with our tokens; flag any values lacking a token and suggest names. Given these tokens, define button variants (size, tone, state) with BEM classes output a table with CSS using only tokens. You can create a dark theme by overriding only color tokens; keep spacing/type identical. Audit these variants for contrast, focus visibility, and hit-target sizes; list failures and token-level fixes. In a nutshell, tokens provide the vocabulary; variants provide the grammar. Together, they yield a scalable, themeable system that stays coherent as your application grows.

Building Button Component with Prompt

Here, we create a versatile and accessible button component that adapts to different use cases. We will define a base button style and variants for primary and small buttons, leveraging design tokens for consistency. This component will be reusable and easy to maintain.

Prompt:

Create an accessible Button component using BEM naming. Deliver: (1) semantic HTML examples; (2) minimal, token-driven CSS; (3) an ARIA pattern for async loading. Requirements:

- **BEM:** *block btn, elements btn__icon, modifiers for* ***variants*** *(btn--primary|secondary|ghost) and* **sizes** *(btn--sm|md|lg), plus* **states***(:hover, :active, [disabled], and a loading modifier btn--loading).*
- **Accessibility:**
  - *Use <button> for actions and [disabled] for non-interactive state.*
  - *Provide visible :focus-visible outline and 44×44px target guidance.*
  - *Include an* ***aria-live="polite" status region*** *for async feedback (for example, "Saving..."), referenced by aria-describedby when loading.*
- ***Tokens:*** *define a* ***CSS variable map*** *(colors, spacing, radius, shadow, typography). All styles must reference tokens; no hard-coded hex/px outside the map.*
- **Behavioral contract (no JS required in output):** *document how the loading state is applied (e.g., add btn--loading, set aria-busy="true", set aria-disabled="true"), and how the live region message is updated by the host app.*
- **Quality:** *support reduced motion (prefers-reduced-motion) and high contrast. Include an examples matrix covering all sizes × variants × states.*

The preceding prompt forces token-first styling and clear BEM semantics, so design changes propagate safely. The ARIA live region and loading contract separate UI from logic, enabling frameworks to toggle states without rewriting CSS. By requiring examples and a state matrix, you get verifiable coverage of sizes, variants, and accessibility behaviors.

Building Card Component with Prompt

Let us build a flexible and reusable card component that showcases content in a clean and organized way. We will define a base card structure with image, title, text, and actions, ensuring that it is accessible and customizable.

Prompt:

Create a responsive, accessible Card component set that supports theme switching by overriding CSS custom properties—no inline styles. Deliver (1) semantic HTML snippets for cards with media, title, meta, body, and actions; (2) embedded, token-first CSS only (no JS required in output).

Requirements

- *Naming: BEM (.card, .card__media, .card__title, .card__meta, .card__body, .card__actions), with modifiers for variants (.card--elevated, .card--outlined, .card--minimal) and sizes (.card--sm, .card--md, .card--lg).*
- *Tokens: Define a CSS variable map (e.g., --surface, --surface-alt, --text, --muted, --border, --accent, --radius, --shadow, --space-*). All styling MUST reference tokens—no raw hex/px outside the map.*
- *Themes: Provide light, dark, and high-contrast themes by overriding the same variables under :root (default) and [data-theme="dark"], [data-theme="contrast"]; optionally respect prefers-color-scheme.*
- *Accessibility: WCAG AA contrast by default; meaningful headings; visible :focus-visible; large tap targets for actions; avoid color-only cues.*
- *Layout: Mobile-first; cards flow in a responsive grid; support content growth (wrapping text, variable media aspect).*
- *States: Hover/focus/selected styles using tokens; disabled action style.*
- *Examples: Output a small gallery showing all variants × sizes across themes, plus the minimal docs for switching themes via data-theme on a parent container.*

Theming is implemented using CSS variables. This allows for a seamless theme switching. You can simply toggle a container attribute, such as `<main data-theme="dark">...</main>`. This approach encourages easy maintenance and customization of light, dark, or custom themes as may be desired, while keeping styles consistent and scalable.

Building Accessible Form Snippet

The foundation of an accessible form lies in proper HTML structure and attributes. The use of **`labels`**, **`fieldsets`**, and **`legends`** provides a clear and navigable experience for screen readers and keyboard users. The form's accessibility is further enhanced with ARIA attributes and a logical tab order. Let us walk you through a production ready form prompt.

Prompt:

Create a mobile-first, accessible form using semantic HTML only (no JS required in output). Include:

- ***Labeled inputs:** each control has a <label for> with matching id; avoid placeholder-only labels.*
- ***Fieldsets& legends:** group related controls (for example, radio/checkbox sets) with <fieldset> + <legend>.*

- **ARIA *for screen readers*:** *use aria-describedby for help text, aria-invalid="true" and aria-errormessage for errors, and an error summary with role="alert" / aria-live="polite".*
- **Logical tab order:** *DOM order matches visual order; all controls keyboard-operable.*
- **Forms best practices:** *meaningful input types (email, tel, and so on), required, pattern where needed, and autocomplete tokens.*
- **Internationalization-ready:** *accessible, translatable text; no color-only cues.*
- **Minimal CSS:** *include visible :focus-visible styles and a small token map (for example, --space-*, --border, --focus, --text-muted) to style spacing, borders, and messages.*
- **Example content:** *name, email, phone, country <select>, newsletter checkbox, contact reason radios, message <textarea>, submit button, help text, and per-field error examples.*

Output a single HTML *snippet with embedded* CSS.

Associating `labels, help text,` and `error messages` via for, `aria-describedby`, and `aria-errormessage` ensures that the screen readers announce the context correctly; the error summary with `role="alert"` provides instant feedback without scripting, while `:focus-visible` and DOM-ordered controls guarantee smooth keyboard navigation.

Now that we have covered foundational components like buttons, let us shift our focus to interactive elements that elevate user experience: Modals, Accordions, and Collapsible Sections. These components help organize content, manage complexity, and improve navigation.

Modals, Accordions, and Collapsible Sections

Interactive disclosure components, such as modals, accordions, and collapsible sections, require careful attention to accessibility and focus management. Modals need to trap focus inside the dialog, announce themselves with accessible names and descriptions, and return focus to the trigger when closed. Accordions and collapsible regions need to implement the WAI-ARIA disclosure pattern with correct roles and keyboard behavior. To ensure a seamless user experience, scrolling should be constrained when overlays are open, and animations should respect reduced motion preferences. With the provision of these precise behavioral requirements, you can generate reusable scaffolding for these patterns. Let us demonstrate that pass keyboard and screen reader checks, exposing hooks for straightforward styling, and theming.

Building Accessible Modal Dialog with Prompt

Now, we will be creating an accessible modal dialog that feels seamless for everyone. We shall follow established accessibility guidelinesusing semantic roles, clear labelling, and logical focusso the dialog is fully operable by keyboard and announced correctly by screen readers. Let us explore the relevant prompt.

Prompt:

Create a mobile-first, accessible modal dialog using semantic HTML + CSS only(no JavaScript in the output).

Structure: *Use either <dialog open> (static example) or a :target pattern (<a href="#modal">Open</a> ... <section id="modal">) with an overlay, a dialog container, a visible* ***title*** *and* ***close*** *control.*

Accessibility:

- *Provide role="dialog" (or native <dialog>), aria-modal="true", aria-labelledby and optional aria-describedby.*
- *Include a* ***visually labeled*** *close control (for example, "Close dialog").*
- *Use autofocus on the first interactive element in the dialog.*

  Keyboard: *Logical tab order; visible :focus-visible styles; close control focusable via keyboard.*

  CSS tokens: *Define and use variables for spacing, colors, radius, shadow (for example, --overlay, --surface, --text, --space-*, --radius, --shadow).*

  Design: *High contrast by default; respect prefers-reduced-motion; center the dialog; overlay blocks page interaction visually.*

  Deliverables: *A single HTML snippet with embedded CSS (no JS), including an* ***open trigger****, the* ***modal****, and the* ***close*** *control.*

It is important to know that without JavaScript, a modal cannot fully trap focus or mark the background as inert for assistive tech. This snippet is as accessible as possible with HTML/CSS, but for production you should enhance it by moving focus into the dialog and restoring it on close, trapping focus within, closing on `<kbd>Esc</kbd>`, and setting inert/aria-hidden on background content while open-added by a tiny JS controller or by using `<dialog>` with `showModal()`.

Implementing Accordion WAIARIA Disclosure

Here, we implementing an accordion using the WAI-ARIA Disclosure pattern. This ensures accessibility and usability. We will pair semantic headings with

`<button>`controls, toggle panels with **`aria-expanded`** and **`aria-controls`**, and expose each panel as a labeled region for screen readers. With clear focus states and robust keyboard support *Tab*, *Enter/Space*, and optional Arrow keys for roving focus, the accordion delivers a predictable and seamless experience for all users. Let us explore the prompt to implement accordion.

Prompt:

Build an accessible accordion using the WAI-ARIA Disclosure *pattern. Deliver:* (1) *semantic* HTML *for a multi-item accordion;* (2) *minimal, token-driven* CSS; (3) *a tiny* JS *controller for state/keyboard.*

Structure and ARIA

- *Each accordion header contains a real <button class="acc__trigger"> with aria-expanded, aria-controls, and an id.*
- *Each **panel** is a <div class="acc__panel" role="region"> with id and aria-labelledby pointing to its trigger.*
- *Wrap items in a container with role="group" and aria-label="Accordion" (or aria-labelledby).*

Keyboard and Behavior

- ***Tab** moves between triggers; Enter/Space toggles a panel.*
- *Optional Arrow Up/Down/Home/End for roving focus across triggers.*
- *Support single-expand **and** multi-**expand** modes (configurable).*
- *Update aria-expanded and panel visibility; keep focus on the triggering button.*

CSS and Tokens

- *Use CSS variables only (e.g., --space-*, --radius, --border, --text, --muted, --accent, --shadow).*
- *Provide visible :focus-visible outlines, high contrast, and prefers-reduced-motion respect.*

Quality and Examples

- *Include at least three items with varied content length.*
- *Pass* WCAG 2.2 AA *for contrast and focus.*
- *Document how to switch single↔multi expand.*

Output: *One self-contained snippet* (HTML, *embedded* CSS, *and ~30–60 lines of* JS).

The WAI-ARIA Disclosure pattern complements, not replaces, semantic HTML. Start with semantic HTML elements, when possible, then add ARIA to convey state changes **`aria-expanded`** and relationships **`aria-controls, aria-labelledby`**. Keep behavior progressively enhanced, the content should remain readable and navigable even if JavaScript fails. Next, we shall explore the designing of a reusable component patterns that can be efficiently generated with precise prompts, streamlining development and ensuring consistency across projects.

Designing Reusable Component Patterns with Prompts

Reusable Component Patterns are a UI design and development approach based on repeatable patterns for building consistent components. Think of it using the same recipe for common UI pieces across your applications. For example, in a shopping web app, the *Add to Cart* button always has the same shape, color, padding, and hover effect, every product card shows an image, title, price, and button in the same layout, the navigation bar keeps the same logo position, menu style, and search box behavior on every page and all forms use the same label style, input fields, error messages, and submit button design. Instead of designing each screen from scratch, you reuse proven UI patterns to keep your app consistent, faster to build, and easier for users to understand. Interestingly, repeatable quality with AI generated codes depends on repeatable prompts. A prompt template captures anatomy, tokens, states, accessibility rules, and testing scaffolds so that each generated component arrives with the same structure. This section defines a template and demonstrates its application to several components. The template enforces BEM naming or utility-first classes, ARIA semantics, and responsive breakpoints. It also asks for Storybook stories or plain HTML demos, and includes test hooks as data-testid attributes. By keeping inputs, elements, and variants predictable, you can swap styles or brands without altering component APIs, which simplifies integration and regression testing across projects.

Building Components with Prompt Templates

You can design a reusable component pattern that can be efficiently generated with well-structured prompts. With predefined templates and clear requirements, you can create consistent components quickly, with accessibility and best practices baked in. Standardized anatomy, naming, and tokens reduce errors, align code across projects, and make maintenance predictable. Instead of reinventing the basics, you can focus on tailoring variants and behaviors to the product's needs. The result is a faster, and a more reliable AI frontend workflow that streamlines development and boosts productivity.

Prompt:

Role: *Senior UI engineer. Produce accessible, responsive* **HTML/CSS/JS *only*** *(no external deps).*

Component name:<COMPONENT_NAME>

Purpose: *One sentence on what it does and when to use it.*

Variants:<LIST_VARIANTS> *(e.g., primary | secondary | ghost).*

States: *hover, focus, active, loading, disabled.*

Requirements

- ***Anatomy:*** *Describe the root element, constituent elements, and any slots/regions (for example, media, title, actions).*
- **Accessibility:** *Specify roles, labels, ARIA mapping, keyboard flows (Tab, Shift+Tab, Enter/Space, Arrow keys if applicable), focus management, and live regions if needed.*
- **Tokens:** *Define CSS variables (colors, spacing, typography, radius, motion, shadows). All styles must reference tokens only.*
- ***Breakpoints:*** *360px (mobile), 768px (tablet), 1024px (desktop). Describe layout changes.*
- ***Behavior:*** *Minimal JS for interaction (what toggles, what attributes change, where focus goes).*
- ***Testing hooks:*** *Add data-testid to key elements.*
- **Constraints:** *Deterministic BEM class names, no inline styles, no frameworks.*

Deliverables (in this order)

1. **HTML:** *Example markup covering all variants/states; include data-testid.*
2. **CSS:** *Token map (:root), component styles, responsive rules, focus-visible styles, reduced-motion.*
3. ***JS (minimal):*** *Event handlers, attribute updates (e.g., aria-expanded), focus management.*
4. ***Usage example:*** *A small, copy-paste page section showing the component in context.*

Acceptance Checklist

- *Uses tokens only (no raw hex/px outside the map)*
- *BEM classes applied consistently*
- *Passes keyboard navigation and visible focus*
- *ARIA attributes reflect state changes*
- *Works at 360/768/1024 without layout breakage*

With the tweaking of the preceding prompt template, start with accessibility to shape structure and minimal JS (roles, labels, focus, live aria-*), and use token-first CSS so every visual choice is a variable, then keep behavior declarative, distinguish variants from states with consistent BEM. Treat breakpoints as explicit contracts. Test real keyboard paths (*Tab/Shift+Tab/Enter/Space*), include data-testid hooks, plan for longer/RTL text and wrapping, and avoid external deps or inline styles so the component stays auditable, themeable, and framework-agnostic.

Conclusion

In this chapter, we explored how to decompose user interfaces into reusable and accessible UI components. From navigation bars and footers to buttons, cards, forms, modals, accordions, and collapsible sections, each element was explored with a focus on structure, behavior, and accessibility. The role of AI in generating prompt-based patterns was emphasized, enabling faster, consistent, and scalable design systems. By leveraging design tokens, BEM naming, ARIA roles, and responsive layouts, you can streamline frontend development workflows while ensuring inclusivity and maintainability. Ultimately, building modular UI components enhances productivity, supports design iteration, and delivers a seamless user experience across applications and devices.

In *Chapter 9: Applied Prompt Workflows*, we aim to explore hands-on projects that simulate real-world scenarios, helping you build a solid portfolio as a frontend developer. By combining everything we have learned so far in this book, we will compose functional, prompt-first interfaces that showcase your skills and help you totransition from theory and isolated components into real-world, prompt-first interface building.

Points to Remember

- UI components are modular, reusable building blocks of interfaces.
- Structure (HTML/CSS) and behavior (interactivity) form a component's anatomy.
- Categories include navigation, input, feedback, and display components.
- Accessibility relies on ARIA roles, semantic HTML, and visible focus states.
- Design tokens ensure consistency in spacing, colors, typography, and shadows.
- BEM class naming promotes maintainability and scalability.
- AI prompts accelerate scaffolding, theming, and generating reusable patterns.
- Components must support responsiveness across devices.
- Reusable templates standardize development and testing.
- Variants and states allow flexibility while preserving consistency.

Multiple Choice Questions

1. What are UI components primarily designed for?
    a. Complex backend logic
    b. Reusable building blocks of user interfaces
    c. Data storage
    d. SEO optimization
2. Which of the two aspects define the anatomy of a UI component?
    a. Tokens and States
    b. Structure and Behavior
    c. Props and Variants
    d. HTML and JavaScript
3. Which category does a progress bar belong to?
    a. Input components
    b. Navigation components
    c. Feedback components
    d. Display components
4. What does BEM stand for in CSS naming?
    a. Block, Element, Modifier
    b. Base, Extension, Module
    c. Button, Event, Marker
    d. Block, Element, Model
5. Design tokens are mainly used to:
    a. Store user passwords
    b. Represent reusable design decisions
    c. Replace JavaScript functions
    d. Build database schemas
6. Which of the following is NOT an input component?
    a. Button
    b. Dropdown
    c. Checkbox
    d. Card

7. Which ARIA attribute indicates whether a section is expanded or collapsed?
    a. `aria-label`
    b. `aria-expanded`
    c. `aria-hidden`
    d. `aria-describedby`
8. Modals require focus management because:
    a. They improve SEO.
    b. Users must remain inside the dialog until closed.
    c. They reduce load time.
    d. They control data flow.
9. Which AI feature helps generate multiple styled versions of the same component?
    a. Tokens
    b. Prompt variations
    c. Accordions
    d. ARIA roles
10. Which of the following is a display component?
    a. Forms
    b. Cards
    c. Checkboxes
    d. Navigation bars
11. Responsive breakpoints typically include which widths?
    a. 360px, 768px, 1024px
    b. 200px, 400px, 600px
    c. 500px, 700px, 900px
    d. 100px, 300px, 800px
12. Which attribute provides screen readers with additional information?
    a. `aria-describedby`
    b. `aria-contrast`
    c. `aria-expand`
    d. `aria-load`

Answers

1. b
2. b
3. c
4. a
5. b
6. d
7. b
8. b
9. b
10. b
11. a
12. a

Key Terms

- **UI Component**: Modular building block combining structure and behavior.
- **Structure**: HTML and CSS defining layout and styling.
- **Behavior**: Interactive response to user actions.
- **Design Tokens**: Named variables for colors, spacing, typography, and so on.
- **BEM Naming**: Block, Element, Modifier convention for CSS classes.
- **Accessibility (ARIA)**: Attributes improving usability for assistive technologies.
- **Variants**: Stylistic alternatives of components (such as primary, secondary).
- **States**: Component conditions like hover, active, disabled, loading.
- **Responsive Design**: Adapting UI to different screen sizes.
- **Prompt Templates**: Structured AI instructions for consistent component generation.

CHAPTER 9
Applied Prompt Workflows

Introduction

In *Chapter 8: Building UI Components*, we explored how you can rapidly generate, customize, and scale interface elements through prompt-based workflows. This chapter dives deep into how to move from an idea to an interface using precise, testable prompts. Applied Prompt Workflows represent the transition from theoretical concepts into practical interface development. Our focus therefore shall be on converting design intent into structured prompts that produce production-ready interfaces. You will learn how to encode layout rules, accessibility requirements, and responsive behavior directly in prompts, reducing the gap between design ideation and coded implementation. Through case studies like an IoT agriculture landing page, a personal bio profile, a fintech landing page, and an IoT dashboard, this chapter demonstrates how prompts act as digital blueprints to compose wireframes and implement designs of interest while enforcing semantic structure and inclusive practices. The discussion extends beyond generation to cover review, refinement, and iteration to guarantee that AI-assisted outputs align with professional standards.

By the end of this chapter, you will be able to author blueprints that translate product goals into component lists, layout rules, and acceptance criteria. You will prompt AI to generate a responsive IoT marketing page, personal bio, a compliant and persuasive fintech landing page, and a scannable IoT dashboard with real-time friendly components. You will direct outputs to use semantic landmarks, accessible patterns, design tokens, and mobile-first Grid and Flexbox. You will review AI code against measurable performance and accessibility targets, capture defects, and iterate with focused prompt that preserve consistency.

Structure

In this chapter, we will cover the following topics:

- Planning UI Blueprint with Prompts
- Designing a Responsive IoT Marketing Landing Page

- Personal Bio Responsive Layout Design
- Designing Fintech Landing Page
- Designing IoT Dashboard Components Layout
- Reviewing and Iterating AI-Generated Interfaces

Planning UI Blueprint with Prompts

Interface design begins with structured planning. This structured planning approach is like building, engineering and planning architecture. Typically, architects create blueprints to plan and visualize a building's layout, structure, and systems, interface designers create wireframes to plan and visualize the layout, structure, and functionality of a digital interface. Before writing a single line of code, you need to plan to establish hierarchy, layout zones, and visual rhythm. The visual hierarchy helps your site users focus on the most important elements and navigate the interface efficiently. This includes organizing content, features, and functionality in a logical and visually appealing manner. With layout zones, you divide the interface into distinct zones or regions that help you to create a clear and organized layout. This can include areas for navigation, content, calls-to-action, and other key elements. In addition, you need to create a consistent visual rhythm that helps your site to guide the user's attention and create a sense of flow. This can be achieved with typography, color, spacing, and other visual elements. Wireframing can be done using digital tools or traditional sketching methods. Creating a low-fidelity sketch or a wireframe helps you to visualize the interface layout and identify potential issues early on. In a nutshell, with these components of the planning process, you can create a solid foundation for your interface design that is user-centered, intuitive, and effective. However, prompt-first workflows replicate this planning process by using descriptive language to generate wireframe-like structures. Instead of the traditional static sketches, prompts act as digital blueprints that AI interprets into layouts. This approach accelerates ideation and creates consistency between design intent and implementation. In this section, you will learn and implement structure withclear, balanced component priorities, and use modular descriptions to guide AI layout engines- ChatGPT or Framer AI. Planning through these prompts sets the foundation for scalable, responsive, and coherent interface systems. Let us get started defining layout hierarchy- heading, navigation, content, and footer.

Defining Layout Hierarchy

As stated earlier, interface design requires clarity before execution. Designers must define zones, flows, and hierarchy. Prompt-first workflows make this planning precise. Instead of sketching, you write structured descriptions that the AI interprets as layouts. These descriptions form digital blucprints that act like interactive wireframes. This layout hierarchy shows where navigation, headers, content, and footers belong. Prompts can also describe spacing, margins, and responsiveness. This planning step avoids any confusion later and enforces a consistent foundation. Let us explore these prompts to instruct ChatGPT to create a hierarchical organization of each project in these sections as follows:

1. **IoT Agriculture Marketing Landing**

   Prompt:

   "Generate a low-fidelity wireframe for an IoT agriculture marketing landing page. Include:

   - *Header with logo on left, nav links in center, and CTA button on right.*
   - *Hero section with large heading, subtext, buttons on left, and illustration placeholder on right.*
   - *Three equal feature boxes below.*
   - *Case study block spanning full width.*
   - *Logos grid with 5–6 partner placeholders.*
   - *Footer with three columns of links."*

   The following screenshot shows the generated wireframe from ChatGPT based on the wireframe prompt:

Figure 9.1: *Screenshot Showing ChatGPT Generated Wireframe*

Note: *Keep all sections in grayscale. Only use simple rectangles for images and text blocks.*

2. **Personal Bio Page**

   Prompt:

   "Wireframe a personal bio page. Include:

   - *Top header with name and subtitle centered.*
   - *Two-column layout with circular avatar placeholder on the left and bio text box with buttons on the right.*
   - *Ensure layout collapses into single column on small screens."*

   Note: *You need to focus on scannability; no colors, just placeholder boxes.*

3. **Fintech Landing Page**

   Prompt:

   "Generate a wireframe for a fintech landing page. Include:

   - *Sticky nav with logo, nav links, and CTA.*
   - *Hero section with heading, subtext, buttons, and illustration placeholder.*
   - *Three feature cards below in a grid.*
   - *Metrics row with three counters.*
   - *Testimonials carousel section with 2–3 placeholder cards.*
   - *Footer with company info and links."*

   Note: *Wireframe should emphasize hierarchy of CTAs and trust signals.*

4. **IoT Agriculture Dashboard**

   Prompt:

   "Create a dashboard wireframe for IoT agriculture. Include:

   - *Sidebar with nav links on the left.*
   - *Top bar with search and icons.*
   - *Three metric cards row.*
   - *Large chart block below.*
   - *Devices table section.*
   - *Alerts section with filters and a table."*

   Note: *Keep the layout clean and modular; only gray boxes and labels, no branding.*

Before you invest your energy in gradients, animations, or advanced styling, wireframes let you validate information hierarchy, navigation flow, and placement of CTAs. Use grayscale boxes, simple text labels, and outlines to design a wireframe for your site project. Do not include animations, gradients, or colors at this stage. Once layout flows are validated, you can the map the wireframes to the full HTML/CSS/JS builds. Planning is where you define the purpose, users, and structure of your design. You identify the target audience like farmers for IoT, investors for Fintech, etc. It is within the planning phase you decide the core flows such as sign-up, request demo, view dashboard. Eventually, you come up with outline of content hierarchy, for example, what goes first: hero, features, or trust signals, constraints setting are also considered like devices, accessibility requirements, branding rules. With wireframe, you can build a *bridge from ideas to design.* Wireframe allows you to answer this question; does this structure work? It allows you to visualize the plan in a tangible way. Next, we will implement the real prompt designed IoT marketing landing page for our imaginary customer who works in the Internet of Things industry.

Responsive IoT Marketing Landing Page

The responsive IoT marketing landing page effectively showcases Internet of Things products or services, capturing attention and driving conversions. The wireframe has been discussed in the previous section; here our focus therefore, is on the actual prompt composition to generate a responsive design, clear value proposition, engaging visuals, and prominent call-to-action. The design is expected to provide a seamless user experience across devices. The simple navigation and intuitive layout of the page encourage visitors to act, thus generating leads and building brand awareness. With this design in mind, businesses can communicate the value of their IoT solutions and drive revenue growth in real life scenario. Let us walk through the prompt structure and use it is or with your custom modifications.

Prompt:

Output: *Single-page* **HTML + CSS + *minimal* JS** *(no frameworks)*

Master Prompt (paste as one block):

*Create a production-ready IoT***agriculture** *marketing landing page. Output* **one HTML file***, embedded CSS, and minimal inline JS for interactions. Follow WCAG AA. Use semantic HTML5, ARIA roles, keyboard navigation, and logical heading order.*

Global: *Use a neutral light background. Primary accent = green. Secondary accent = warm yellow. Typography is legible with clear hierarchy. Respect prefers-reduced-motion.*

Header / Navigation: *Fixed top navbar with role="navigation" and aria-label="Main Navigation". Left: SVG leaf logo (inline SVG, descriptive <title>). Right: links "Solutions", "Products", "Case Studies", "Contact". Far right: CTA button "Request Demo". Provide hover and focus states with visible outlines. On touch and click, use a subtle ripple effect via JS. Collapse to an accessible hamburger menu on mobile (aria-expanded, aria-controls).*

Hero: *Full-width* ***gradient background*** *(green → light yellow). Left column:* H1 *"Smart Farming with* IoT *Data." Short subline about improved yield and reduced waste. Two buttons: Primary "Get Started" (gradient fill, hover glow, ripple on tap), Secondary "Learn More" (outline, hover underline). Right column: Inline SVG illustration of a farm with sensor icons. Give the SVG role="img" and <desc> describing the scene. Animate hero content with a gentle fade-in on load; respect reduced motion.*

Features: *Three-column grid of feature cards (SVG icon, bold title, short description). Cards have hover lift and soft shadow. Keyboard focus shows solid outline. Define spacing tokens and consistent 24px gaps. On mobile, stack vertically with generous spacing.*

Case Study: *Full-width background image of crops with a top-to-bottom gradient overlay for text legibility. Include a testimonial quote, name, and role. The image uses alt text and aria-describedby for the quote. Animate on scroll with a mild fade-up.*

Logos / Partners: *Row of grayscale partner SVG logos. On hover, fade to brand color. Ensure sufficient contrast and accessible names (aria-label).*

Footer: *Dark, high-contrast section. Company info, quick links, social icons (inline SVG with titles). Links have hover underline and visible focus. Include small compliance text (privacy, terms). Provide a "Back to top" link with aria-label.*

Responsiveness: *Define breakpoints for mobile, tablet, and desktop. On mobile: stacked sections, full-width buttons, collapsed nav. Ensure CTAs remain prominent.*

Accessibility: *Alt text for all images and SVGs. Color contrast AA. Focus styles on all interactive elements. Landmarks (header, nav, main, footer). Forms and buttons have accessible names.*

Performance / SEO: *Use <meta> for description and social cards (Open Graph). Defer noncritical JS. Inline critical CSS for above-the-fold.*

Micro-interactions:

- *Buttons: 150–200ms hover/focus transitions; ripple on click/tap.*
- *Cards: 100–150ms lift with shadow; no large motion.*
- *Section reveals: gentle fade-in; disabled for reduced motion.*

Deliverables: *One file containing HTML structure, <style> for CSS, and minimal <script> for menu toggle and ripple. No external libraries.*

The design concept shown below closely matches the requirements and visual elements described in the prompt, providing a clear representation of the desired IoT landing page. The generated design output might be slightly different from your output. Further prompting can ensure that the missing right-side image in the hero section appears.

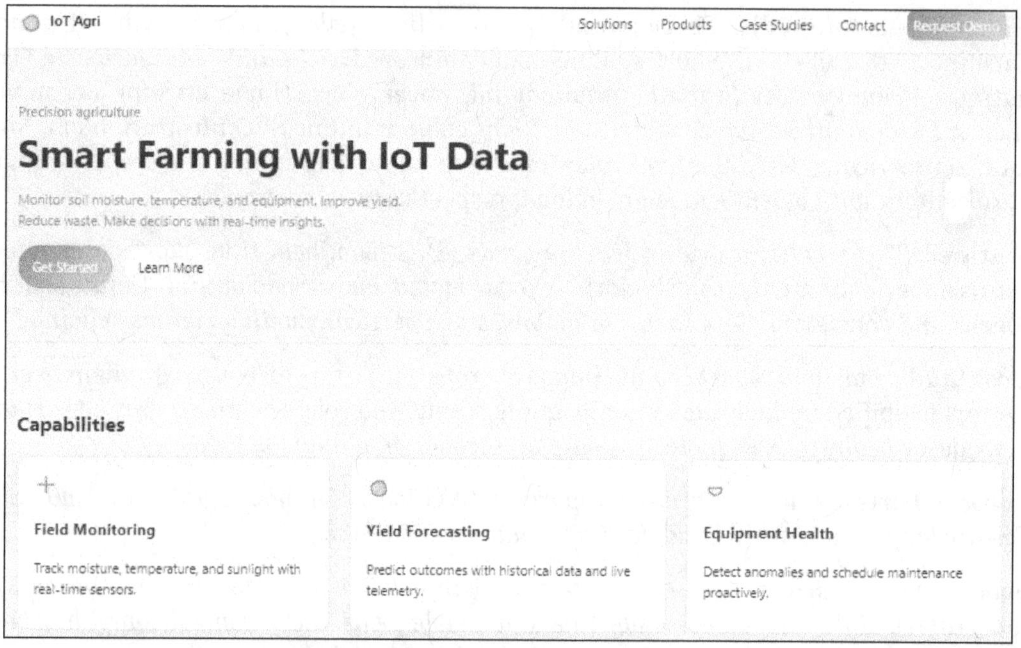

***Figure 9.2**: Screenshot Showing ChatGPT Generated IoT Marketing Landing Page*

So, with the preceding prompts and design output, we have a production-ready, single-page HTML/CSS/JS IoT agriculture marketing landing page that adheres to WCAG AA accessibility standards. It incorporates various design elements, including a responsive layout, semantic HTML5, ARIA roles, and keyboard navigation. The design features a neutral light background, green and warm yellow accents, and legible typography with a clear hierarchy. The solution consists of a single HTML file with embedded CSS and minimal inline JavaScript, without any external frameworks or libraries.

Now, we proceed with building our portfolios with the prompt-based designs of projects. Here is where we build personal bio page thatreflects the unique personality and brand of an individual.

Designing a Responsive Personal Bio Layout

The personal bio page design is centered on the individual identity while balancing the supporting content. The design elements are expected to include a profile image, name, description, and external links. Prompting lets these elements be placed logically and responsively. Unlike static design tools, AI system responds to structured language about alignment and flow. The following prompt ensures a visual balance, and also accessibility like `alt` text for images and button focus states with a clear expectation of polished and responsive designs suited for professionals and creatives.

Prompt:

Output: *Single-page* **HTML + CSS** *(no JS required, optional tiny JS for menu skip link)*

Master Prompt (paste as one block):

Produce an accessible, responsive **personal bio** *page. Output a single HTML file with embedded CSS (no frameworks). Use semantic structure, WCAG AA, and strong keyboard navigation.*

Header: *Centered name as H1 with subtle* **gradient text**. *Subtitle below in a muted tone. Provide a skip-to-content link for accessibility.*

Profile Section: *Two-column layout on desktop. Left: circular profile photo (high-res). Add descriptive alt. Provide a soft shadow and a gentle hover zoom (transform scale 1.02). Right: professional summary in short paragraphs, consistent line height. Include bullet highlights if necessary.*

Social / Actions: *Row of 2–3 action buttons (LinkedIn, GitHub, Twitter). Inside each button, inline SVG icon with a <title>. Buttons have clear hover/focus states (color shift + slight scale). On small screens, buttons expand full width. Provide visible focus outlines.*

Color / Type / Spacing: *Use a light background, dark text. Ensure contrast ratios are AA or better. Apply a scalable spacing system (8px or 4px base). Headings have consistent rhythm (H2, H3).*

Responsiveness: *At mobile breakpoints, stack photo above text. Maintain padding and breathing space. Constrain max width for readability.*

Optional Sections: *Skills list as chips with accessible labels; recent work or publications list with semantic lists and external link indicators.*

Accessibility:

- *All icons and images have titles/alt.*
- *Focus styles are visible on every interactive element.*
- *Landmarks and headings logical.*
- *Respect reduced motion (disable hover zoom on reduced-motion).*

Animations: *Subtle fade-in on hero and social buttons; disable if reduced motion.*

Deliverables: *Single HTML with <style> CSS. No JS except optional skip-link focus helper if needed.*

The design concept provided in the succeeding figure closely aligns with the prompt's requirements and visual specifications, accurately capturing the desired layout, aesthetics, and functionality.

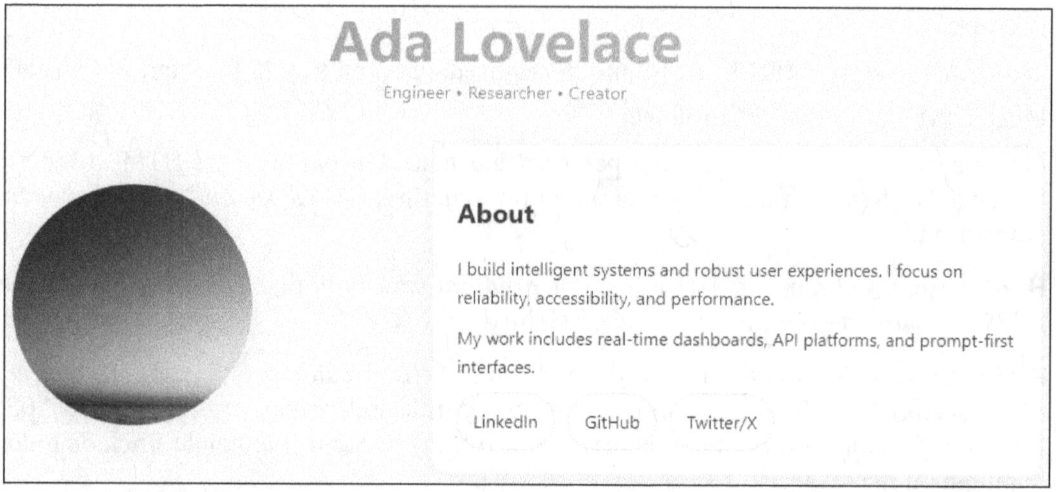

Figure 9.3: *Screenshot Showing ChatGPT Generated Bio Profile Page*

The preceding prompts and screenshot illustrate a single-page personal bio design that embodies accessibility, responsiveness, and semantic structure, adhering to WCAG AA standards and prioritizing strong keyboard navigation. The key design elements include a centered header with subtle gradient text, a two-column profile section with soft shadows and hover effects, and action buttons with distinct hover and focus states. This design is achieved through a single HTML file with embedded CSS, and optionally, a tiny JavaScript for menu skip link functionality.

Designing Fintech Landing Page

Fintech products thrive on trust and clarity. Landing pages need to communicate value quickly while guiding users toward conversion. The design key sections include a strong hero message, trust signals, and calls to action. Prompting allows these marketing messages to be described with precision. AI systems then translate these prompts into structured sections, such as feature grids and customer testimonial rows. This prompt-first approach streamlines workflows, reducing iteration cycles, and enabling you to rapidly test and refine multiple page versions. This section shows how to write fintech-specific prompts that emphasize security, reliability, and conversion.

Prompt:

Output: HTML + CSS + JS *(single page). JS only for menu, counters, and carousel.*

Master Prompt (paste as one block):

*Create a modern **fintech** landing page focused on trust and conversion. Output one HTML file with embedded CSS and minimal JS for navigation, animated metrics, and a testimonial carousel. Follow semantic HTML5 and WCAG AA.*

Header / Nav: *Fixed top bar with company logotype (inline SVG shield icon). Nav links to "Features", "Pricing", "Security", "Contact". Prominent CTA "Open Account". Touch ripple on buttons. Hamburger menu on mobile with ARIA attributes and focus trapping.*

Hero:*Gradient background (blue → purple). Large H1: "Secure Transactions at Scale." Subline explaining reliability. Primary CTA "Open Account" (gradient fill, hover glow, ripple on tap). Secondary "Learn More" (outline). Add inline SVG illustration of a secure payment shield with <title> and <desc>. Gentle fade-in on load.*

Features: *Three-column grid of cards. Each card includes a finance SVG icon, concise headline, and benefit text. Hover lift and shadow; visible focus rings.*

Metrics: *Row of three animated counters (uptime %, total transactions, clients). Counters increment using JS with aria-live="polite" for screen readers. Provide accessible labels and fallback static values if JS is disabled.*

Testimonials: *Carousel with 3–5 client quotes, names, and photos (descriptive alt). Use JS for slide navigation. Provide accessible controls (prev/next buttons with labels, current slide status via aria-live). Smooth but subtle slide transition; respect reduced motion.*

Trust Signals: *Grayscale partner logos (SVG). On hover, gradually reveal brand color. Provide aria-label for each logo.*

Security / Compliance: *Section listing security badges and short compliance note (for example, SOC 2, PCI DSS). Link to detailed policy pages.*

Footer: *Dark high-contrast footer with links, social icons (SVG with <title>), and legal text. "Back to top" anchor with aria-label.*

Responsiveness: *Collapse grids to single column on mobile. Preserve CTA visibility. Limit line lengths for readability.*

Accessibility: *Alt text for all images. Keyboard accessible carousel and menus. Visible focus outlines. Color contrast AA.*

Micro-interactions:

- *Buttons: 150–200ms transitions and ripple.*
- *Cards: 120ms hover lift.*
- *Metrics: 1.0–1.5s ease counter animation.*
- *Respect reduced motion preference.*

Deliverables: *Single HTML with embedded CSS and minimal JS modules for menu toggle, counters, and carousel. No external libraries.*

The design concept below effectively translates the prompt's requirements into a visual representation. The design closely matches the specified elements and overall vision.

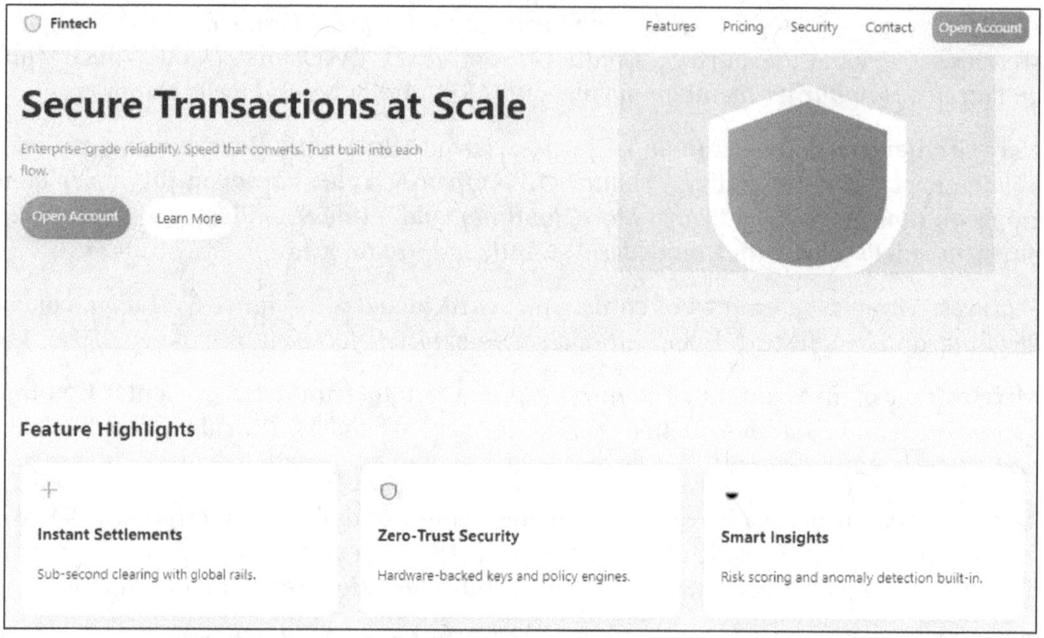

Figure 9.4: *Screenshot Showing ChatGPT Generated Fintech Page*

In the aforesaid prompt and screenshot, the expected outcome is a responsive fintech landing page that effectively communicates trust and drives conversion. The key sections are hero messaging, feature highlights, animated metrics, customer testimonials, and security assurances. The design is built with accessible HTML, CSS, and minimal JavaScript. This design ensures a seamless user experience across devices.

Next, we shall discuss the last project for this section, which is designing IoT dashboard to showcase the dashboard design capabilities of AI system prompt engineering.

Designing IoT Dashboard Components Layout

IoT dashboards display complex data. They need to balance clarity with density. Prompt-first workflows help test layouts before implementation. Instead of sketching, prompts describe panels, widgets, and navigation zones. AI outputs structured dashboards with modular blocks. This supports rapid prototyping of monitoring tools. Designers can explore how data flows across charts, lists, and alerts. Prompting ensures reusability by defining components clearly. Dashboards also demand responsive behavior, as they are often used on tablets and desktops. A well-prompted IoT layout reveals data without overwhelming users. This section shows how modular descriptions create functional dashboards through AI-driven design. Let us explore the prompt for the components of an IoT dashboard.

Prompt:

Output:HTML + CSS + JS *(single page). JS for sidebar toggle, chart stubs, and live updates mock.*

Master Prompt (paste as one block):

Build a responsive IoT agriculture dashboard. Output one HTML file with embedded CSS and minimal JS. Use semantic structure, ARIA roles, and WCAG AA. Include placeholder data and chart stubs (canvas or SVG), with accessible descriptions.

Layout: *Left sidebar navigation with icons for Dashboard, Devices, Reports, Settings (inline SVG with <title>).* **Top** *header bar with search input, notifications button, and profile menu. Use role="navigation" and label landmarks. Provide keyboard navigation and focus order. Hamburger button collapses the sidebar on mobile with aria-expanded.*

Status Cards: *Row of three metric cards (Temperature, Soil Moisture, Battery). Each card has an SVG icon, bold metric, unit label, and trend arrow. Hover zoom and soft glow. Keyboard focus outline. Provide aria-label describing the metric and current value.*

Charts:

- *Primary line chart for "Device Activity (Last 24h)".*
- *Secondary sparkline charts in cards for quick trends.*
- *Use gradient strokes and tooltips on hover or focus (JS).*
- *Provide <figcaption> and ARIA description for each chart. Respect reduced motion (static rendering fallback).*

Device List: *Table or card list of devices with status (green/yellow/red), location, and last check-in. Use icon badges with sufficient color contrast and accessible text labels (e.g., aria-label="Status: Warning"). Row hover highlight and focusability.*

Alerts Panel: *Table of active alerts with timestamp, device, issue, and severity. Provide filter controls (All / Warning / Critical) with aria-pressed toggles. Ensure focus management and keyboard support.*

Responsiveness:

- *Sidebar collapses on mobile.*
- *Cards stack vertically.*
- *Charts fill width and remain legible on small screens.*
- *Preserve touch targets ≥44px.*

Accessibility:

- *Alt text for all visuals.*
- *Focus indicators for all interactive controls.*

- *Forms with labels and aria-describedby.*
- *Color contrast AA or better.*

Micro-interactions:

- *Cards: 100–120ms hover scale + shadow.*
- *Buttons and toggles: ripple on click/tap.*
- *Section reveal: soft fade-in; respect reduced motion.*

Performance: *Defer noncritical JS. Keep CSS lean. Provide ARIA live regions only where necessary.*

Deliverables: *Single HTML file with CSS and minimal JS for sidebar toggle, tooltip behavior, chart stub rendering (no external libs), and basic filtering.*

The design concept shown in the following figure effectively translates the prompt's requirements into a visual representation. The design closely matches the specified elements and the overall vision.

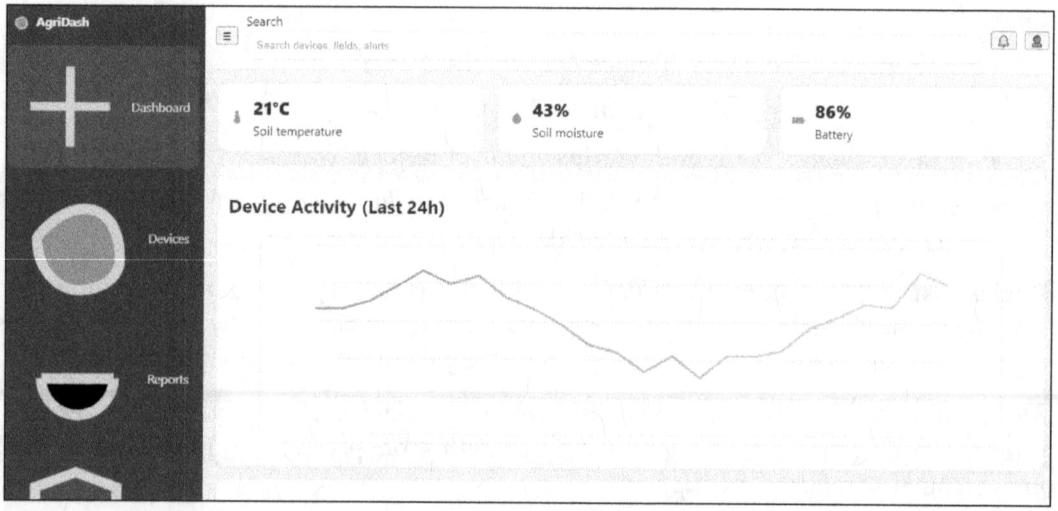

Figure 9.5: *Screenshot Showing ChatGPT Generated IoT Dashboard Component*

In the preceding prompt and screenshot, the expected outcome is a user-friendly and accessible IoT dashboard that provides real-time insights into agricultural metrics. It features a responsive design, interactive charts, and device monitoring. The dashboard is built with HTML, CSS, and minimal JavaScript, prioritizing accessibility and performance.

With the design requirements and expectations established, let us move on to an important phase of reviewing and iterating AI-generated interfaces, where we refine and perfect the output to meet user needs and project goals.

Reviewing and Iterating AI-Generated Interfaces

As discussed previously, AI system designs are not final outputs. They need review and refinement. Prompt-first workflows rely on iteration cycles. Each cycle improves clarity, hierarchy, and usability. A review process checks for alignment, accessibility, and responsiveness. Errors often occur in spacing, contrast, or component sizing, even with missing placeholders. Like the previous IoT agriculture marketing page example, the current design lacks an image in the hero section, which was a key element in the original prompt. You then need to rewrite prompts with precise adjustments. Iteration also adds missing accessibility features, such as alt text and ARIA roles. Reviewing makes AI a co-creator rather than a one-time generator. This section presents a systematic approach for analyzing outputs and refining them until they meet professional standards. In this section, we will review and refine the ChatGPT-generated prompts for each project, starting with the IoT agriculture marketing landing page. We will analyze the original prompts, identify areas for improvement, and create enhanced versions to optimize their effectiveness.

Improving IoT Marketing Landing Page

In the IoT agriculture marketing landing page, the missing hero image happened because the original prompt asked for an "*Inline SVG illustration of a farm with sensor icons*" without describing the actual shapes, composition, or forbidding placeholders. Models often default to generic boxes when instructions are not specific. To fix this, you should explicitly require real inline SVG markup (no placeholders), describe the farm scene in detail like crop rows, sensor nodes, a drone, and a satellite, and include accessibility tags like `<title>` and `<desc>` with aria-labelledby. Similarly, partner logos and feature icons should be defined as inline SVGs or data-URI images rather than *logo* text blocks. Adding a global rule like "*Do not render placeholder image boxes or X marks – embed inline* SVG *or data-*URI *only*" ensures all visuals appear correctly. Finally, clarify animations apply to content, not image substitution, so the SVG remains visible during load. Next, we shall explore an improved prompt.

Prompt:

Produce a production-ready IoT *agriculture marketing landing page. Output a single .html file with embedded* <style> CSS *and minimal inline* <script> *(no frameworks, no external resources).*

Follow semantic HTML5 *structure,* WCAG AA *standards, and strong keyboard navigation.*

Global requirements:

- *No placeholder images, boxes, or text.*
- *All illustrations, icons, and logos must be embedded as* ***inline <svg> markup*** *or* ***data-URI SVG <img>*** *(no external files).*

- *Every SVG includes <title> and <desc>, referenced with aria-labelledby.*
- *All interactive elements have visible focus styles.*
- *Respect prefers-reduced-motion (disable fades/animations when set).*
- *Inline critical CSS for above-the-fold; defer noncritical JS.*
- *Neutral light background with green as the primary accent and warm yellow as the secondary accent.*
- *Clear typographic hierarchy, legible spacing.*

Header / Navigation:

- *Fixed top navbar with role="navigation" and aria-label="Main Navigation".*
- *Left: Inline SVG leaf logo (<title> + <desc>).*
- *Center/right: Links "Solutions", "Products", "Case Studies", "Contact".*
- *Far right: CTA button "Request Demo".*
- *Hover/focus states with outlines. Subtle ripple effect on click (JS).*
- *Collapsible hamburger menu on mobile with aria-expanded and aria-controls; keyboard trap managed.*

Hero:

- *Full-width gentle gradient background (green → light yellow).*
- *Left: <h1> "Smart Farming with IoT Data" + short subline. Two buttons:*
    - *Primary "Get Started" (gradient fill, glow on hover, ripple on tap).*
    - *Secondary "Learn More" (outline, underline on hover).*
- *Right:* **Inline SVG illustration** *(no placeholders). Must show: crop rows, three sensor nodes with antennas, a drone, a satellite, and subtle data grid lines.*
- *SVG: black stroke-only line art, responsive with viewBox, <title> + <desc>, aria-labelledby, role="img".*
- *Animation: gentle fade-in for text + SVG on load; disabled if reduced motion.*

Features:

- *Three-column grid of feature cards.*
- *Each card: Inline SVG icon, bold title, short description.*
- *Hover: lift + soft shadow (100–150ms). Keyboard focus: solid outline.*
- *Consistent 24px gaps. Stack vertically on mobile.*

Case Study:

- *Full-width background image/illustration (inline SVG or data-URI).*

- *Gradient overlay for text contrast.*
- *Include testimonial quote + name + role.*
- *Image area must have alt or aria-describedby.*
- *Fade-up animation on scroll; disabled for reduced motion.*

Logos / Partners:

- *Grid/row of partner logos (inline SVGs only).*
- *Default grayscale, fade to brand tone on hover.*
- *Each logo has aria-label for accessibility.*
- *Maintain AA contrast.*

Footer:

- *Dark, high-contrast section.*
- *Company info, quick links, and inline SVG social icons (with <title>).*
- *Compliance text: privacy + terms.*
- *Links underline on hover, visible focus styles.*
- *Include "Back to top" link with aria-label="Back to top".*

Responsiveness:

- *Define breakpoints for mobile, tablet, desktop.*
- *Mobile: stacked sections, full-width CTAs, collapsed nav.*
- *Optionally sticky primary CTA at bottom of viewport with accessible controls.*

Micro-interactions:

- *Buttons: 150–200ms hover/focus transitions; ripple effect on click/tap (JS).*
- *Cards: 100–150ms shadow lift.*
- *Section reveals: fade-in; disabled if reduced motion.*

Deliverable:

- *A single .html file.*
- *Inline <style> CSS.*
- *Minimal inline <script> for menu toggle and ripple.*
- *No external libraries or links.*
- *Include <meta> description + basic Open Graph tags.*

With these small changes, your prompt will reliably output a user-friendly design that includes actual illustrations, accessible markup, and avoids empty placeholders.

Improving Personal Bio Page

The main risk with this prompt is that the AI system may still insert the placeholder images for the profile photo or icons if not instructed otherwise. To avoid this unwanted output, explicitly require a real inline SVG for social icons with `<title>` and `aria-label` and a circular `<img>` with descriptive `alt` text for the profile photo, not a blank box. Similarly, specify that optional sections skills, publications listshould use semantic HTML elements and not generic placeholders. Adding a global instruction like "*Do not output placeholder images or text blocks; embed actual inline* SVGs *or data-*URI *images directly in the* HTML" ensures necessary visuals render correctly. For accessibility, make sure the skip-to-content link is focusable and visible, and that hover/zoom animations respect prefers-reduced-motion. Here is an improved prompt.

Prompt:

Produce an accessible, responsive personal bio page. Output a single .html file with embedded <style> CSS (no frameworks).

Follow semantic HTML5 structure, WCAG AA standards, and strong keyboard navigation.

Global Requirements:

- *No placeholder images or icons.*
- *Embed actual inline SVGs for social icons (with <title> and aria-label).*
- *Use a real <img> element for the profile photo with a descriptive alt.*
- *All interactive elements must have visible focus styles.*
- *Respect prefers-reduced-motion (disable animations/hover zoom when set).*

Layout and Content:

- ***Header:***
  - *Centered <h1> name with subtle gradient text.*
  - *Subtitle <p> below in muted tone.*
  - *Provide a "Skip to content" link that becomes visible on focus.*
- ***Profile Section:***
  - *Two-column layout on desktop.*
  - ***Left:** Circular profile photo with soft shadow + hover zoom (transform: scale(1.02)), but disable zoom if prefers-reduced-motion.*
  - ***Right:** Professional summary in short paragraphs with consistent line height. Allow bullet highlights where relevant.*
- ***Social / Actions:***
  - *Row of 2–3 buttons (LinkedIn, GitHub, Twitter).*
  - *Each button contains inline SVG icon + <title>.*

    - *Clear hover/focus states: color shift + slight scale.*
    - *On small screens, buttons expand full width.*
- ***Optional Sections:***
    - ***Skills:*** *Display as accessible chips (<ul> with <li>).*
    - ***Recent Work / Publications:*** *Semantic list (<ul> or <ol>), external links marked with an indicator (for example, "↗").*

Color / Type / Spacing:

- *Light background, dark text with AA contrast.*
- *Scalable spacing system (4px/8px multiples).*
- *Headings (h2, h3) follow consistent rhythm.*
- *Constrain max-width for readability.*

Responsiveness:

- *Mobile: stack profile photo above text, maintain padding and breathing space.*
- *Desktop: two-column layout maintained.*

Animations:

- *Subtle fade-in for header and social buttons.*
- *Disable animations if reduced motion is requested.*

Deliverable:

- *A **single HTML file** with inline <style> CSS.*
- *No JavaScript, except an optional helper for skip-link focus handling.*

With these refinements, the prompt will consistently produce a clean, accessible bio page with actual icons and images, logical heading order, and a responsive layout rather than an output with missing visuals.

Improving Fintech Landing Page

The prompt fintech landing page requires refinement to guarantee higher-quality output. While it calls for inline SVG icons and logos, it does not forbid placeholder text like *logo* which risks wireframe-style visuals instead of polished assets. Carousel accessibility is also underspecified: it mentions controls, but not whether `aria-live` should announce the active slide, or if keyboard arrow navigation is supported, leaving room for inaccessible implementations. The counter section notes static fallbacks but lacks structural guidance; requiring `<span>` elements with `data-target` and fallback text would prevent empty values when JavaScript is disabled. Animation requirements are clear as well. Without explicitly enforcing prefers-reduced-motion, accessibility may be overlooked. Key SEO and performance essentials are missing as well, such as

<meta> descriptions, Open Graph tags, and inline critical CSS, which were included in stronger prompts. Lastly, while JavaScript is limited to menu, counters, and carousel, the restriction is not explicit enough, risking unnecessary scripts and bloated output. Let us explore an improved prompt.

Prompt:

Produce a modern fintech landing page focused on trust and conversion. Output a single .html file with embedded <style> CSS and minimal inline <script> (no external libraries). Follow semantic HTML5 structure, WCAG AA standards, and strong keyboard navigation.

Global requirements:

- *No placeholder images or icons.*
- *All illustrations, logos, and icons must be embedded as inline <svg> markup or data-URI SVG <img>.*
- *Every SVG includes <title> and <desc> with aria-labelledby.*
- *All interactive elements have visible focus styles.*
- *Respect prefers-reduced-motion (disable animations/transitions when set).*
- *Inline critical CSS for above-the-fold.*
- *Include <meta> description and Open Graph tags for SEO/social.*
- *JS must only be used for menu toggle, counters, and testimonials carousel.*

Header / Navigation:

- *Fixed top bar with inline SVG shield logo (<title> + <desc>).*
- *Nav links: "Features", "Pricing", "Security", "Contact".*
- *Prominent CTA button "Open Account".*
- *Buttons have hover/focus states and ripple effect on click/tap.*
- *Mobile: hamburger menu with aria-expanded + aria-controls, focus trapping for accessibility.*

Hero:

- *Gradient background (blue → purple).*
- *Large <h1>: "Secure Transactions at Scale."*
- *Subline with short descriptive copy.*
- *Two buttons:*
  - *Primary: "Open Account" (gradient, glow on hover, ripple).*
  - *Secondary: "Learn More" (outline, underline on hover).*
- *Inline SVG illustration of a secure shield + payment elements. Must have <title>, <desc>, role="img".*

- *Gentle fade-in on load; disabled if reduced motion.*

Features:

- *Three-column grid of feature cards.*
- *Each card: inline SVG icon, bold headline, short description.*
- *Hover lift (120ms) + soft shadow.*
- *Keyboard focus shows solid outline.*
- *Stack vertically on mobile.*

Metrics:

- *Row of three animated counters (uptime %, total transactions, clients).*
- *Each counter inside <span data-target="...">fallback</span>.*
- *JS increments numbers with aria-live="polite" for screen readers.*
- *Fallback values remain visible if JS is disabled.*

Testimonials:

- *Carousel of 3–5 client quotes, names, and photos.*
- *Photos include descriptive alt.*
- *JS navigation with "Prev"/"Next" buttons.*
- *Active slide announced via aria-live.*
- *Support keyboard arrow navigation + focusable controls.*
- *Subtle slide transition; disabled if reduced motion.*

Trust Signals:

- *Row of partner logos (inline SVGs).*
- *Default grayscale, transition to color on hover.*
- *Each logo has aria-label.*
- *Maintain AA contrast.*

Security / Compliance:

- *Section with inline SVG security badges (for example, SOC 2, PCI DSS).*
- *Short compliance note + links to policy pages.*

Footer:

- *Dark, high-contrast section.*
- *Company info, quick links, and inline SVG social icons (with <title>).*
- *Legal text (privacy, terms).*
- *"Back to top" link with aria-label="Back to top".*

Responsiveness:

- *Breakpoints for mobile, tablet, desktop.*
- *On mobile: single-column layout, stacked sections, full-width CTAs.*
- *Ensure CTA buttons remain visible.*
- *Limit line lengths for readability.*

Micro-interactions:

- *Buttons: 150–200ms hover/focus transitions + ripple.*
- *Cards: 120ms hover lift.*
- *Counters: 1.0–1.5s easing animation.*
- *Carousel: smooth but subtle transitions.*
- *Disable all motion if prefers-reduced-motion.*

Deliverable:

- *One .html file with inline <style> CSS.*
- *Minimal inline <script> for menu toggle, counters, and carousel.*
- *No external libraries or resources.*

In the preceding prompt, the structure and explicit intent of the requirement guarantee a more predictable outcome.

Improving IoT Dashboard Components

The problem with IoT dashboard component is mainly in the flow and clarity. The wording is somewhat repetitive, and details like aria-live, ripple, and reduced motion are scattered rather than grouped. The deliverables could be sharper by clearly stating what JS should handle versus what remains static. The charts risk misinterpretation without libraries, they should be clarified as canvas/SVG stubs, not fully interactive visuals. Let us examine an improved prompt.

Improved prompt

Output: *Single HTML file with embedded CSS + minimal JS. JS only for sidebar toggle, tooltip behavior, chart stubs, and filtering.*

Goal: *Build a responsive IoT Agriculture Dashboard with placeholder data and accessible chart stubs. Prioritize semantic HTML5, WCAG AA accessibility, and efficient performance.*

Layout:

- ***Sidebar Navigation (Left):*** *Links for Dashboard, Devices, Reports, Settings. Use inline SVG icons with <title>. Provide role="navigation" and labeled landmarks. Collapsible on mobile with hamburger toggle (aria-expanded, focus trapping).*

- **Top Header:** *Includes search input, notifications button, and profile menu. Ensure clear keyboard focus order and role landmarks.*

Components:

- **Status Cards (Row of 3):** *Temperature, Soil Moisture, Battery. Each includes:*
    - *SVG icon, bold metric, unit label, trend arrow.*
    - *Hover zoom + glow; keyboard focus outline.*
    - *Accessible aria-label with current metric value.*
- **Charts:**
    - *Primary line chart: "Device Activity (Last 24h)".*
    - *Secondary sparklines embedded in cards.*
    - *Gradient strokes, tooltips on hover/focus.*
    - *Provide <figcaption> + ARIA description.*
    - *Static fallback (no animation) if prefers-reduced-motion.*
- **Device List:** *Table or card grid showing: device status (green/yellow/red), location, last check-in.*
    - *Status shown via icon + text (aria-label="Status: Critical").*
    - *Row hover highlight and keyboard focusable.*
- **Alerts Panel:** *Table of alerts (timestamp, device, issue, severity).*
    - *Filter controls (All / Warning / Critical) as aria-pressed toggles.*
    - *Ensure focus management + keyboard navigation.*

Responsiveness:

- *Sidebar collapses on mobile.*
- *Cards stack vertically on smaller screens.*
- *Charts scale fluidly.*
- *Maintain minimum 44px touch targets.*

Accessibility:

- *Alt text for all icons/visuals.*
- *Visible focus indicators.*
- *Forms with labels + aria-describedby.*
- *Ensure color contrast AA+.*
- *Use aria-live sparingly (only for updates that must be announced).*

Micro-interactions:

- *Card hover: 100–120ms scale + shadow.*
- *Buttons/toggles: ripple effect.*
- *Section reveal: soft fade-in (disabled if reduced motion).*

Performance:

- *Defer noncritical JS.*
- *Inline, optimized CSS.*
- *Keep assets lean and SVG-based.*

Deliverables:

- *One HTML file with embedded CSS.*
- *Minimal inline JS for sidebar toggle, chart stub rendering, tooltips, and alert filtering.*
- *No external libraries.*

In the preceding prompt, a block-based structure layout, components, interactions, responsiveness, accessibility, performance and deliverables in this systematic approach would make the requirements more digestible and production-ready.

Conclusion

This chapter demonstrated how prompt-first workflows can streamline web design processes from idea to interface. By planning UI blueprints, practicing structured prompt design, and reviewing generated outputs, you have acquired the skills to guide AI as a design co-creator. Each example in this chapter reinforced the value of hierarchy, responsiveness, and accessibility in professional layouts. Importantly, iteration was highlighted as a critical practice. It allows outputs to evolve toward clarity, compliance, and usability. Applied prompt workflows enable designers and developers to collaborate more efficiently, producing maintainable, standards-aligned interfaces with reduced overhead. As AI becomes integral to digital product development, understanding this workflow provides a competitive advantage in speed, precision, and scalability. In the next chapter, we will discuss the blending of visual design tools and prompt engineering to deliver a professional website.

Points to Remember

- Prompts are like digital blueprints for wireframe creation.
- Planning hierarchy, zones, and flows before coding to ensure design clarity.
- Embed accessibility in prompts in your like semantic landmarks, alt text, ARIA roles, and reduced-motion support.

- Prioritize mobile-first design with Grid and Flexbox.
- Prompt output must be reviewed and refined, not accepted blindly.
- In frontend development, use inline SVGs and gradient backgrounds for lightweight, accessible visuals.
- Always include measurable success criteria such as contrast ratios, keyboard navigation, and performance constraints.

Multiple Choice Questions

1. Which of the following is the main purpose of applying prompt-first workflows?
   a. To replace developers completely
   b. To accelerate ideation while maintaining design intent
   c. To generate only static mockups
   d. To avoid accessibility practices
2. Which of the following should be avoided in professional prompt outputs?
   a. Semantic HTML5
   b. Inline SVG icons
   c. Placeholder images or "X" marks
   d. ARIA labels for navigation
3. What role does iteration play in applied prompt workflows?
   a. It eliminates the need for planning.
   b. It allows refinement of outputs to meet professional standards.
   c. It ensures outputs are always correct on first attempt.
   d. It replaces accessibility reviews.
4. In a responsive IoT agriculture landing page, which accessibility feature is critical for the navigation menu?
   a. ARIA roles and aria-expanded for collapsible menus
   b. Bright gradient colors
   c. Placeholder partner logos
   d. Only hover effects without keyboard support
5. Which is the deliverable format for most designs in this chapter?
   a. PowerPoint slides
   b. HTML + CSS + minimal JS (single file)

    c. JSON schemas
    d. External JavaScript frameworks

6. Why should wireframes be kept in grayscale at early stages?
    a. To hide accessibility problems.
    b. To emphasize structure without distractions from styling.
    c. To replicate brand guidelines immediately.
    d. To test animations early.
7. What is the role of micro-interactions in prompts?
    a. To confuse users.
    b. To improve usability with subtle animations like hover, ripple, and fade-in.
    c. To increase file size unnecessarily.
    d. To replace semantic HTML.
8. Which is a recommended practice for testimonial carousels in fintech landing pages?
    a. Use automatic autoplay only.
    b. Provide accessible prev/next controls with aria-live updates.
    c. Use images without alt text.
    d. Remove keyboard navigation.
9. In IoT dashboards, what ensures that users are not overwhelmed?
    a. Using random colors for alerts.
    b. Modular component design with clear zones.
    c. Avoiding responsive layouts.
    d. Disabling semantic markup.
10. Which design token is emphasized in prompts for spacing?
    a. Randomized values
    b. 24px gap tokens and scalable spacing system
    c. Hard-coded absolute pixels
    d. No spacing system

Answers

1. b
2. c
3. b
4. a
5. b
6. b
7. b
8. b
9. b
10. b

Key Terms

- **Applied prompt workflow:** A structured approach to building interfaces by encoding design rules and hierarchy into natural language prompts.
- **Wireframing:** Low-fidelity representation of layouts that establishes structure before applying styling.
- **Semantic HTML5:** HTML elements that convey meaning and improve accessibility like `<header>`, `<nav>`, `<main>`.
- **ARIA Roles:** Attributes that define accessibility roles for screen readers and assistive technologies.
- **Design Tokens**: Reusable values like spacing, color, typography that enforce consistency across components.
- **Micro-interactions:** Subtle animations or feedback such as hover, ripple, fade-in that enhance usability without distraction.
- **Iteration:** The process of refining AI-generated outputs by rewriting or adjusting prompts.
- **WCAG AA:** Accessibility standard ensuring sufficient contrast, keyboard navigation, and inclusive design.
- **Scalable Vector Graphics (SVG):** Lightweight, accessible, and resolution-independent graphics embedded directly in markup.
- **Mobile-First Design:** An approach that prioritizes small-screen usability before scaling layouts for larger screens.

CHAPTER 10
Visual Prompting in Design Tools

Introduction

In *Chapter 9: Applied Prompt Workflows*, we had translated our intent into repeatable applied prompt workflows, scoping goals, encoding constraints, and iterating with tight feedback loops. In this chapter, you are introduced to visual prompting in design tools, the emerging practice of guiding design tools such as Framer AI, wix, and Webflows to use natural language commands in design creations. This approach blends design thinking with the conversational User Experience (UX), allowing you to prototype layouts and UI flows directly from prompts without writing code.

This chapter picks up from that system-level foundation and shows how to steer visual outcomes in AI design tools such as Framer AI using precise, testable prompts. You will, moreover, learn to express structure, tokens, and responsive rules so that generated layouts respect accessibility, performance, and brand. In addition, we aim to examine the limitations of the AI-generated UI and how to counter them with acceptance criteria, human review, and prompt deltas. The outcome is a predictable path from ideas to shippable, standard-aligned interfaces. We will start the conversation with the importance of visual prompting in today's frontend development.

After reading this chapter, you will be equipped to translate product goals into clear prompts, generate accessible and responsive layouts, and specify tokens, grids and breakpoints for consistent theming. You will direct micro-interactions and motion with performance. You will implement constraints and prompt reusable components and editable layers for easier maintenance. You will review outputs using acceptance criteria like semantics, keyboard flow, contrast, responsiveness, and load time. Finally, you will iterate with focused prompt feedback, documenting decisions for hand-off to ensure AI-assisted interfaces stay aligned with brand systems, accessibility standards, and measurable success metrics.

Structure

In this chapter, we will cover the following topics:

- Why Visual Prompting Matters
- Prompting in Framer AI
- Prompt-Friendly Design Habits
- Limitations in AI Designs

Why Visual Prompting Matters

Visual design tools with AI capabilities like Framer, Wix, Webflow are collapsing the distance between an idea and something that you can click. Teams can now work faster by describing their intent in prompts and receiving production-ready layouts in seconds, eliminating the need for schedule coordination, handoffs, and file management. The speed does not just save a few hours; it fundamentally changes how products begin, evolve, and align across functions. Business minded designers and developers are testing markets before breakfast. In this section, we are heading to discuss the four ways visual prompting matters in this evolving digital ecosystem. We will explore rapid prototyping, improving communication and collaboration, democratizing design, and impacting productivity. Let us start with prototyping with speed.

Prototyping with Speed

Design prototyping is the process of creating a preliminary version of a product, service, or system to test and refine its design. It helps to visualize concepts, test assumptions, gather feedback, iterate and refine based on the feedback and testing results. Let us examine a classic business case scenario where a business executive can write a prompt as follows: "`Make a landing page with a hero section, call-to-action button, and pricing cards.`" In less than a minute, an AI system layout returns a responsive page, a hero with headline/subhead/visual, a primary CTA, and a pricing grid with three tiers, feature checklists, and a secondary CTA for enterprise leads. It arrives with semantic HTML that already maps to common ARIA roles. The power here is not just the time saved; it is the feedback velocity. When a model can draft the 80% solution instantly, the team can spend its attention on the 20% that drives outcomes: messaging, offer framing, social proof, and the one friction that blocks signups.

Improving Collaboration and Communication

AI system narrows the gap that exists between designers and developers. Instead of a long handoff documents with page-long specs, redlines, and ambiguous annotations, designers can smoothly write prompts encoded with system intent: *"Use our spacing scale (4, 8, 12...), font tokens (Title/Body/Caption), and a 12-column grid; compose a dashboard with a left nav, KPI strip, and table with sortable columns."* The output respects these constraints and describes the components in a way that maps to a code. Developers, in turn, do not just receive a flat mock. They get a layout aligned with intended component hierarchies –`<Page>→<Sidebar>→<NavItem>, <Header>→<KPIGroup>→<KPI>, <Table>→<TableHeader>→<TableRow>→<TableCell>.` Variants (default/hover/active/disabled) are clearly enumerated. Spacing is expressed in tokens rather than arbitrary pixels. If your stack uses utility classes or a component library, the model can target that dialect: *"Render with our Button, Card, and Input components; prefer semantic tags; keep class names BEM-style.* "This makes reviews cheaper and sharper. The collaboration and communication work both directions: engineers can compose prompts back to design like refactoring of cards to use the new elevation tokens; swap inline SVGs for icon components; reduce DOM depth in hero. The AI turns the request into updated layouts and code snippets; the design and engineering converge without tedious documentation.

Democratizing Design

One of the game-changing impact of visual prompting is the ability for anyone to start designing, regardless of technical skills. A marketer can now say: *"Build a dark-mode newsletter signup page with an image background"* and get started. The AI system would simply return an HTML/CSS-ready page with specs output as follows:

- A dark, high-contrast palette that passes baseline accessibility checks (for example primary text on background ≥ WCAG AA contrast).
- A hero image with a subtle overlay so the form remains legible.
- A concise value proposition, an email field with validation hints, a primary CTA, and privacy reassurance.
- Sensible mobile breakpoints and keyboard-navigable controls.

For the marketer, this removes two historic barriers in development: *dependence*, waiting for dev/design cycles and *risk*, fear of breaking production. They can preview, tweak copy, try three different hero images, and publish a campaign-specific page without touching a CSS file. When they are ready, they can hand the output to engineering as structured artifacts: semantic HTML, a stylesheet with tokens, and a checklist of states with success, error, and loading. Engineering team can then integrate auth, analytics, consent, and localization work that truly benefits from human oversight. The eventual net effect is that the subject-matter experts can express intent directly, and the organization benefits from more experiments with less design bureaucratic bottlenecks.

Vibe coding and Low-Code/No-Code (LCNC) tools push this idea even further by making prompt-driven apps and landing pages easier to produce and refine. Rather than beginning with an empty design file, a user can describe the page in the natural language, define the vibe, structure, and purpose, and receive a working draft that is ready for review and iteration. This means a campaign page, signup flow, or lightweight product interface can move from concept to prototype in minutes. Teams can test different headlines, layouts, CTA placements, and visual treatments with less friction, while still preserving a path for engineering to step in later with analytics, authentication, localization, and stronger production controls. In practice, these tools do not replace careful design or development, but they greatly reduce the distance between intent and implementation. And this is what makes prompt-driven creation so powerful.

Improving Productivity

Visual prompting in design enables teams to iterate live, propose changes in natural language, see instant updates, streamlining the feedback process and boosting productivity.AI system has transformed how teams meet. Instead of a 90-minute design review with static slides, the group iterates live with prompts. You can project the working draft while stakeholders propose adjustments in natural language. AI system renders updates in seconds. Ambiguities that would normally lead to follow-up meetings are resolved in the room. For instance, a fintech team is refining a dashboard. Let us examine a first prompt idea *"Executive overview with a KPI strip (Balance, NPL ratio, Net interest margin), recent transactions, and a risk heatmap."* The output is good, but compliance asks for clearer audit trails. Then, the prompt is updated with *"Add an activity log with timestamped events; make every KPI drill-down accessible via keyboard; include explanatory tooltips with definitions from our glossary."* In addition, legal wants disclaimers on modeled values. Once again, the prompt is updated as follows: *"Mark simulated projections with a striped badge and an info tooltip; add 'last updated' timestamps; include export buttons with progress feedback "*. In three cycles, all the parties see their concerns reflected in the interface, not just minutes. The designer guides visual clarity and information hierarchy. The product manager safeguards scope and acceptance criteria. Engineering spots complexity like heatmap rendering performance and proposes alternatives on the fly. Compliance validates disclosures. The meeting ends with aligned artifacts: updated layout, component tree, and a backlog of integration tasks tied to visible UI changes. This prompt-driven approach brings in two advantages, shorter latency between idea, and proof. The stakeholders do not have to imagine how a change might look; they see it, which prevents misalignment and traceable decisions. The prompt history functions like a living spec. Each revision explains the rationale why the audit log exists, and why projections are marked, with their inherent values in onboarding and auditing. In a nutshell, the organizations that benefit most will not be the ones who generate the prettiest first prompt drafts. They will be the ones who treat AI as a co-pilot for clarity, iteration, and shared ownership. Next, we explore how you can use Framer AI to assist with your visual designs.

Note: *Visual prompting matters because it compresses design cycles, reduces miscommunication, and empowers non-designers.*

Prompting in Framer AI

Framer AI makes the jump from idea to interactive layout feel easy. You describe the page you want like **`"portfolio with a bold hero, tagline, and three project cards",`** and a working draft appears, ready to drag, resize, and refine. This is not just a faster wireframe; it is a new creative loop where prompts become the handoff, the spec, and the prototype all at once. You can explore options without restarting from scratch. With minimal effort, you can inherit a cleaner structure, and the non-technical teammates finally can get a safe runway to try ideas respectively. In this section, we will break down a practical, end-to-end workflow for prompting in Framer using its AI feature: starting from creating an account to initiating with a blank canvas, scaffolding with wireframe elements, writing effective prompts, previewing and iterating live, and exporting to shareable or production-ready output with an example to ground it all. Let us dive in!

Step 1: Setting up an Account

Creating account and login is the first step to using Framer. Go to framer.com, click sign up and go through the account setup process. After that, you can log in.

Step 2: Starting with a Blank Canvas

Start by writing a clear, one-sentence goal for your page: What job should this page do? For example, you may want to build a landing page for your fintech product or capture newsletter emails. This intent guides your prompts and iterations. In Framer, start fresh to avoid inherited styles. Name the page meaningfully like **`MarketingPage Home - v0`** to track progress. Load brand colors and typography as tokens or set defaults upfront to align Framer AI outputs with your visual language from the start. That small prep step ensures that your AI output aligns with your visual language from the first render.

Step 3: Setting the Foundation

Add essential elements like logos, approved CTAs, or social icons to Framer AI before prompting. These elements act as anchor that guide the model's outputs. Keep it light; two or three elements are enough. Over-specifying can limit creativity. Name elements clearly like Primary CTA, Logo to preserve them in later iterations. This sets the stage for a collaborative process where the tool proposes structure, and you steer with intent.

Step 4: Composing Focused Prompt

Now, compose your prompt and paste in the Framer AI box. Crafting effective prompts by including three key elements: *structure*- sections, components, *purpose or goal of the page*, and *constraints* like accessibility, responsiveness, tone. For example, "*Create a fintech marketing page with a hero section, feature list, and call-to-action button in a responsive layout to drive sign-ups, keeping it accessible with clear typography.*" Focus on intent first, and layer in styles direction later. Use tone words like "fintech" or "minimal" to shape the design.

Step 5: Previewing the Output

When Framer AI generates the layout, skim it for overall shape and check if it meets key expectations: requested sections are present, visual hierarchy is clear, interactive elements are in expected places, and headings and body text feel balanced. Then, make quick edits on the canvas to refine the draft: adjust spacing, swap placeholders, and label edits clearly. The goal is to achieve enough coherence for the targeted prompts, such as "*increase hero heading*" or "*add card hover states*" to further refine the design.

Step 6: Refining with Iteration

Refine your design with iteration. Use clear, one-dimensional prompts to tweak elements like typography *increase hero text size*, alignment *center primary button*, background *add subtle gradient*, states *add hover states to project card*, and responsiveness *stack project cards on mobile*. With fast re-renders, maintain a creative flow: prompt, glance, tweak, repeat. Save versions at milestones and restate prompts more precisely if changes go off track, ensuring a smooth design process.

Step 7: Styling without Breaking Usability

Prioritize accessibility to ensure that usability is not compromised for aesthetics. Add accessibility constraints into your prompts or checklist, such as enforcing WCAG AA contrast, using semantic headings, adding visible focus rings, including `alt` text placeholders, and providing inline validation messages for forms. By making accessibility a non-optional constraint, you avoid costly rework and create an inclusive design from the start. Framer AI will respect these guidelines when asked, allowing you to design with both form and function in mind.

Step 8: Designing with Real Content

Use a realistic copy to test your layout. Replace `lorem ipsum` with proto-content: a concise tagline, project descriptions that highlight the problem and outcome, and actionable CTAs. If your copy is not ready, prompt Framer AI for placeholder content with specific constraints, such as "*Write a 10-word tagline for a fintech product designer.*" Then, refine the tone and language to ensure that the design holds up to real content. A layout that works with realistic copy will translate well to production.

Step 9: Adding Micro-Interactions

Add micro-interactions thoughtfully to improve user understanding, and not just for visual appeal. Use motion and feedback to guide users: like a subtle card lifts on hover, pressed states and loading spinners on clicks, and gentle section reveals on scroll. For empty states, provide helpful copy and clear next steps. Use prompts like "*apply consistent 150-200ms ease to hover and focus states*" to systematize interactions, and fine-tune with Framer's visual controls if needed.

Step 10: Publishing Your Design

When your page is ready, choose the right output for your next step: share a link for feedback, live publish or export code-ready artifacts for development. Before exporting, run a final checklist to ensure accessibility and quality: verify headings, alt text, contrast, CTAs, and mobile layout. Label your export clearly to indicate scope and readiness.

The real magic with Framer AI is not that it is fast, it is that it makes feedback visible. Instead of debating options in a slide deck, you test them live, someone in your team may says "*center the CTA, bump the hero, add a gradient,*" you prompt, and everyone sees the result. That shared artifact shortens cycles, reduces misinterpretation, and builds a prompt history that doubles as documentation.

Next, we aim to discuss essential to develop prompt-friendly design habits that translate effective prompts to production user interfaces.

Prompt-Friendly Design Habits

Prompt-friendly design is now a creative craft. You are teaching an AI system to think like a product designer with a clear intent, strong hierarchy, and enough constraints to avoid guesswork. James Clear, author of Atomic Habits writes, "*You do not rise to the level of your goals. You fall to the level of your systems.*" Clear's point is that outcomes follow processes. Goals set direction, but your daily routines, checklists, and environment determine what happens. If your system is weak, motivation and big goals will not save you. If your system is solid, results become the natural by-product. In prompt-driven development, treat great AI system outputs as the by-product of a repeatable system, your workflow, templates, and environment, not one-off clever prompts. Let us explore how you build a system that accelerates time to production and improves the quality of your design outcome.

Prompting with Constraints

AI model thrives on constraints. The loose prompts such as "Make a homepage" is an invitation to invent random sections. What about *"Make a homepage with a hero banner, navigation bar with four links, testimonial section, and footer with social icons"*? This approach narrows the search to proven patterns with a better output.

Not Preferred

"*Make a homepage.*"

Preferred

"*Make a homepage with a hero banner (headline, subhead, primary* CTA), *a top navigation with four links* (Home, Features, Pricing, Contact), *a testimonial section (3 quotes with avatars), and a footer with social icons.*"

Unspecific prompts like "*Make a homepage*" yield poor results, while detailed specifications ensure the output meets your needs. The latter preferred example demonstrates how clear direction and setting the boundary enables precise execution, thereby saving time and reducing revisions.

Thinking in Hierarchy

When composing effective prompts, you mirror the structure of the DOM: header, main, and footer, with sections within the main content area. Start by defining the skeleton of your design, outlining the layout and sections in order like header with logo and nav, hero, features grid, testimonials, pricing, FAQ, and footer. Once the structure is locked in, you can add details like visual styling, typography, and spacing, with precise instructions like "*apply a soft diagonal gradient to the hero*" or "*increase* H1 *scale by* 20%." This approach ensures that every stylistic change produces expected outcome, without reshuffling the entire layout. By following this prompt pattern, you will achieve better results. Define the layout skeleton, populate sections with minimal content, apply visual styling, and finally, add interactive states like hover and focus.

Leveraging Action Verbs

Let us consider prompts with action verbs. Verbs eliminate ambiguity. To compose effective prompts, use action verbs that clearly direct the action, like "create," "align," "apply," and "replace." This approach eliminates ambiguity and guarantee precise results. By using specific verbs like "center," "increase," "resize," and "group," you can define exactly what you want to achieve. For best results, treat each sentence as a single operation. You need to keep prompts re-rendering small and predictable. This verb-driven approach streamlines the design process and yields more accurate outcomes.

Prompting with Responsiveness in Mind

When designing for responsiveness, it is vital to define breakpoints upfront to avoid broken layouts on smaller screens. Embed responsive behavior into your prompts by specifying how elements should adapt across different screen sizes. For example, you can instruct the system to "*collapse a 3-column grid to 2 columns at 768px and 1 column at 480px*" or "*keep the CTA above the fold on mobile and stack hero content.*" Do not forget to consider key factors like grid behavior, image treatment, navigation, and form functionality. A well-composed prompt looks like this: "*Generate responsive variants for desktop, tablet, and mobile, collapsing grids and maintaining readable type scale, with primary CTAs visible without scrolling on mobile.*" If you do not specify, you are likely going to get a pretty desktop design with a broken mobile device display. Always bake behavior into your design prompt.

Improving Prompt Flow

Prompting is a step-by-step process that refines the output with each iteration. By breaking down design requirements into manageable chunks, you can achieve precise and polished results. Let us explore a system that streamlines your design process, reducing iterations and improving prompt flow.

v0 – Skeleton

"Create a SaaS homepage with header (logo + nav: Features, Pricing, Customers, Sign in), hero (headline, subhead, primary CTA), 3-card benefits grid, pricing (Starter, Pro, Enterprise), testimonials (3), FAQ (5 items), and footer with social icons. Goal: drive free trial signups. Ensure semantic headings and accessible contrast."

v1 – Content

"Use exact copy:

Hero H1: 'Build Faster with AI.'

Hero subtext: 'Design, preview, and publish in minutes.'

Primary CTA: 'Start free trial'.

Pricing: Starter $9, Pro $29, Enterprise $99 (monthly)."

v2 – Responsiveness

"Make the 3-card grid collapse to 1 column on mobile; ensure CTA stays above the fold. Add hamburger nav at <768px."

v3 – Style

"Apply a subtle top-left gradient, increase H1 by 20%, center the hero CTA, and add 150ms hover elevation to cards."

v4 – States

"Add loading states to CTA, focus outlines to links/buttons, and an empty FAQ state with a contact link."

As you can see, each pass is small, testable, and reversible. Thev0 to v4 represent different versions of a prompt or design iteration. Each version builds upon the previous one, refining the design requirements as follow:

- **v0:** Initial skeleton or structure
- **v1:** Adds content
- **v2:** Adds responsiveness
- **v3:** Adds styling
- **v4:** Adds interactive states

Interestingly, this design approach is not cast in stone. You can extend this process further to include additional stages, like v5: *adds animations or micro-interactions as this enhances user engagement and feedback*, v6: *refines accessibility features to ensure usability for diverse users and complies with accessibility standards*, v7: *implements dark mode or theme switching as this provides user preference options and improves readability*, v8: *adds error handling or edge cases to enforce robustness and reliability*, and v9: *finalizes and refines all design elements to guarantees a polished and cohesive user experience*. You can clearly adapt and expand this versioning system to fit your specific design needs and priorities. As we leverage AI to generate designs, it is important to acknowledge the limitations that come with relying on algorithms and models, a co-pilot engine. Now, we shall explore some of the challenges and constraints of AI-driven design, and how to work effectively within these obvious boundaries.

Limitations in AI Designs

It is easy and convenient to assume that AI will deliver production-ready interfaces on issuing a command. While AI-powered design tools can accelerate the process, they often require refinement and oversight to achieve the desired outcome. AI tools does well at recombining existing patterns, but often struggle with innovation, consistency, accessibility, and adaptability. Visual prompting can sketch a direction, but the translation to robust HTML/CSS/JS still needs your judgment, adjustments, and tests. As discussed previously, treat AI system like co-creator, an engine that is awesome at blocking in layouts and generating options while you are responsible for the standards, structure, and polished outcome. The goal is not to avoid AI system, it is to build a system around it that catches errors, closes gaps, and channels speed into production shippable quality. In this section, we will examine some of the limitations in visual prompting tools.

Gaps in Visual Prompting

The challenge with visual prompting lies in its inherent ambiguity. Instructions like "*make it modern and minimal*" can mean different things to different people, and even specific directives, such as "*create a three-tier pricing table*," leave room for loose interpretation. Visual prompting tools aim to streamline process with natural language, but they often struggle to fully grasp the subtleties of intent. Should the layout follow a strict grid system or a more fluid design? How many characters should the hero copy wrap at for optimal readability? Without precise design tokens, such as specific design system names, spacing scales, or semantic component labels, the AI system is left to make assumptions. While these assumptions can accelerate the initial design phase, they often introduce inconsistencies that require later refinement.

Inconsistency in Outputs

AI system like ChatGPT, Framer AI outputs can be unpredictable, even with identical prompts. The same instruction might yield different results across runs or model versions, affecting DOM structures, CSS class names, and spacing. For instance, asking for a three-column grid could produce perfectly aligned columns one time and inconsistent gutters the next. These small discrepancies can accumulate, resulting in visual noise like misaligned baselines, uneven padding, and inconsistent typography. In the code, this manifests as duplicated styles, deviations from your design system, and conflicting breakpoints. Without strict schema enforcement, such as specifying "*columns: 3, gap: token.spacing.md*," the time spent fixing inconsistencies can outweigh the benefits of using an AI-generated code.

The Limits of AI Creativity

In the AI ecosystem, creativity is often measured by the model's ability to generate novel combinations of existing patterns, but true originality and artistic intent can be harder to quantify. AI thrives in familiar territory like grids, cards, and standard layouts. However, when tasked with something more innovative, like "a fashion brand hero that feels abstract and editorial," it often defaults to safe, familiar patterns. The result might be a grid of tiles, carousel, or card stack, reflecting the model's training data rather than true creativity. To achieve a more art-driven design, you need to think overlapping typography, asymmetry, or kinetic interactions. You will need to provide specific guidance, like "*asymmetric layout with oversized typography and dominant negative space.*" Even then, a designer's touch is often necessary to push the AI beyond its comfort zone of familiar, predictable layouts. Even with its limits, AI creativity opens important opportunities for transformation. It helps teams explore more ideas faster, prototype with less friction, and shift effort from repetitive first-draft work toward refinement, judgment, and strategic direction. This makes creativity more iterative, collaborative, and accessible across both technical and non-technical teams.

Understanding Accessibility Challenges

Sometimes, AI-generated outputs often fall short on accessibility standards. Common issues include missing ARIA roles, skipped landmark semantics, and inadequate color contrast, which can become more pronounced when placeholder content is replaced with real data. Buttons might be incorrectly implemented as styled `<div>`elements, modals might lack focus traps, and heading levels might be used inconsistently for stylistic purposes rather than semantic structure. Color choices that look good in one context can fail WCAG AA compliance in others, such as during hover states or on different backgrounds. Features like screen reader text, skip links, and proper form labels are often inconsistent unless explicitly prompted. To ensure accessibility, you need to thoroughly review AI outputs using automated audits like Lighthouse, validate heading structures, verify focus order, and conduct manual testing with keyboard navigation and screen readers.

Understanding Superficial Responsiveness

While many AI design tools claim to generate responsive layouts, they often stop at surface-level adjustments. A grid might collapse into a single column at an arbitrary breakpoint, or media and text sections might stack without consideration for content hierarchy, readability, or user experience. True responsiveness requires a deeper understanding of content, type scales adjusting dynamically, spacing adapting to screen size, complex components reorganizing or simplifying, and images are directed for each breakpoint. AI-generated CSS often creates a mess of custom media queries that may not match your design system's standard breakpoints. To achieve cohesive responsiveness, you will need to refactor these into a logical set of breakpoints and rewrite layout logic using container queries, min/max clamps, and other techniques that ensure a smooth experience across devices.

Overall, use AI design tools for speed, ideation, scaffolding, and repetitive markup, but never surrender a careful output review. The productive pattern is the AI draft; you set up automated checks, then implement human in the loop system for human critique and system merge. Start by encoding your rules, tokens, components, accessibility into the prompt and the validator so quality becomes the default. Expect to refactor, normalize spacing, align semantics, tune breakpoints, and swap proprietary bits for your system. Over time, you tend to keep a golden set of examples and failures, promote only those prompts that pass acceptable accessibility, responsiveness, and portability standard. This is how you carefully leverage AI's velocity while shipping designs you can maintain in production.

Conclusion

In this chapter, we discussed how effective visual prompting turns AI from novelty into dependable design muscle. When you encode structure, tokens, interactions, and acceptance criteria, tools such as Framer AI produce layouts that read well, adapt across viewports, and respect accessibility. Pair disciplined prompts with rigorous review and small, targeted iterations, and you will ship faster with clearer collaboration and interfaces users can trust. In the next chapter, we shall turn an AI-generated code into a fully functional, publicly accessible website. With this step, you can bridge the gap between the theoretical AI-generated code and practical, real-world application development and deployment.

Points to Remember

- Start every prompt with purpose, audience, and success metric.
- Use tokens (color, roles, spacing, type) instead of hard-coded values.
- Specify sections, components, states, and acceptance criteria explicitly.
- Enforce accessibility: single H1, logical headings, focus visibility, WCAG AA contrast.
- Declare responsive behavior and breakpoints up front.
- Favor action verbs; one operation per sentence; version in small deltas.
- Audit before export: semantics, keyboard flow, contrast, responsiveness, and performance.
- Keep a prompt history as living documentation for hand-off.

Multiple Choice Questions

1. Which of the following is the primary benefit of visual prompting?
    a. More decorative effects
    b. Clear translation of intent into structured outputs
    c. Fewer layout options
    d. Elimination of reviews
2. Which item should be included in a Framer AI prompt?
    a. Random color names
    b. Page purpose, sections, tokens, and acceptance criteria
    c. Only screenshots
    d. File system paths
3. Which practice improves accessibility in generated layouts?
    a. Multiple H1 elements per page
    b. Single H1 with logical heading levels

   c. Headings styled as paragraphs
   d. Removing headings
4. Which token choice best preserves theming?
   a. Hex values embedded everywhere
   b. CSS variables mapped to roles and scales
   c. Inline styles per element
   d. Images for text
5. Which acceptance criterion is most relevant for color?
   a. Brand hue only
   b. Contrast ratios that meet or exceed standards
   c. Long gradients on every section
   d. Randomized palettes
6. What should a guided hero prompt require for CTAs?
   a. Vague labels
   b. Accessible text and focus styles
   c. Hidden buttons
   d. Image-only buttons
7. Which statement about AI limitations is accurate?
   a. AI always matches brand nuance.
   b. AI may produce inaccessible interactions.
   c. AI never repeats defaults.
   d. AI guarantees perfect semantics.
8. Which iteration tactic is most effective?
   a. Rewrite the entire design each time.
   b. Issue small, targeted prompt deltas.
   c. Avoid documenting changes.
   d. Ignore acceptance tests.
9. Which performance note is appropriate for hero images?
   a. Disable responsive images.
   b. Require srcset and size constraints.

   c. Use full-resolution images on mobile.
   d. Block rendering for analytics.

10. Which prompt element best supports reuse?
    a. Flattened layers
    b. Reusable components with named parts
    c. Rasterized text
    d. Absolute positioning everywhere
11. What should review checklists verify?
    a. Only visual alignment
    b. Semantics, keyboard flow, contrast, responsiveness, and load time
    c. Animation count
    d. File name length
12. Which constraint guards motion-sensitive users?
    a. Longer animations
    b. Disabling focus outlines
    c. Reduced-motion handling with simplified states
    d. Hover-only interactions

Answers

1. b
2. b
3. b
4. b
5. b
6. b
7. b
8. b
9. b
10. b
11. b
12. c

Key Terms

- **Applied Prompt Workflow:** A repeatable process for scoping goals, encoding constraints, and iterating prompts toward production-ready outputs.
- **Visual Prompting:** Using natural-language instructions to direct AI design tools to create layouts, components, and states.
- **Tokens:** Named design variables (for example, color roles, spacing scale, type scale) used to ensure consistency across outputs.
- **Acceptance Criteria:** Measurable checks (semantics, contrast ratios, keyboard flow, responsiveness, and performance budgets) used to evaluate AI outputs.
- **Prompt Delta:** A small, targeted change to a prompt that modifies one aspect of the design to keep iterations predictable.
- **Component Tree:** The structured hierarchy of UI parts (such as `<Page>→<Header>→<Nav>`), mirroring implementation semantics.
- **Micro-interaction:** Small, purposeful UI motions or feedback (hover, focus, loading) that clarify state changes.
- **WCAG AA:** Accessibility contrast and behavior standards ensuring legibility and operability for diverse users.
- **Responsive Rules:** Declarative behaviors across breakpoints that govern stacking, scaling, and layout adaptation.
- **Prompt-Friendly Habits:** Practices (constraints, hierarchy, verbs, versioning) that yield consistent, high-quality AI design outputs.

CHAPTER 11
From AI Code to Live Website

Introduction

In *Chapter 10: Visual Prompting in Design Tools*, we introduced visual prompting and the emerging best practice of guiding design tools like Framer AI and others using natural language commands to execute design ideas. In this chapter, you are guided through the deployment pipeline that turns AI-generated code into a fully functional, publicly accessible website. While AI tools can generate functional HTML and CSS, production-ready deployment still requires a developer's attention to detail, cleanup, and environment setup. You will learn how to export, review, and clean up AI-generated code to meet industry standards. This chapter introduces GitHub basics, showing how to organize your project repository and push updates to version control. It then guides readers through deploying with Vercel, a popular platform for hosting frontend projects. You will end up with a live, mobile-responsive website built using prompt-driven development.

After reading this chapter, you will be able to export AI-generated code, refine and optimize it through cleanup and best practices, understand the fundamentals of GitHub for deployment purposes, and successfully deploy your project using Vercel, resulting in a live and mobile-responsive web application.

Structure

In this chapter, we will cover the following topics:

- Exporting AI-Generated Code
- Cleaning up the Code
- GitHub Basics for Deployment
- Deploying with Vercel

Exporting AI-Generated Code

In the current era, AI tools can compose your UI components, no doubt. Yet, the export stage sets the tone for everything that follows. In *Chapter 9: Applied Prompt Workflows*, we had generated a fintech landing page from ChatGPT. Now, your goal is to start the process of going live, you extract cleancode in a format suitable for integration and deployment. In this section, we will focus on exporting pure HTML and CSS, ideal for simple static websites. The fintech landing page will be deployed live.You will start by choosing the export that best matches your stack like plain HTML/CSS that this book focuses on. One of the significant advantages of pure HTML and CSS exports is the lack of dependencies or frameworks. This reduces the risk of compatibility issues or version conflicts. This approach also allows for effortless customization, as you can directly edit the HTML and CSS files without worrying about complex build processes or compilation steps. It is important to note that search engines tend to favor static sites, which can improve your page's visibility and ranking. There are a couple of best practices when exporting pure HTML and CSS like determining the export format, verifying your asset packaging and mobile responsiveness. Let us start a brief discussion on acceptable format for our project and how this is done.

Exporting the Right Format

While our focus in this book is pure HTML and CSS output, it appears noteworthy that other export formats can be suitable for specific use cases as well. For instance, if you plan to add interactivity to your fintech marketing page, such as pricing toggles or lead capture forms, a JavaScript-heavy approach like Vue or React might be more suitable. Similarly, if you are building a more complex application that requires server-side rendering, image optimization, or internationalization, Next.js can be considered a better fit. Now that you have decided on the static HTML/CSS, open VS code, copy and paste the code snippet from ChatGPT, then save your file as .html for the webpage and .css for the styles. You can also instruct ChatGPT to make the final output a download HTML and/or CSS file, depending on your preference. With this right away download, you do not need to copy and paste code snippets anymore. Next, we shall explore how you handle your digital assets, typography and brand color.

Verifying Assets, Typography, and Brand Color

It is essential to ensure that your assets, including logos, icons, and device renders, are correctly linked to their respective paths. This step is vital in preventing broken links and guaranteeing your page renders flawlessly across various environments. Next, define your brand's typography and color palette to maintain consistency throughout the exported code. Use stable font names and hex codes to ensure visual coherence. By doing so, you will be able to create a professional-looking web page that is not only visually appealing but also easy to maintain and deploy. This attention to detail will ultimately improve your brand's overall image and user experience. Overall, make sure that your AI generated output adheres to the best practices as follows:

- To maintain a clean and efficient project structure, it is important to keep static assets in designated folders. Store assets like images, favicons, robots.txt
  In the **`/public/`** folder
- Optimize your images for web use by converting hero images to WebP/AVIF and keep a PNG fallback if needed.
- Check relative paths like **`./images/device.webp`** and make sure they resolve locally. This is crucial because it ensures that your assets, such as images, are correctly linked and loaded.

This approach ensures easy access, clear organization, and simplified deployment, making it easier to manage your web project.

Mobile Responsiveness

Mobile responsiveness is one another key aspect to consider. Since most users access websites through mobile devices, testing your exported code on smaller screens is vital to ensure a seamless user experience. To achieve this, use relative units like percentages or viewport units to define layout dimensions. Additionally, make sure your media queries are correctly set up to handle different screen sizes. If you are looking for a simple, fast, and lightweight solution that gives you full control over your code, pure HTML and CSS is an excellent choice. By following the best practices which includes validating asset paths, locking down fonts and colors, and testing on small screens, you will be able to maintain and deploy your website project. Ultimately, exporting pure HTML and CSS can be a straightforward and efficient way to bring your UI components to life. By understanding the strengths and limitations of this approach, you can create fast, lightweight, and easily maintainable web pages across different projects and industry.

Note: *From raw snippets (ChatGPT), copy HTML/CSS/JS into separate files; avoid inline <style> if possible.*

Now you have got a working export format, assets links path set correctly, and a folder that builds locally; next, we will clean the code, so it is semantic, accessible, and production-grade.

Cleaning up the Code

Cleaning up the code is a vital step in taking an AI-generated code draft and turning it into a professional-grade build.As for the fintech marketing page, prioritize semantics like screen reader clarity, accessibility such as focus states, contrast, and performance based on image format, and how fonts are served. Replace generic **`<div>`** piles with **`<header>`**, **`<nav>`**, **`<main>`**, **`<section>`**, and **`<footer>`**. Avoid inline styles and put your CSS code into a shared stylesheet. Make the hero responsive with fluid typography and keep the device imagery crisp with object fit. Ensure the lead form uses native inputs, labels, and helpful error messages. Finally, wire up a minimal toolchain like *Prettier*, *ESLint*, and *Stylelint* enforce consistency in your projects even before you touch Git. With this approach, your clean code will be easier to review, deploy, and roll back if something goes south ways. Next, we ensure that the final output pass sematic and accessibility checks.

Semantic and Accessibility

Semantics in web development means using HTML elements according to their real meaning and purpose. For instance, using **`<header>`**, **`<nav>`**, **`<main>`**, **`<section>`**, **`<article>`**, and **`<footer>`** provides structure to a page in a way that browsers, screen readers, and search engines can understand. This directly supports the Search Engine Optimization (SEO) layer because search engines use semantic structure to better interpretcontent, hierarchy, and relevance of a page. In other words, good semantics improves accessibility for users, and resultant clarity for search engines, making your site easier to navigate and easier to discover. A well-structured codebase is vital for accessibility and search engine optimization. These are some key considerations to ensure AI generated codes follow the semantic structure and accessibility essentials:

- Use one **`<h1>`** tag and maintain a logical heading order (H2, H3, etc.) to improve screen reader clarity.
- Bind labels to inputs using the **`for`** attribute and **`id`**, provide clear error text, and ensure visible focus rings for better accessibility.
- Use **`aria-live="polite"`** to provide feedback to screen readers during form submission.
- Use native **`<button>`** and **`<a href>`** elements. These are keyboard-friendly by default.

To improve accessibility, use semantic HTML elements correctly, as landmarks like **`<header>, <nav>, <main>,`** and **`<footer>`** help assistive tech navigate the page. Headings **`<h1>-<h6>`** should form a logical outline, with one `<h1>`per page and no skipped levels. By incorporating these elements, along with properly structured lists, buttons, images, tables, and forms, you can create a more accessible and user-friendly experience for all users. Additionally, web accessibility means building content and interfaces that everyone can perceive, operate, understand, and use regardless of ability, device, or context. Start with semantic HTML, proper labels and `alt` text, predictable keyboard focuses and interactions, sufficient color contrast, and resilient layouts that work with zoom, dark mode, and reduced motion. Use ARIA only to fill gaps, never replace native elements, provide clear errors and status messages, and test with keyboard, screen readers, and automated checkers.

CSS Consolidation and Fluid Layout

CSS consolidation is about creating a lean, predictable, and reusable stylesheet. This approach not only simplifies maintenance but also improves the performance of your website. In the present era, building websites that are both visually appealing and highly functional across various devices and screen sizes is vital. Two key strategies that can significantly improve the maintainability and responsiveness of your code are CSS consolidation and fluid layouts. When you adopt best practices in these areas, you can ensure that your websites are adaptable, efficient, and provide a smooth user experience. These are some best practices that increase maintainability and improve responsiveness:

- Store colors and spacing as CSS variables to promote consistency and reusability. For instance, storing colors, spacing, and other design elements as CSS variables in the `:root` pseudo-class as follows.

  ```
  :root {
  --primary-color: #333;
  --secondary-color: #666;
  --spacing: 1rem;}
  ```

  This approach promotes consistency across your website and makes updates more manageable.

- Replace fixed widths with max-width and margin-inline: auto to create a responsive layout.
- Use **`font-size: clamp()`** to create fluid typography that adapts to different screen sizes. For example:

Fluid layouts allow your website's components to adapt gracefully to different screen sizes and devices. Grid is ideal for creating complex, two-dimensional layouts. While flexbox is better suited for one-dimensional layouts that allow elements to adapt and align properly. Take a look at this example:

```
.container {display: grid; grid-template-columns: repeat(12, 1fr); gap:
var(--spacing);}
.item {grid-column: span 6;}
```

The preceding code creates a 12-column grid layout with a gap between cells defined by the **`-spacing`** variable. Each **`.item`** element will occupy 6 columns of the grid, effectively taking up half of the available width since 6 columns out of 12 is half. For example, if the **`.container`** is 1200px wide, each column would be approximately 100px wide (1200px / 12 columns). The **`.item`** element would then occupy 600px (6 columns x 100px per column). This grid layout is commonly used in responsive design to create flexible and adaptable layouts that work well on different screen sizes. With our code now optimized for performance and maintainability, let us add collaboration and version control mix with GitHub. By leveraging GitHub's features, we can further improve our development workflow, code quality, and ensure a seamless deployment process.

GitHub Basics for Deployment

GitHub is a cloud-based platform for version control and collaboration, allowing developers to host, manage, and track changes to their codebase using Git. It simply allows developers to work together, track changes, and contribute to projects, while also providing features like bug tracking, project management, and code review tools. GitHub is your deployment control room. You will initialize the repository, push your fintech marketing page, and adopt a lightweight branch strategy that pairs well with Vercel's deployments. The main branch represents production. This workflow makes feedback fast and safe, and it is perfect for marketing iterations. With GitHub wired, deployments become routine instead of stressful. Before we push our code to GitHub and eventual deployment to Vercel, let us explore some of the core concepts in software version control and collaboration as follows:

- **Commits:** A commit is a snapshot of changes made to the codebase. When you make changes to your web page, you commit the changes. In essence, you are recording a new version of the code. Best practices for commits include writing clear and concise commit messages, keeping commits small and focused on a single change, using imperative mood in commit messages like *fix bug* instead of *fixed bug.*

- **Pull Requests (PRs):** A pull request is a way to propose changes to a repository. It allows you to review changes, discuss them with others or your team, and ensure that the changes are tested and validated before they are merged into the main codebase. To create a PR, you will need to create a new branch for your changes, commit your changes to the branch, then open a pull request to merge your branch into the main branch.

- **Issues:** In GitHub, issues are a way to track bugs, enhancements, or other tasks in a repository. They can be used to report bugs or issues, propose new features or enhancements, track progress on tasks, and assign tasks to team members.

- **Branches:** In GitHub, branches are separate lines of development in a repository. They allow you to work on different features or fixes independently without affecting the main codebase. Common branch types are feature branches like **`feat/new-feature`** for developing new features, fix branches like **`fix/bug-fix`** for bug fixes, and release branches like **`release/v1.0`** for preparing and maintaining releases.

In a nutshell, all these concepts allow developers to track changes to their codebase, making it easier to collaborate and manage different versions of their software.

Now, we will open fintech marketing page directory in a terminal and push codes to GitHub. We will start with installing Git. A git is a tool on your system that manages versions.

For linux OS:

Open terminal and run **`sudodnf install git-all`** or **`sudo apt install git-all`** if you are using Debian / Ubuntu linux derivatives.

For a macOS

Open terminal and run **`git -version`** or you download and install from **`https://git-scm.com/downloads/mac`**

For windows OS

Download Git for windows from the Git website and run the installer, default options are fine for most users: **`https://git-scm.com/downloads/win`**

Next, we will push web page-index.html to repository.

Step 1: Run **`git -version`** to make sure Git is properly installed

The create account if you are a new GitHub user. Then, go to repositories and create new repository. The following screenshot shows the last page of repository creation as follows:

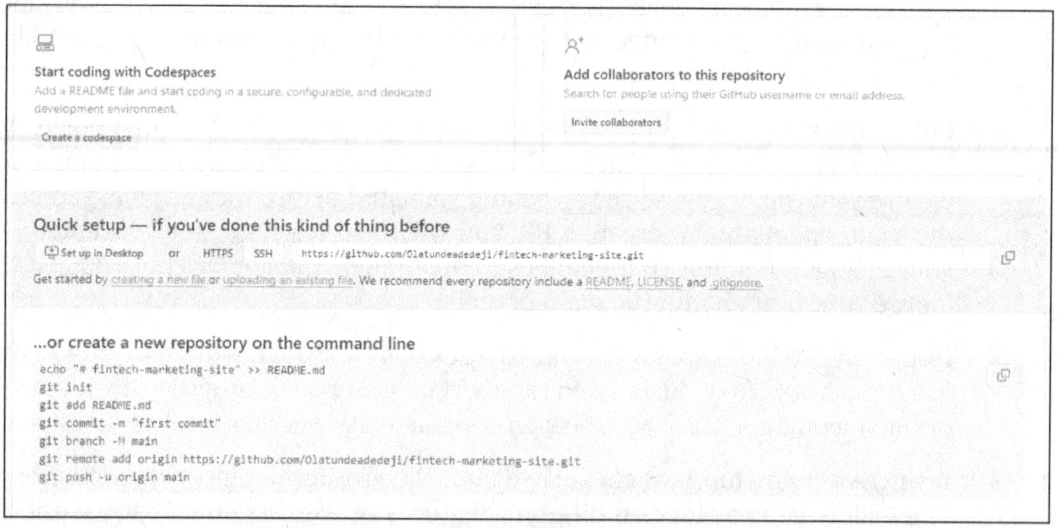

Figure 11.1: *Screenshot Showing GitHub Repository Setup*

Note the repository URL or path, https://github.com/<yourusername>/fintech-marketing-site.git. You will need it later.

Step 2: Initialize, commit, push

Open your terminal in your project directory and run the following:

- `gitinit&&git branch -m main`
- `git add .`
- `git commit -m "core: import fintech marketing page "`
- `git remote add origin https://github.com/<yourusername>/fintech-marketing-site.git`
- `git push -u origin main` (If your repository is not found, you will get error, `remote: Repository not found.`)

In the preceding steps, you are able to initialize a Git repository and push your project to GitHub. By following these GitHub basics, you now have a solid foundation for the fintech marketing page enabled for fast feedback, safe deployments, and efficient collaboration.

Now that GitHub is set up, we will integrate it with Vercel, allowing for efficient and secure production deployment.

Note: *In GitHub, a well-structured commit message is vital for effective version control and collaboration, as it clearly communicates changes to team members and helps track project history.*

Deploying with Vercel

Deployment simply refers to the process of making a website or application live and accessible to users. It involves uploading code to a server, configuring settings, and ensuring everything works as expected. Vercel is a smart choice for quick deployment due to its seamless integration with GitHub, automatic code optimization, and secure HTTPS provisioning. With Vercel, you can deploy fast, scalable, secure websites and applications with ease. You can leverage features like preview deployments, rollbacks, and performance monitoring. With these features, you are able to focus on building website while Vercel handles the deployment complexity. In this section, we ship fintech marketing page to production steps as follows:

1. **Step 1: Creating a Vercel Account or Login**

   Go to *www.vercel.com*and sign up for a new account or log in if you already have one.Choose your preferred sign-up method like email, GitHub, GitLab, or Bitbucket.

2. **Step 2: Importing fintech marking page project**

   Create a new project in Vercel with `Add new` button and import your GitHub repository.Ensure your **`index.html`** file is in the root directory.

3. **Step 3: Configuring settings**

   In Vercel Project Settings, set the **Output Directory** to the folder containing your `index.html` file.

4. **Step 4: Deploy**

   i. Vercel will automatically deploy your site on push to the main branch.

   ii. Preview deployments will be generated for every branch push.

   iii. A live link is generated like https://fintech-marketing-site.vercel.app/

The preceding steps ensure automatic HTTPS provisioning, and fast and secure deployment. With these steps, your static HTML site will be live and accessible by public users.

Conclusion

In this chapter, we guided you through how to transform AI-generated code into a live, reliable website. We started by selecting the right export format, such as HTML/CSS for simple static sites, and verified assets and brand tokens to ensure consistency. To make the code semantic and accessible, we implemented proper landmarks, headings, labels, and focus states. We then consolidated CSS using variables, adopted fluid typography, and built responsive layouts with grid and flexbox. With version control in place using Git and GitHub, we maintained clear commits and a simple branch model. Finally, we connected the repository to Vercel, enabling automatic deployments to production and preview deployments for branch pushes. The outcome is a lightweight, maintainable, and mobile-first marketing site, along with a repeatable pipeline for future projects. This streamlined process sets the foundation for efficient development and scalability.

In the next chapter, we will discuss AI hallucinations and dive deeper into a pivotal process of refining an AI-generated frontend code.

Points to Remember

- Use plain HTML/CSS exports for simple static sites to minimize dependencies and avoid unexpected issues.
- Keep assets organized in a dedicated folder like /public and use relative paths such as `./images/device.webp` for seamless maintenance.
- Define typography and color tokens with stable font names and hex codes to ensure design consistency.
- Design mobile-first and test on narrow viewports to prioritize user experience on smaller screens.

- Implement semantic HTML landmarks and maintain a logical heading outline with one `<h1>` per page for better accessibility.
- Bind labels to inputs, preserve focus rings, and use native controls to enhance form accessibility.
- Use CSS variables for design tokens and avoid fixed widths; instead, use max-width and auto margins for flexible layouts.
- Apply **`clamp()`** for fluid typography and combine Grid and Flexbox for responsive, adaptable layouts.
- Make small, focused commits with clear and descriptive messages to track changes effectively.
- Initialize a Git repository, add a remote, and push to GitHub, then use pull requests for code review and collaboration.
- Connect your GitHub repository to Vercel to enable automated previews and production deployments.
- Test your site with keyboard and screen readers and use ARIA attributes only when necessary to fill accessibility gaps.

Multiple Choice Questions

1. For a simple static marketing site, which export is usually best?
    a. React + Redux SPA
    b. Next.js SSR
    c. Plain HTML/CSS
    d. Vue + Vuex
2. Why verify relative asset paths like `./images/device.webp`?
    a. Faster DNS
    b. Prevent broken images across environments
    c. Smaller CSS
    d. HTTP/3
3. Which practice most improves form accessibility?
    a. Placeholder-only context
    b. Custom div inputs
    c. Hiding focus rings
    d. Labels bound with for/id + visible focus

4. Recommended `<h1>` usage per page:
    a. Many
    b. Zero
    c. Exactly one
    d. Depends on design
5. When should ARIA be used?
    a. To replace native elements
    b. Only to fill semantic gaps
    c. For styling
    d. SEO only
6. Best way to centralize design tokens:
    a. Inline styles
    b. Many !importants
    c. IDs everywhere
    d. CSS variables in :root
7. Best tool for two-dimensional layouts:
    a. CSS Grid
    b. Flexbox
    c. Absolute positioning
    d. Tables
8. Good pattern for fluid typography:
    a. font-size: 16px everywhere
    b. Only media queries
    c. font-size: clamp (min, pref, max)
    d. VW units only
9. A focused commit message example:
    a. Update
    b. Stuff
    c. core: import fintech marketing page
    d. Fixed

10. If gitinit put you on master but you want main:
    a. Do nothing.
    b. Delete repo.
    c. git branch -m main.
    d. git checkout master -b main.
11. Which of the following GitHub feature is used to discuss and review changes before merge?
    a. Issues
    b. Pull Requests
    c. Releases
    d. Actions
12. How are Vercel preview deployments typically created?
    a. Automatically for every branch push
    b. Manual only
    c. Tags only
    d. Not supported

Answers

1. c
2. b
3. d
4. c
5. b
6. d
7. a
8. c
9. c
10. c
11. b
12. a

Key Terms

- **Export format (HTML/CSS):** Framework-free markup and styles for simple static hosting, ensuring lightweight and fast page loads.
- **Semantic HTML:** Using structural elements like `<header>`, `<nav>`, `<main>`, `<section>`, and `<footer>` to define content hierarchy and improve accessibility for assistive technologies.
- **Accessibility (a11y):** Best practices to ensure content is usable by everyone, including proper labels, focus management, contrast ratios, and strategic use of ARIA attributes.
- **CSS Variables:** Tokenizing design elements like colors and spacing for consistency and easy maintenance, allowing for global style updates with minimal code changes.
- **Fluid Typography (clamp):** Scaling text between minimum, ideal, and maximum sizes to create responsive typography that adapts to different screen sizes and devices.
- **Grid vs. Flexbox:** Grid for two-dimensional layouts and Flexbox for one-dimensional alignment, choosing the right tool for the job to create flexible and responsive designs.
- **Commit:** A snapshot of changes with a clear and focused message, providing context and tracking progress in version control.
- **Branch:** A separate line of development like feat/*, fix/*for isolating features or fixes, enabling parallel development and organized workflows.
- **Pull Request (PR):** A proposal to merge changes, facilitating discussion, review, and feedback before integrating code into the main branch.
- **Issues:** GitHub's built-in bug and task tracker for managing project tasks, tracking progress, and collaborating with team members.
- **Vercel:** A hosting platform that integrates seamlessly with GitHub, providing automated previews for branch pushes and production deployments from the main branch.
- **GitHub Push:** The basic steps to push code to GitHub: `gitinit, git add ., git commit, git remote add origin <url>,`and `git push -u origin main,` establishing a connection between local and remote repositories.

CHAPTER 12
Refining AI-Generated Code

Introduction

The Chapter 11: *From AI Code to Live Website*, proves that we can ship an AI generated code to live production where other users can view our craft. AI can sketch a usable page in seconds, but production-ready frontend code still requires a careful human in the middle approach. In this chapter, you will level up with turning AI-generated HTML and CSS into robust, semantic, accessible, and fast pages. You will learn to spot common AI hallucinations and subtle inconsistencies; apply systematic fixes for semantics, ARIA, color contrast, and responsive layout; and tune performance with practical, low-risk optimizations. You will also refine your prompts, so the next AI code starts getting closer to your acceptable standards. By the end of this chapter, you will have a repeatable prompting approach to reviewing, refining, and verifying with humans in the loop that converts raw AI composition into a polished production-grade frontend.

After reading this chapter, you will be able to understand how to spot and prevent structural issues in HTML, such as invalid elements, duplicate IDs, and broken labels, ensuring robust and reliable web development. You will also learn to refactor AI-generated HTML/CSS into semantic, accessible, and performant components, leveraging clear landmarks, correct ARIA attributes, and valid properties. Additionally, you will discover how to apply prompt revision patterns with guardrails, constraints, and self-checks to iteratively improve output quality. You will also become proficient in using quick validation routines, such as HTML validators and DevTools, to catch potential risks and errors. Finally, you will learn to effectively divide work in a human-AI collaborative workflow, where humans set intent, review edge cases, and provide feedback, while AI composes, self-audits, and refines its output based on updated rules.

Structure

In this chapter, we will cover the following topics:

- Understanding AI Hallucinations
- Prompt Revision Patterns
- Human versus AI Comparison

Understanding AI Hallucinations

AI hallucinates when it produces an output that looks possible, but is false. The model is not lying. It is predicting the next tokens. Typically, AI model predicts the next most likely tokens based on patterns, not facts. In coding, this yields fake properties, elements, or patterns. Eventually, you have code output that compiles in your head, but not in the browser. The page can break, or sometimes it and fails silently. This is a behavior that we do not expect from our code. Early language models had good time with hallucination. They were trained to continue next token or text, not to verify facts. As training corpora and parameters grew, models' fluency improved, and confidence increased, but precision did not keep up. Tools were added like retrieval, function calling, and code interpreters, yet the core hallucination behavior remains. If the model doe does not know, it will guess, and it will guess based on the patterns in the data. This behavior is the seed of hallucination, where models generate possible sounding but inaccurate information. Interestingly, coding tools have definitely helped with formatting, linting, and unit testing. However, when it comes to HTML and CSS, the lack of rigorous testing can be risky. A single error can cascade, and model self-created attributes or elements might look right but are not grounded in knownW3C (World Wide Web Consortium) standard. It is like the model is tempted to even create custom elements that sound possible, but do not exist. The complexity of HTML and CSS evolution contributes to hallucinations. Mixed signals in training data, where specs propose features, browsers implement them unevenly, and blog posts showcase different possibilities. All these mean models learn patterns, not implementation status. When you have not too clear prompts, they lead to assumptions, causing models to fill in gaps with possible but potentially incorrect details. Next, we will discuss the challenge of structural hallucinations where AI models generate code that appears possible but violates vital structural rules that affect semantics and accessibility expectations.

Structural Hallucinations

Structural hallucinations in HTML refer to issues like incorrect semantic markup, duplicate IDs, and broken label/input associations or heading skips. These problems hinder screen reader navigation, form usability, and website outline structure, which consequentially may affect site Search Engine Optimizations (SEO). Fixing these errors improves user experience, website accessibility, and search engine rankings. This ensures websites are functional and accessible to everyone. Let explore both the structural hallucination in HTML and how to spot and fix them. Proper HTML structure is essential. AI model can output a bad HTML example-hallucination. The issues are identified in red as follows:

```
<!DOCTYPE html>
<html>
<head>
<meta charset="utf-8">
<!-- bogus meta -->
<meta name="viewport" content="responsive">
<!-- phantom component and attribute -->
<card theme="glass" elevation="3">
<title>Acme</title>
</card>
</head>
<body>
<!-- invented element and invalid nesting -->
<stack>
<a href="/pricing">
<button>Pricing</button>
</a>
</stack>

<!-- framework bleed and duplicated ids -->
<div id="hero" class="container mx-auto btn btn-primary">
<p id="hero">Welcome!</p>
</div>

<!-- invented ARIA role -->
<nav role="navigation-bar">
<div role="menuitem">Home</div>
</nav>

<!-- lazy on div does nothing -->
<div loading="lazy">Big image soon</div>
</body>
</html>
```

The preceding code shows that the HTML code has issues with non-standard elements and attributes, such as **`<card>`** and **`theme="glass"`.** There is also invalid nesting, like a **`<button>`** inside an **`<a>`** tag. The code has a duplicated id attribute "hero" and framework class bleed. Additionally, the ARIA roles used are invalid, and the loading attribute on a div element is ineffective.

Now, let us examine how we fix it.

Fixed HTML Output:

```
<!DOCTYPE html>
<html lang="en">
<head>
<meta charset="utf-8">
<!-- correct meta -->
<meta name="viewport" content="width=device-width, initial-scale=1">
<title>Acme</title>
<!-- remove phantom components; keep head clean -->
</head>
<body>
<!-- valid nesting; link styled like a button via CSS -->
<nav aria-label="Primary">
<ul>
<li><a class="btn" href="/pricing">Pricing</a></li>
</ul>
</nav>

<!-- unique IDs; avoid framework classes unless included -->
<section id="hero">
<p>Welcome!</p>
</section>

<!-- correct ARIA role usage -->
<nav aria-label="Utility">
<ul>
<li><a href="/">Home</a></li>
</ul>
</nav>

<!-- use <img> for lazy loading -->
<figure>
<img src="big.jpg" alt="Product hero" loading="lazy">
<figcaption>Our latest release.</figcaption>
</figure>
</body>
</html>
```

In the preceding code snippet, the HTML code is well-structured and follows best practices. The head section is clean, and the body contains valid nesting, unique IDs, and correct ARIA role usage. The link is styled like a button via CSS, and lazy loading is properly implemented using the **img** tag with the loading attribute. The code is also semantic and accessible.

Now, we explore styling and layout hallucinations where AI models create visually appealing but structurally inconsistent designs, deviating from specified styles and layouts.

Styling and Layout Hallucinations

Styling and layout hallucinations occur when CSS targets non-existent elements or uses overly complex selectors, those selectors that are dependent on a specific HTML structure. This can lead to styles silently failing and small edits causing unintended regressions. To avoid this, it is vital to match CSS selectors with actual markup and flatten specificity. With this, styles become more maintainable and less prone to errors. Let us explore some the typical hallucinations in CSS and how to fix them.

```
.hero {text-color: #222; display: inline-block-flex; border-radius-y:
12px;  gap-y: 24px; }
.nav {  & a {    color: var(--link);}}.card {  background: var(--
surface);  backdrop-filter: blur(10px);}
.gallery {display: grid;grid-template: masonry;}
```

The preceding CSS code contains non-existent properties like **`text-color`**, **`border-radius-y`**, **`gap-y`**, invalid syntax (Sass-style nesting in a **`.css`** file), undeclared variables (**`--surface`**), and experimental properties without fallbacks (backdrop-filter). The grid masonry syntax is also not supported in standard CSS, resulting in potential layout issues.

Now, let us examine a fixed example as follows:

```
.hero {  color: #222; display: inline-flex;   border-radius: 12px;  row-
gap: 24px; }
.nav a {  color: var(--link, #0a58ca); }
:root {  --surface: rgba(255, 255, 255, 0.6);}
.card {  background: var(--surface);  background-color: rgba(255, 255,
255, 0.85);  backdrop-filter: blur(10px);}
.gallery {  display: grid;  grid-template-columns: repeat(auto-fill,
minmax(16rem, 1fr));  gap: 1rem;}
```

The aforesaid fixes address the issues by using valid CSS properties and syntax. Key changes include replacing non-existent properties with correct ones, defining the --surface variable, providing a fallback for var(--link), and adding a supported grid layout for the gallery. The backdrop-filter now has a fallback background-color for better compatibility.

Moreover, it is important to know how to detect hallucinations in HTML and CSS. Always perform simple and repeatable checks on HTML ad CSS code. Validate HTML using the W3C validator (https://validator.w3.org/) to catch errors like unknown elements and duplicate IDs. Lint CSS with Stylelint identify unknown properties and values. Use DevTools to inspect console errors, crossed-out styles, and computed styles. Also, check for framework bleed, audit ARIA roles and attributes, and ensure that CSS variables have declarations or fallbacks. Cross-browser testing with tools like Playwright (https://playwright.dev) and simplifying over-specific selectors can also help uncover hidden bugs. Ultimately, you need to understand that it is not just about generating code from ChatGPT or any Large Language Model, you also need to understand the subtleties of compatibility, defaults, and assumptions that come with it.

Next, we shall discuss prompt revision patterns. Addressing structural hallucinations, styling inconsistencies, and other issues requires a strategic approach to prompt design. By refining prompts through targeted revision patterns, you can significantly improve the quality and reliability of AI-generated outputs.

Prompt Revision Patterns

Prompt revision patterns are a response to a predictable failure mode whereby Generative AI model generates a good-looking UI code that fails silently on semantics, accessibility, and maintainability. The solution is not a well-structured longer prompt or post-prompt linting alone; it is an iterative, contract-driven prompt that embeds guardrails, budgets, and self-checks. This review evaluates how and when these patterns work, where they break, and how to operationalize them for HTML5/CSS3. You need to start with guardrails, add constraints with specific limits, and include verification asks. Iterate by comparing old and new prompts, retaining what is helpful and removing unnecessary parts. This process yields cleaner HTML, valid accessibility, lean CSS, and optimized images. This can effectively author a reliable contract for the model.

Guardrails for Reliable Outputs

In the context of AI-driven development, guardrails refer to the explicit constraints and rules that guide the output of a model to ensure it meets specific standards, requirements, and best practices. This approach often involves Human in the Loop (HITL) practices, where people review, or approve sensitive or high-impact outputs. The guardrails and humans in the loop practices are part of ethical and responsible AI. Responsible AI aims to make AI fair, transparent, accountable, and safe in real-world use. In practice, guardrails encourage a set of non-negotiables that the model must adhere to, preventing common errors and inconsistencies in the generated code. With clear guardrails, you can significantly improve the quality and reliability of AI-generated outputs. Guardrails are particularly useful when you want to force AI models to prioritize essential aspects of web development, such as semantics and accessibility. Semantics play a crucial role in structuring web content, making it more interpretable by both humans and machines. Accessibility, on the other hand, ensures that web applications are usable by people with disabilities, complying with standards like the Web Content Accessibility Guidelines (WCAG). By front-loading semantics and accessibility rules, guardrails narrow the output space, making it more likely that the model will produce high-quality, standards-compliant code. One of the key benefits of guardrails is that they help prevent unnecessary downstream refactoring. When you require specific semantic elements, like `<header>`, `<nav>`, `<main>`, and `<footer>`, and enforcing proper heading order, you can avoid structural issues that might arise later in the development process. Similarly, accessibility invariants, such as "*do not remove focus outlines*" and "*associate <label> with inputs*," prevent common regressions that visual review might miss. Let us examine an example to illustrate the concept of guardrails template as follows:

"*Use HTML5 landmarks (<header>, <nav>, <main>, <footer>) and ensure one <h1> per page with strictly descending headings. Meet WCAG AA standards by maintaining focus outlines and using real lists (<ul>/<ol>) for grouped items. Associate <label> with inputs and include aria-current on active navigation items when applicable.*"

By incorporating such guardrails into AI prompts, you create a reliable contract for the model to follow, resulting in cleaner, more accessible, and maintainable code. Over time, this approach yields significant benefits, including reduced refactoring needs, improved code quality, and enhanced user experience.

Optimizing with Constraints and Budgets

In addition to establishing guardrails, applying constraints with budgets can further refine AI-generated outputs. This ensures that the AI-generated codes are lean, efficient, and maintainable. Budgets are limits set on specific aspects of the output, like CSS size, selector depth, or token usage, which force the model to make deliberate choices about code structure and performance. By imposing these constraints, you can prevent common issues like CSS bloat, deep selectors, and excessive token usage.

When applied effectively, budgets promote best practices such as using variables to avoid duplication, utility classes to manage cascades, and component scope to prevent global leakage. For instance, limiting selector depth to two or fewer helps curb specificity wars and improves code reusability. In the same vein, capping CSS at a certain number of lines, for instance, 150 lines encourages the consolidation of styles into `:root` variables and logical properties, resulting in more efficient and maintainable code. Consistent naming conventions, such as BEM or a well-documented token scheme, also play an important role in maintaining stable mental models across iterations. This consistency is not just about your website look and feel, it directly impacts the performance and scalability of the codebase. By requiring the use of `:root` variables for colors, spacing, and other design elements, you can ensure that styles are applied uniformly and can be easily adjusted globally if needed.

Moreover, budgets have a direct link to performance. When you push the AL model toward lcancr DOM structures, fewer blocking resources, and consistent image handling practices like including width and height attributes and using loading="lazy", budgets can contribute to better *First Contentful Paint times* and *Layout Shift stability.*

When dimensions and font strategies are declared thoughtfully, the user experience becomes more predictable and responsive. To maximize the effectiveness of budgets, they should be scoped and tiered, tied to component counts or supported modes rather than a universal ceiling. This approach allows for flexibility while maintaining overall control over the output's quality and performance. For instance, a well-composed budget might specify: "*Limit CSS to 150 lines, with no selector chains deeper than 2. Define colors and spacing in :root variables and use them throughout. Allow an additional 30 lines for RTL support and 50 lines for dark mode.*" By setting such clear and reasonable constraints, you can ensure that AI-generated code is not only functional but also optimized for performance and maintainability. Ultimately, the goal of constraints and budgets is to strike a balance between flexibility and control, allowing you to create high-quality, efficient outputs that meet their needs without sacrificing performance or scalability. With the application of these principles, you experience full potential of AI-driven development while maintaining the quality and reliability of their code.

Improving Reliability with Self-Checks

Self-checks are a mechanism that requires AI models to verify their own output against specific criteria. This ensures that the generated code meets essential standards and requirements. This approach helps improve the accuracy and quality of AI-generated code. Self-checks can take various forms; typical examples are as follows:

- Landmarks present: *[yes/no]*
- Headings: one <h1>, descending: *[ok]*
- Labels match inputs: *[ok]*
- Image width/height + loading="lazy": *[count]*
- Any contrast risks found: *[list]*

These checks provide immediate feedback on the code's adherence to specific requirements. Additionally, highlighting potential issues, such as contrast risks, allows for targeted review and improvement. While self-checks are valuable, they are not without limitations. Models may exhibit overconfidence in their assessments or drift in their reporting format. To counter these issues, requesting evidence snippets like "*List the <h1> and <h2> texts you found*", and versioning the audit schema can improve the reliability and consistency of self-checks. You can maximize the effectiveness of self-checks by combining them with external linters and ensure that the audit process is well-structured and consistent. With the self-integrating checks into the development process, you significantly improve the quality and reliability of AI-generated code, ensuring that it meets the required standards and best practices.

Revising prompts transforms one-off fixes into standard patterns by establishing guardrails, enforcing lean code budgets, and incorporating self-checks. Through continuous iteration based on review feedback, these prompts evolve to prevent recurring issues, allowing consistent quality and reliability in AI-generated outputs.

Next, we will pair these smarter prompts with a Human versus AI Division of Labor department, so the model handles breadth while you apply judgment where it matters the most.

Human versus AI Comparison

AI models like ChatGPT can quickly generate HTML and CSS code, but it is not always perfect. Humans are better at making sure that the code is meaningful, accessible, and user-friendly. The best approach is to have humans design and edit, while AI builds the code based on clear instructions. This way, humans can refine the code and teach AI models what to do differently next time. In the previous section, we discussed some of the core concepts to ensure AI model outputs align with standardized HTML/CSS structures, and expectations. We explored guardrails, what must always be true to protect structure and accessibility, constraint and budget, a strict limit to force choices that prevent bloat and instability, and ways to improve self-checks. All these are essentials to prevent AI models from misrepresentation or hallucinations at best. In this section, we will examine the roles of humans in the loop in collaborative workflow where the humans take the lead in defining intent and meaning, composing a detailed mini-spec that outlines guardrails, constraints and budgets.

Typically, in an AI-Human workflow, humans review edge cases, such as dark mode and right-to-left layouts, and refine the design by converting every useful edit into a new rule. Meanwhile, AI generates HTML and CSS code quickly according to the spec, utilizing tokens and shallow selectors, and even conducts a basic self-audit to ensure compliance, reporting on details like proper heading structure and image optimization.

The following screenshot depicts the collaborative workflow between AI and humans and explains best practices to achieve optimal results:

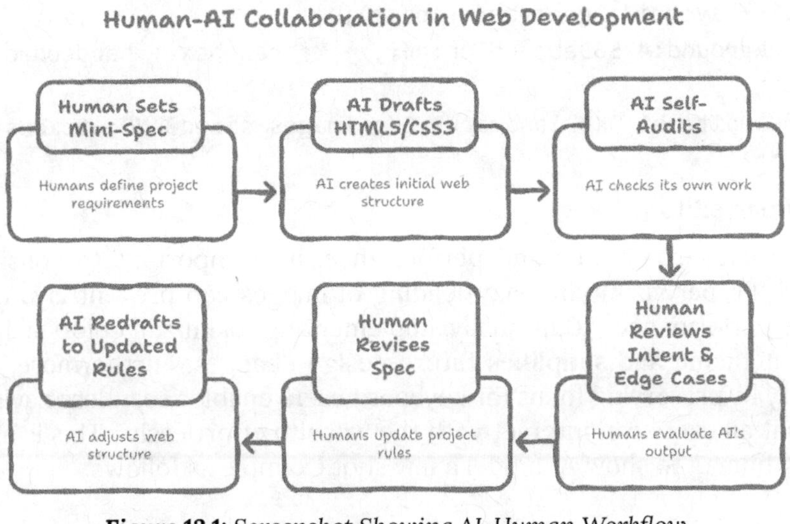

Figure 12.1: *Screenshot Showing AI-Human Workflow*

The preceding screenshot image showcases a looped workflow showing how humans and AI co-build web projects: humans set a mini-spec, the AI drafts HTML/CSS and self-audits, then humans review edge cases and revise the spec. The AI redrafts to the updated rules, continuing the cycle until the site meets the requirements.

Let us explore a practical example of a prompt and see how humans and AI collaborate in a web development workflow, explaining the distinct roles each plays in the process. We start with writing a mini- spec as follows:

Step 1: Writing the mini-spec

Prompt:

"*Use header, nav, main, footer. One <h1> per page; headings descend. Keep focus outlines. Use real lists for grouped items. Use :root tokens—no raw hex or ad-hoc spacing. Selector depth ≤ 2. All images must declare width and height and loading="lazy". Append a 5-bullet self-audit confirming these items.*"

Step 2: Demonstrating AI first draft

```
<header><h1>Products</h1></header>
<main>
<section class="card">
<img src="shoe.jpg" alt="Blue running shoe">
<h2>Velocity Runner</h2>
<button class="btn">Add to cart</button>
</section>
</main>
<style>
:root { --brand:#2563eb; --space:1rem; }
.card { display:grid; gap:var(--space); }
.btn { background:#2563eb; color:#fff; } /* raw hex + hardcoded white */
</style>
<!-- Self-audit: h1 OK; landmarks OK; images sized? NO; tokens? partial;
depth OK -->
```

Step 3: Human edits

To improve user experience and performance, it is important to consider several key factors. Proper sizing and lazy-loading of images can prevent layout shifts and boost page performance. Additionally, implementing tokenized colors helps maintain a consistent theme and simplifies future design changes. Furthermore, prioritizing accessibility by preserving focus for keyboard users enables seamless navigation. This ensures that all users can interact with the website effortlessly. This is an improved tweak with human to show AI model a few shot example as follows:

```
<imgsrc="shoe.jpg"alt="Blue running shoe"
width="320"height="180"loading="lazy">
<style>
:root { --brand:#2563eb; --fg:#111; --bg:#fff; --space:1rem; }
.btn { background:var(--brand); color:var(--bg); }
.btn:focus-visible { outline:2px solid currentColor; outline-offset:2px;
}
</style>
```

Step 3: Spec revision

With these best practices in mind, the next step is to refine the specification in Step 1. A revised spec might read: "*Images must have width, height, and loading="lazy" to prevent layout shifts and optimize performance. No raw color values are allowed—only tokens like --bg, --fg, and --brand can be used to maintain a consistent theme. Additionally, focus outlines must remain visible to ensure accessibility for keyboard users.*" As the AI model learns from these guidelines, it will automatically incorporate them into future generations, streamlining the review process and reducing the need for manual edits. Over time, the reviews will get smaller and more focused, as the AI model becomes more proficient in meeting the specified requirements.

Interestingly, when you provide AI model a tiny, testable brief and then act as careful editors, you get the best of both worlds: AI speed with human judgment. Guardrails keep structure and accessibility intact; budgets keep CSS lean and predictable; tokens keep design consistent; the self-audit keeps reviews factual. Over a few iterations, the AI models inevitably learn your rules, and you shift from fixing basics to shaping better user experiences. That is the human versus AI partnership at its simplest and most effective in HTML/CSS.

Note: *Human sets intent, AI drafts and self-checks, humans review and refine, and the AI redrafts, thus maintaining an iterative loop that turns specs into a finished site.*

Conclusion

While AI can rapidly sketch out UI concepts, reliability and precision require a more deliberate approach. With the integration of robust guardrails that enforce semantic and accessibility standards, imposing lean budgets on selector depth, CSS size, and tokens, and incorporating self-checks, you can transform rough first AI model drafts into robust, standards-compliant frontends. When paired with regular human review, particularly for critical aspects like intent, edge cases, and accessibility, this iterative process enables AI-generated code to become increasingly refined and reliable. As the human-AI collaboration cycle repeats, the feedback loop tightens, and each iteration yields smaller and more incremental changes. Ultimately, this yields a production-ready site that meets the highest standards of quality and usability.

In the next final chapter, we will build on the knowledge covered in this book to outline a path to AI-driven frontend mastery and explore the essential habits that will keep you future-ready in the age of artificial intelligence.

Points to Remember

- Hallucinations look factual on the surface but violate specs, treat them as predictable failure modes to guard against.
- Prefer HTML5 landmarks, one **`<h1>`** with descending headings, real lists, and proper label/input associations.
- Keep CSS valid and shallow (selector depth ≤ 2), avoid raw values by using **`:root`** tokens, and provide fallbacks.
- Require images to include width/height + loading="lazy" to reduce layout shift.
- Back claims with automated checks (validators, linters) and the AI's self-audit report.
- Turn every useful human edit into a new rule so the next draft comes out closer to spec.

Multiple Choice Questions

1. Which best describes an AI "hallucination" in UI code?
    a. A runtime crash due to network latency
    b. Plausible-looking but invalid or unimplemented markup/styles
    c. Any warning in DevTools
    d. Minified CSS
2. Which is a correct fix for an invented element like `<card>`?
    a. Keep it; browsers will polyfill it.
    b. Wrap it in <stack>.
    c. Replace with semantic elements and classes.
    d. Add role="card".
3. Which ARIA usage is recommended in primary navigation?
    a. `role="navigation-bar"`
    b. `aria-label="Primary" on <nav>`
    c. `role="menuitem"` on every link
    d. No labels allowed

4. Which heading pattern is correct?
    a. Multiple <h1> per page
    b. <h1>→<h3>→<h2>
    c. One <h1>, then strictly descending levels
    d. Headings in any order
5. Which CSS is invalid in a .css file (not a preprocessor)?
    a. inline-flex
    b. row-gap
    c. Sass-style nested rules with &
    d. border-radius
6. A lean CSS budget primarily helps with:
    a. Reducing image file formats
    b. Preventing specificity wars and bloat
    c. Auto-generating JS bundles
    d. Disabling DevTools
7. Which image rule helps prevent layout shift?
    a. decoding="sync"
    b. Omitting alt
    c. Explicit width and height
    d. Using SVG for everything
8. The guardrail "`selector depth ≤ 2`" aims to:
    a. Speed up JavaScript execution.
    b. Encourage shallow, maintainable CSS.
    c. Disable dark mode.
    d. Allow deep component theming.
9. Which tool combination is recommended to catch HTML/CSS issues early?
    a. W3C Validator + Stylelint + DevTools
    b. Only manual visual testing
    c. Database profiler
    d. Package manager audit

10. In the self-audit, which item is appropriate to report?
    a. CDN uptime
    b. Count of images with width/height and loading="lazy"
    c. Number of JS functions
    d. Server response codes
11. Why avoid raw hex colors in component styles?
    a. They are deprecated.
    b. Tokens in :root improve consistency and theming.
    c. Browsers cannot parse hex in 2025.
    d. Hex breaks ARIA.
12. In the Human ↔ AI loop, humans should focus primarily on:
    a. Writing all CSS by hand
    b. Edge cases, intent, accessibility, and updating rules
    c. Disabling validators
    d. Hosting infrastructure

Answers

1. b
2. c
3. b
4. c
5. c
6. b
7. c
8. b
9. a
10. b
11. b
12. b

Key Terms

- **Hallucination (UI)**: AI output that appears plausible but violates standards or reality (including invented elements/properties).
- **Structural Hallucination**: Errors that break semantics or accessibility (duplicate IDs, incorrect nesting, heading skips, bad ARIA).
- **Guardrails**: Non-negotiable prompt rules ensuring semantics, accessibility, and consistency (such as landmarks, single <h1>, focus outlines).
- **Budgets**: Explicit limits (CSS lines, selector depth, and token usage) that curb bloat and improve performance.
- **Self-Checks (Self-Audit)**: Model-generated verification list confirming adherence to the spec (landmarks present, headings order, image sizing).
- **Framework Bleed**: Stray utility/framework classes included without the framework, causing unpredictable styles.
- **Tokens**: Design variables in `:root` (for example, `--brand`, `--bg`, `--space`) used instead of hard-coded values.
- **Specificity Wars**: Escalating selector complexity to override prior rules, leading to fragile CSS.
- **Landmarks**: HTML5 structural elements (`<header>`, `<nav>`, `<main>`, `<footer>`) improving structure and navigation.
- **Accessibility Invariants**: Rules that must always hold (labels tied to inputs, visible focus, valid ARIA).

CHAPTER 13
AI-Driven Frontend Mastery and Future Readiness

Introduction

In *Chapter 12, Refining AI-Generated Code*, you learned to refine AI-generated frontend code to meet real-world standards because AI outputs often require review and enhancement to ensure quality, accessibility, and performance. In this chapter, we aim to systematize how AI fits into that frontend workflow. We begin by focusing on the clean-code practices that keep complexity low over time: cohesive modules, descriptive naming, and automated quality gates that catch regressions early. From there, you will build a personal prompt library, templates with purpose, constraints, tokens, and acceptance criteria, that enable AI model suggestions to arrive already shaped to your standards.

This chapter closes with a pragmatic look at the developers' job market: how AI shifts effort from boilerplate to orchestration, review, governance, and ethical decision-making. The through-line is simple: treat the AI output as a *draft*, encode your standards in both code and prompts, and let continuous integration enforce them. This allows you to move faster without accruing tomorrow's technical debt. When this is done well, AI models become a force multiplier for clarity, maintainability, and career durability.

After reading this chapter, you will be able to structure prompts as modules for readability, testability, and low complexity using the Don't Repeat Yourself approach. You will build a versioned prompt library with templates, variables, and few-shot examples that encode tokens, naming conventions, and acceptance criteria, review AI outputs critically, refactor regularly, and integrate changes through tests and human code review, and explain how AI re-allocates developers' effort toward orchestration, quality assurance, accessibility, and governance, while identifying the skills that compound as AI model tools evolve.

Structure

In this chapter, we will cover the following topics:

- Clean Code and Maintainability
- Creating Your Own Prompt Library
- The Role of AI in the Developers' Job Market

Clean Code and Maintainability

Clean code refers to code that is easy to read, understand, and modify. Even in an AI-assisted workflow, maintaining clean, well-structured code is vital for the long-term sustainability of projects. AI can accelerate code creation, but without developers' oversight, it may also introduce technical debt, a term used in software development cost of fixing and improving existing software due to shortcuts or suboptimal design choices. This concept has improved developers' awareness and made human attention to code maintainability more important than ever.

AI coding assistants such as GitHub Copilot and ChatGPT can produce a lot of code quickly. In fact, many developers report significant productivity gains from these tools. In Stack Overflow's 2024 Developer Survey, 81% of respondents identified increasing productivity as the biggest benefit of AI tools[1]. However, more code does not automatically mean better code. AI coding tools can be super helpful, but they can also lead to messy code if not used carefully. Sometimes, these tools suggest quick fixes that work but are not the best solution. This can result in duplicated code, more rework, and less focus on refining existing code, ultimately affecting code quality. It is all about finding a balance between speed and quality. To counteract these tendencies, it is important to apply clean code practices diligently when using AI. Have it in mind that maintainability is how easily a code can be understood and modified by you or others later. It is a top priority for any long-lived project. Studies and expert guidelines stress that adhering to the Don't Repeat Yourself (DRY) principle, and writing modular, well-documented code are essential for sustaining project velocity over the year. In an AI-augmented environment, this advice holds true more than ever. You should treat AI-generated code as a first draft, not a final product. Even GitHub's own guidance clearly states: "*Review Copilot's suggestions carefully. Consider not just the functionality and security of the suggested code, but also the readability and maintainability of the code moving forward.*" (GitHub Docs, "Best practices for using GitHub Copilot"). If you treat it as a rough draft that engineers then polish, you can keep quality high. But if you are indulging in copying AI output verbatim without review, those rough edges turn into tomorrow's technical debt. Now, let us explore some of the best practices to make sure you maintain a clean code with AI AI-assisted workflow.

---

1. www.survey.stackoverflow.co/2024/ai

- **Review AI outputs critically**

  Do not assume the AI's suggestion is the best solution. Treat AI-generated code as a draft. Read it with a reviewer's eye: Is this the simplest, clearest solution? Will others understand it? If the code is convoluted, refactor—break large functions into focused units, simplify conditionals, and remove redundancy.

- **Enforce your coding standards**

  AI does not know inherently your project's conventions or style guide unless you prompt it to. AI-generated snippets often come back with uneven names or formatting. Run them through your linter and formatter to normalize style and tell the model what you expect, like *use semantic HTML tags*, and *follow our CSS naming rules*. This clear guidance, plus automated checks, and keeps your codebase consistent.

- **Stay DRY and modular**

  If an AI model suggests writing a chunk of code that duplicates existing functionality, rethink it. It is easy to unknowingly create duplicate code because the AI may not have full coverage of your entire codebase. Whenever you use an AI model like ChatGPT, double-check if there is already a function or component that does something similar. Encourage reuse, and you can even prompt the AI model with something like *refactorto use existing components/functions if possible*. Keeping functions small and focused will also help the AI model and other developers understand where to slot in new code without creating redundancy.

- **Use AI for quality assurance**

  Paradoxically, an AI model can be a part of the solution to the quality problem if used wisely in software development. Modern AI tools can assist in writing unit tests, spotting potential bugs, and suggesting code improvements. For instance, you can ask ChatGPT to review a block of code for bugs or edge cases to essentially act as a pair programmer who double-checks your work. Some AI systems and IDE extensions can scan for security vulnerabilities or bad practices and alert you in real time. Leverage these code quality assurance features to turn an AI model into a partner in keeping your code clean and secure.

- **Refactor regularly**

  It is advisable to regularly refactor your code, including AI-generated parts, to keep it clean and maintainable. Use an AI model like ChatGPT and GitHub Copilot to help with tasks such as simplifying functions, improving readability, and extracting repeated logic. After making these changes, run your test suite to catch any issues.

- **Maintain security and best practices**

  When using AI coding tools, be aware that suggestions might include hidden issues such as security vulnerabilities or bad practices. Always review and test the AI-generated code as stated earlier, especially in critical parts. Use security linters, audits, and your own expertise to ensure that the code is secure, accessible, and follows best practices. As one large user study found, "*participants who had access to an AI assistant wrote significantly less secure code than those without access*[2]."

In a nutshell, writing a clean code is a non-negotiable requirement, even when a Large Language Model is helping you write it. Think of the AI as a co-worker; it can do the legwork, but you are the senior developer who must review and guide its work. By vigilantly enforcing clarity, consistency, and good architecture, you ensure that the codebase remains healthy. When working with AI-generated code, it is a good idea to review and refine it before integrating it into your project. This way, you can leverage AI's productivity benefits while maintaining clean and robust code. Consider flagging AI-composed code for extra scrutiny in code reviews to ensure it meets best practices and your standards.

Now that we have covered best practices when working with AI coding tools, let us explore how to create a personalized prompt library to further boost productivity and get the most out of these AI tools.

Creating Your Own Prompt Library

As you incorporate AI tools into your development workflow, you will notice that composing an effective prompt is an art in itself. This section explores how to build a personal prompt library for the frontend, a curated collection of prompts that you have refined and found useful. By saving and organizing these prompts, you can increase your productivity and maintain consistency in your AI-assisted frontend tasks.If you have ever found yourself typing similar requests into ChatGPT or another coding assistant repeatedly, a prompt library is the solution. In simple terms, a prompt library for developers is a collection of ready-made AI prompts tailored for common coding and debugging tasks. Think of it as a toolbox of questions/commands you can copy and paste to get immediate help from AI models, instead of formulating a new prompt from scratch each time. For instance, rather than typing out "Explain what this CSS snippet does and how I can improve it" every time you need that, you can save that prompt once and reuse it whenever needed. By doing so, you focus on the core problem and let the AI handle the routine parts. The prompt library provides the phrasing that you already know works well.

Why do you need a prompt library? First, it saves time and mental energy. Just as you might have a library of code snippets or reusable templates for common HTML structures, having a library of prompts means you are not re-thinking how to ask the AI for something every single time. It speeds up your workflow because you have a starting point for the AI model query. Second, it brings consistency. If you and your

2 *Neil Perry, Srivastava, Kumar &Boneh*, ACM CCS 2023, *https://dl.acm.org/doi/10.1145/3576915.3623157*

team use standardized prompts for certain tasks, you are likely to get more uniform results. For instance, consistent coding style or documentation format from the AI. Third, using a prompt library helps you improve prompt quality over time. The prompts in the library are expected to be battle-tested. They must have yielded good results in the past and often are refined to avoid misinterpretation. Over time, as you add to this library, you also get better at prompt engineering by learning from these examples.

Building and Curating Your Prompt Library

As stated previously, a prompt library is your reusable toolkit of well-tested instructions you feed into an AI model like ChatGPT to speed up every day HTML/CSS tasks, without sacrificing accessibility, semantics, or maintainability. Treat it like a design system in plain English words: organized, versioned, and tailored to the way you build user interfaces. Now, let us explore some of the ways you can build a battle-tested prompt library, starting with a collection of winning prompts.

- **Collecting winning prompts**

  Begin to save prompts that yield impressive results. Let us take this prompt as an example: "*Generate a responsive navigation bar in pure* HTML/CSS *with a dropdown menu*". When you compose a prompt that generates exactly what you need, add it to your library. This collection will grow faster than you think. Keep a document for storing your prompts. Note the prompt, the output, and any tweaks you made. Review and refine your collection regularly. By collecting successful prompts, you will develop a valuable resource for future projects and improve your prompt-crafting skills.

- **Organizing prompts by category**

  Create a clear category to organize your prompts. You need to keep your growing list of prompts manageable, organize them by purpose into clear categories such as *HTML/CSS Layouts*, *CSS Debugging*, *Accessibility Checks*, *Code Explanations*, *Bug Fixing*, and *Optimization/Refactoring*. This thoughtful structure makes it easy to find the right prompt when you need it most. For instance, when a CSS issue arises, you can quickly navigate to your CSS *Debugging* category and use a saved prompt to troubleshoot the problem.

- **Leveraging template variables**

  As you create prompts, you will notice some patterns. Often, parts of the prompt can be abstracted. For instance, a prompt like "*Explain what the following code does and identify any potential issues: [code snippet]*" could be reused for any code snippet by replacing the bracketed part. You can design prompts as templates where you plug in the specifics each time. Mark placeholders clearly like *[code snippet]* or *[error message]* so that when using the library, you know what to replace. This makes prompts reusable and reduces the chance of forgetting to include important details.

- **Maintaining a shared repository for teams**

  If you are working with others, consider keeping the prompt library in a place, from where everyone can access, such as a shared markdown file in your repo. A shared prompt library becomes a valuable reference for the whole team over time. It improves the onboarding experience for junior developers. For instance, junior developers or new team members can benefit from the refined prompts that other team members have developed. It also means the team's usage of the AI model becomes more standardized. One developer might discover a great way to ask an AI model to generate documentation comments for functions, and by sharing that prompt, all team members can uniformly produce high-quality comments with the AI model's help.

- **Refining prompts through feedback**

  As you know, building a prompt library is not a one-and-done task. It is an iterative process. After using a prompt from the library, evaluate the AI model's response. Did it solve your problem? Could it be better with a slight tweak? For instance, maybe your prompt "*Explain this code*" tends to give too much detail;you might refine it to "*Explain this code at a high level*" for more concise answers. You need to regularly refine your prompts based on the output quality and feedback from usage. Over time, each prompt in your library can be fine-tuned to perfection.

- **Leveraging tools for prompt management**

  You can manage a prompt library with simple tools, even a plain text file or notes app works, but there are also browser extensions and apps specifically designed for storing and injecting prompts. For instance, some Chrome extensions like *Saved Prompts- https://chromewebstore.google.com/detail/nbfhlbpkebiejihbipapniegllacifhb* lets you save prompts and insert them into ChatGPT with a click. Using tools can integrate the library seamlessly into your workflow. The exact tool matters less than the system that works for you; the goal is quick access to your curated prompts whenever you need them. By creating your own prompt library, you essentially build a personal knowledge base for AI interactions. It is more like having a coding cheat-sheet, but for an AI model. This encourages you to use the AI model more effectively: rather than typing ad-hoc requests and hoping for the best. Ultimately, a prompt library boosts both productivity and consistency in your workflow. It reduces repetitive effort, minimizes the chance of forgetting an important detail in a prompt, and standardizes the way you and your team interact with AI.

Note: *Keep your prompt library lean by grouping by intent, naming for action plus outcome, templating with variables and rich metadata, embedding context/constraints and acceptance criteria with examples/tests, versioning and pruning regularly while removing any sensitive data.*

The Role of AI in the Developers' Job Market

Large Language Model is not removing frontend jobs so much as it is rearranging them. Code generation is getting cheaper and faster, but teams still win or lose the human work of shaping semantics, guaranteeing accessibility, enforcing performance budgets, and integrating changes safely into real products. This shift is visible in the data; the developer adoption of AI assistance has gone from mainstream to default, with Stack Overflow's surveys showing 76% of respondents using or planning to use AI tools in 2024 and 84% in 2025[3]. AI models handle baseline tasks; humans are expected to focus on high-value work. GitHub's controlled experiments and field studies reported faster task completion, famously a 55% speedup for a targeted coding exercise and shorter time-to-merge when AI model assistance is used appropriately-*https://github.blog/news-insights/research/research-quantifying-github-copilots-impact-on-developer-productivity-and-happiness*. The lesson for frontend teams is not that the machine *does the job*, but that it accelerates draft work, so humans can spend more iterative time on review, testing, and user-visible polish. As companies continue to adopt AI, frontend practices are being integrated into broader AI workflows and governance structures. According to McKinsey's 2025 State of AI report, nearly three-quarters of organizations now leverage AI in at least one business function, marking steady growth over the past year. This shift brings new responsibilities and expectations. Legal and security teams are focused on AI usage, data leaders are concerned with prompt inputs, and engineering managers prioritize measurable, traceable value from using data-driven insights instead of relying on personal experiences to make decisions. In frontend work, the best results come from combining AI's speed with strict quality controls, starting with accessibility. Tools like axe-core *https://github.com/dequelabs/axe-core*, can automatically scan for violations and reference WCAG criteria. AI can then draft fix proposals and comments, while developers maintain oversight of semantic correctness. This approach leads to clearer code changes, faster reviews, and a clear audit trail that satisfies stakeholders.

Performance is another key area where AI can be leveraged effectively. By setting clear thresholds based on Google's Core Web Vitals like *Largest Contentful Paint* (LCP ≤ 2.5s), Cumulative Layout Shift (CLS < 0.1), and Interaction to Next Paint (INP ≤ 200ms), teams can tie the release of features to measurable benefits for users. AI can suggest optimizations like reducing render-blocking work, but these should be verified with tools like Lighthouse before implementation. To future-proof frontend development, integrate AI responsibly with strict quality controls. You need to focus on accessibility by using tools like axe-core to scan for violations and leverage AI to draft fixes while maintaining human oversight. For performance, set clear thresholds based on Core Web Vitals and use Lighthouse CI to enforce performance budgets. Tools like Playwright help ensure visual stability by detecting UI changes and regressions, while

3 *https://survey.stackoverflow.co/2025/ai*

AI can assist in identifying and prioritizing issues. With the blend of AI efficiency with human oversight, you can achieve better code quality, faster development, and more reliable user experiences. To achieve optimal results, maintain governance by making AI outputs reviewable and treating generated code like third-party dependencies. Focus on small, measurable improvements and clear documentation to ensure reliable and user-friendly results. In a nutshell, AI models are transforming the developers' job market, shifting focus to strategic, high-level work. To thrive, you should leverage AI as a tool, fine-tuning meta-skills like analysis, design, and communication while deepening core coding skills. By striking a balance, AI models like ChatGPT, GitHub Copilot, Gemini, Llama, and Grok can accelerate growth. Stay adaptable, continuously improve, and you will ride the wave of change.

Conclusion

As we conclude this chapter on AI-driven frontend mastery, the key takeaway is balance. Leverage the incredible capabilities of AI to assist in writing code, brainstorming solutions, and automating tedious tasks – these tools can dramatically speed up development and even help you learn new techniques. But at the same time, double down on the human aspects of software development: creativity, clean coding, critical review, and lifelong learning. The future of frontend development will not be AI *or* humans; it will be AI *and humans working together*. By writing maintainable code, curating your prompt library, and cultivating a future-ready mindset, you are not just preparing for changes – you are positioning yourself to lead in this new era. The fact that you have focused on HTML and CSS fundamentals means you have a strong foundation; now, with AI as part of your toolkit, you can build on that foundation higher and faster than ever before. Stay curious, stay critical, and do not fear the evolution of the field. If you carry forward the lessons of clean code and continuous improvement, you will remain an invaluable part of the web development ecosystem – no matter how much AI is woven into it. Here is your future-ready frontend career, powered by both human insight and AI innovation!

Points to Remember

- Treat AI suggestions as first drafts, review for simplicity, readability, and security.
- Readability beats cleverness, prefer small, single-purpose modules, and descriptive names when building your prompt library.
- Enforce linters/formatters/types/tests on every push, block merges when gates fail.
- Stay DRY and modular, refactor duplicated logic instead of pasting AI snippets.
- Encode tokens and conventions in prompts; parameterize, do not hard-code.
- Use AI for quality assistance, tests, and bug-spotting, but keep human oversight as required.

- Track and pay technical debt explicitly; small, steady refactors win.
- Prioritize accessibility and ethics; AI speeds drafts, you safeguard users.

Multiple Choice Questions

1. Which practice most improves long-term maintainability?
    a. Deep inheritance trees
    b. Small, single-purpose modules with tests
    c. Global mutable state
    d. Commenting on every line
2. What should a prompt template always include?
    a. Random examples
    b. Constraints and acceptance criteria
    c. Only visual mockups
    d. Proprietary secrets
3. Which CI step best prevents style churn?
    a. Manual formatting
    b. Prettier and a linter on every push
    c. Screenshots in PRs
    d. Weekly cleanups only
4. How should tokens be handled in a prompt library?
    a. Hard-code colors/spacing
    b. Parameterize tokens and document scales
    c. Ignore tokens
    d. Store tokens in comments only
5. Which statement about AI and developer roles is most accurate?
    a. AI removes human review.
    b. AI increases the value of system design and governance.
    c. AI eliminates testing.
    d. AI guarantees accessibility.
6. Which approach reduces cognitive load in functions?
    a. Many mixed-type params
    b. Pure functions with clear inputs/outputs

   c. Hidden global dependencies
   d. Deeply nested conditionals

7. Best place to store and evolve prompts?
   a. Private notes only
   b. Versioned repo with changelogs
   c. Chat history without backups
   d. One undocumented file

8. Which gate should block merges of AI-generated code?
   a. Screenshot approval
   b. Passing automated checks and human review
   c. A green background color
   d. A long commit message

9. Most useful metric for prompt library quality?
   a. Lines per prompt
   b. % generations passing acceptance tests
   c. Number of emojis
   d. Repo file size

10. Which naming guidance best supports maintainability?
   a. Short, context-free names
   b. Consistent, descriptive names aligned to domain language
   c. Randomized identifiers
   d. Duplicated abbreviations per team

11. Which ethical concern belongs to team guidance?
   a. Ignore license notices
   b. Data privacy, attribution, and bias mitigation
   c. Emoji usage rules
   d. Monitor size preferences

12. Habit that turns AI from a draft generator into a partner?
   a. Accept outputs without review.
   b. Encode standards in prompts and enforce them in CI.
   c. Disable tests to speed up merges.
   d. Avoid documenting decisions.

Answers

1. b
2. b
3. b
4. b
5. b
6. b
7. b
8. b
9. b
10. b
11. b
12. b

Key Terms

- **Clean Code**: This is a readable, simple, and maintainable code that minimizes complexity.
- **Technical Debt**: This is the future rework costs from shortcuts or suboptimal design.
- **Don't Repeat Yourself (DRY)**: An approach to eliminate duplication via reuse and refactoring.
- **Cyclomatic Complexity**: A measure of decision paths; lower is easier to reason about.
- **Prompt Library**: Curated, versioned prompts with variables, constraints, and examples.
- **Acceptance Criteria**: Observable, testable conditions for "done," used in prompts and CI.
- **Tokens/Design Tokens**: Named values, color, spacing, typography used consistently in UI and prompts.
- **Quality Gates (CI)**: Automated checks, format, lint, tests, a11y/security scans that block merges on failure.
- **Accessibility (a11y)**: It refers to inclusive design, ensuring that the products are usable by people with disabilities.
- **Governance**: Policies and review practices for safe, compliant AI/code usage

Index

A

F

G

H

I

V

W

X

www.ingramcontent.com/pod-product-compliance
Lightning Source LLC
LaVergne TN
LVHW060446061126
851857LV00016B/1744
* 9 7 8 9 3 4 9 8 8 7 7 4 9 *